The Hunt for "Tokyo Rose"

The Hunt for "Tokyo Rose"

Russell Warren Howe

MADISON BOOKS
Lanham • New York • London

P6

Published by Madison Books
4720 Boston Way
Lanham, Maryland 20706

3 Henrietta Street
London WC2E 8LU England

Distributed by National Book Network

The paper used in this publication meets the minimum
requirements of American National Standard for
Information Sciences—Permanence of Paper for
Printed Library Materials, ANSI Z39.48–1984. ∞™
Manufactured in the United States of America.

5   4   3   2   1

Library of Congress Cataloging-in-Publication Data

Howe, Russell Warren, 1925–
The hunt for "Tokyo Rose" / Russell Warren Howe.
p.   cm.
Includes bibliographical references.
1. Tokyo Rose, 1916–   .
2. United States—Biography.
3. Japanese Americans—Biography.
4. World War, 1939–1945—Japan.
5. Trials (Treason)—California—San Francisco.
I. Title.
CT275.T717H68   1989
940.54'88752'092—dc20   89–35273 CIP
[B]

ISBN 0–8191–7456–4 (alk. paper)

British Cataloging in Publication Information Available

Contents

CONTENTS

Twelve pages of photographs follow page 176.

Foreword

THE AUTHORS OF THE CONSTITUTION of the United States were aware of the excesses and injustice that often flow from the emotional accusation, "TREASON." James Wilson of Pennsylvania, one of the wisest and most influential delegates at the convention, insisted on defining this ultimate crime against the state in the charter. He hoped to prevent political abuses of power against government-proclaimed enemies of the patria. He wanted the new nation to avoid the "numerous and dangerous excrescenses" that disfigured the English law of treason.

Had the definition of treason been adequately limited, this book with its tragic story might not exist. The prosecution and imprisonment of a fiction on false charges involving only speech that was harmless, if not helpful, to the U.S. war effort by "a solitary American patriot" requires, after all, a crime so horrible as to paralyze the power of reason. Treason served this need.

The Constitution incorporated two definitions of treason used by the legal system from which independence had been wrested: "levying War" against the United States, or "adhering to their enemies, giving them Aid and Comfort." Curiously, they actually made it extremely difficult to convict those charged with actually "levying War" against the government by requiring two witnesses to the same act of war. Thus the early trial of Aaron Burr failed. But it made absurdly easy the treason charge of "adhering to their Enemies, giving them Aid and Comfort," even with the two witness requirement. Those who engage in armed aggression against their own country are protected, while those who seem disloyal, including possibly the peacemakers, are endangered.

So greatly did leadership fear the power of the word and hate those they believed abused it that, from among the millions of American participants in all the tumult of World War II, seven of the twelve persons indicted for treason were radio announcers. We should recall Eugene V. Debs' observation on his way to prison in 1918 that it is a very dangerous thing to exercise the right of free speech in a country fighting to make the world safe for democracy. The constitutional definition of treason serves the cause of war by protecting those who wage it while placing those who resist at risk.

A myth called "Tokyo Rose" offers a classic study of irrationality in war and its wake. It is a woeful tale of contempt for truth, corruption of justice, failure of character, indifference to principle, arrogance of power and the endless horrors of war. There are only traces of lonely courage and faith, all among the victims, in this further evidence that "justice is the fugitive from the winning camp."

Russell Warren Howe, a prodigious and relentless seeker of fact, presents a vast tapestry of places, events and people that, stitched together, offers stunning historical insights and powerful truths about war, law and human nature. The places are the western Pacific, Australia, Japan, the Philippines, the United States, Watts in south central Los Angeles, prisoner of war camps such as Suragadai in Japan, which supplied language skills for its broadcasting, the studios of Radio Tokyo and the capital before, during and after World War II. Later we are taken to a courtroom in San Francisco, then to a federal prison in West Virginia and finally to Chicago.

The events are Japanese immigration to America's west coast; the difficulties of cultural and racial integration; the attack on Pearl Harbor described to a Japanese American in Tokyo; the Bataan death march; the surrender of Singapore; the capture of Americans, Australians, Filipinos and others on Wake Island from downed aircraft, sunken ships and land battles; the misery of prison camps; the turning tide of war; the bombing of Japan; Hiroshima; the pervasive inhumanity of war.

The people are Issei and Nisei, Australians, Americans, heroes and survivors in Japanese war prisons, the Japanese people in wartime, lonely American GI's in the far-flung, war-torn islands of the Pacific, Hirohito, Tojo, Truman, MacArthur, an array of U.S., Japanese and other government officials, the major figures of the U.S. Department of Justice, Attorney General Tom C. Clark, FBI Director J. Edgar Hoover, U.S. prosecutors, investigators, judges, witnesses, the American press, Walter Winchell, the New York Times, the staff and administration of Japan's wartime radio stations. Hovering over the whole vast scene is the spectre of Tokyo Rose, alluring, poisonous, false, treacherous traitor.

Tokyo Rose, Howe tells us, was as famous as Emperor Hirohito. When the American press first arrived in Japan after the long deadly years of war, four persons were most avidly sought for interviews: Hirohito, Tojo, MacArthur and Tokyo Rose.

But there was no Tokyo Rose. No one, absolutely no one, ever used that name on any Japanese radio. There were at least twenty-seven women disc jockeys who broadcast in English for Japan: fourteen on its government station, NHK, from Tokyo; many more from other cities occupied by Japan throughout the Pacific, but no Tokyo Rose. Long before the trial, high officials for the U.S. government conceded this "legendary seductress" was a myth. Tokyo Rose never existed. It became necessary, therefore, to invent her.

Nor was the nonexistence of Tokyo Rose merely a matter of misnomer, or mistaken identity. What's in a name? No one, by any other name, made the statements or said anything that had the consequences attributed to the hated words of Tokyo Rose. We must ask whether mere words, the worst fantasized, can ever be a crime. Even if so, here there was no criminal word and no *corpus delicti*. For all the prosecution's efforts at "ear witness" identification, joined by such eminences as *The New York Times* which appealed for persons able to identify an infamous voice, no meaningful or reliable memory and no tape whatsoever of an incriminating nature supported the claims of treason. From all the monitoring and recording of Japanese radio, not one sound was found that records an utterance by the woman indicted as Tokyo Rose that was even hostile to the United States. The siren song that broke the hearts of homesick GI's, convinced them their wives and girlfriends were unfaithful, paralyzed them with fear of imminent attack, defeat or capture, accurately forecast air raids and land assaults, and falsely described losses of ships, battles and islands was never sung. The woman accused was thin, scurvied, not pretty, with a rough, deep voice and almost masculine style.

From an enormous archive of effort to find the evil word, Howe extracts statements as diverse as a SeaBee on Saipan, a Marine lieutenant in the jungles of the South Pacific islands, and General Robert Eichelberger ordering favorite records dropped by parachute from American bombers striking Tokyo to be played for GI's over NHK, to support the proposition that "Tokyo Rose" was popular entertainment who improved American military morale. With acerbic, but instructive wit, he suggests the only possible value the extensive search for victims of the wicked tongue of the non-existent Rose of Tokyo is for sociologists studying how myths are born.

Also instructive, Howe, who in another book successfully demythologized Mata Hari, in his exhaustive pursuit of this myth succumbs to another. He refers to FBI agents in 1948 as being "famous for their long campaign against the vicious leaders of organized crime." It was another decade before J. Edgar Hoover admitted organized crime existed. We may need some myths and illusions, but a people who want to be free should be every wary of myths that subvert their basic principles.

Like George M. Cohan, Iva Toguri, accused as Tokyo Rose, was born on the fourth of July. This should have been the ninth count in her indictment. It, at least, was true. From her birth in 1916 in Watts, an area of south central Los Angeles where the first major race riot of the 1960's erupted, Iva moved on to graduate from UCLA and voted for "One World" Wendell Wilkie to be president in 1940.

In the fateful summer of 1941 she was sent to Japan by her parents for the first time in her life to help a sick aunt. She was miserable there, finding the pre-war diet, customs, language and discipline strange and difficult. She received parental consent and tried to schedule her return home on a ship departing for Los Angeles on December 2 which was forced to return to Japan.

Hearing of the attack on Pearl Harbor and commencement of war from her Japanese cousins, she applied for a U.S. passport to return home. She renounced the Japanese citizenship conferred on her by Japanese law, but never claimed by her. An alien, not fluent in Japanese, she was not interned but was placed under surveillance and with her American clothes was viewed suspiciously by neighbors. Urged by authorities to become a Japanese citizen, she refused.

The war years were terrible for her. She experienced hunger, scurvy, beri-beri, malnutrition. The money she had to pay for her trip home was quickly exhausted. She could not afford transportation to a neutral port when repatriation became possible for a brief period.

She answered an ad in the *Nippon Times* for English-language typists at Radio Tokyo and was hired. She worked part-time at the Danish Consulate to make ends meet. In mid-November of 1943, long after American GI's claimed to hear Tokyo Rose broadcasts, she was ordered to be transferred from the typing pool to radio broadcasting at station NHK as a temporary employee. She had been chosen for a broadcast job there by an Australian POW. He assured her the program was "straight entertainment." On the radio she read scripts prepared by POW's and played records. She was chosen by the POW's who produced the programs for two reasons. Her voice was bad so listeners would not take her seriously and she was known to be sympathetic to the American side and would not betray the POW's with whom she worked to the Japanese. They acknowledged they trusted her with their lives. She liked working with them, felt a bond and thought she was doing the right thing. Calling herself Annie, sometimes Orphan Annie, Iva read short scripts written by POW's and played records.

Altogether, Iva broadcast little more than a year, a twenty minute entertainment segment on an hour program. After Australian POW Major Cousens, who first conscripted her for the program, left NHK following a heart attack, Iva tried to end her temporary employment in broadcasting.

Toward the end of the war, she converted to Catholicism and married a Eurasian in April 1945, with whom she shared her anti-Japanese feelings. The Danish mission closed in early 1945, thus leaving her with no other support but Radio Tokyo, where she worked sporadically during 1945 until shortly before the end of the war. The Danish minister confirmed her pro-American commitment, as did Major Cousens and other POW's.

In fact, throughout her time with the POW's she rendered them heroic service at personal risk and sacrifice. She brought them fruit, vegetables and other food she needed herself, aspirin, quinine and other medicine and news from the Danish mission.

Iva Toguri never adjusted to the Japanese culture. She remained an alien, an enemy alien at that. While she was an American citizen "heroine working behind enemy lines," her parents were interned in concentration camps in California. Her mother, never strong, died at the Tulare Assembly Center early in the war.

At the end of the war, as American reporters poured into Japan looking for "Tokyo Rose," Iva Toguri, not understanding how the wartime mythology had created a monster, volunteered her story and accepted entreaties and proffered contracts for a story that named her "Tokyo Rose."

She was arrested in October 1945, and held for three months without any visits from family or friends, or any lawyer. She had no change of her own clothes, and underwent lengthy interrogation and frequent viewing by curious American dignitaries. After a year during which the military Counter Intelligence Corps found no evidence against her, military investigators for G2 recommended her release, a United States Attorney and Assistant Attorney General recommended against prosecution, she was released.

Having suffered only another year for the crime of helping a sick aunt, Iva Toguri struggled vainly to return home to her father and brother and sisters. In October 1947, the Department of Justice finally approved issuance of a U.S. passport to her. But the emotions of war flamed anew. The Los Angeles City Council passed a resolution opposing her return there. Walter Winchell, the famous radio commentator and columnist, in a sick display of journalistic demagoguery began to taunt the government for its failure to prosecute her. Another journalist who had earlier obtained a contract for her story, thus contributing to the false notion there was a Tokyo Rose, announced he had handed Attorney General Clark a "signed confession" to her treasonous acts.

By the summer of 1948, as Iva Toguri was still seeking permission to return to her family, an American presidential campaign was heating up. On August 16, 1948, over virtually uniform recommendations from investigators who found no evidence of crime and prosecutors who saw no case against her, Attorney General Clark ordered the arrest of Tokyo Rose. This was the decisive act in a long course of wrongful and sometimes criminal conduct that led to Iva Toguri's conviction for treason. There was no basis in law or fact for the charges brought against her.

In a desperate effort to develop evidence of guilt, investigators threatened witnesses until they perjured themselves. Exculpation evidence was destroyed. Witnesses and evidence favorable to the defense was not permitted to be brought from Japan. Statements she made there which would benefit her defense were classified secret and she was denied copies. At least one witness committed perjury before the grand jury. An important witness brought to the U.S. by the prosecution was spirited out of the country when he insisted on testifying to the truth.

FBI witness statements reveal that two persons interviewed separately provided identical testimony, over 2,000 words in length, an impossibility. To assure the constitutional two witness standard would be met, a witness was compelled to say he was present at all times testified about by another witness.

A reluctant grand jury insisted that a POW who supervised Iva be presented for indictment and was assured he would be. But evidence of POW's writing her script, and directing her programs or participating in propaganda activity was never presented to a grand jury. Still two grand jurors voted against Iva Toguri's indictment, highly unusual in a system where prosecutors boast they can secure the indictment of a "ham sandwich."

When Iva was brought to San Francisco to stand trial, the FBI tried to interview her on arrival, knowing legal counsel retained by her father was waiting to see her. They wanted one last chance to trick her into incriminating statements. Earlier the FBI tried to destroy a defense of coercion by getting her to admit no one held a gun to her head when she broadcast, an image she took literally.

Howe's passion for justice became so inflamed, he urged, ". . . every child should be taught at school: do not answer questions from an FBI agent, even a friendly one, without an attorney present." It is an obvious civics lesson from the sad history he is relating, but no encouragement to those who would like to be able to love their country and still love justice.

Repeated bail applications were denied though there was no evidence Iva would flee if released.

The defense was denied subpoena power and expenses for witnesses needed from Japan while the government brought nineteen witnesses from there. When defense witnesses were made known to the government, the FBI interviewed them, discouraging some from testifying and causing some to change their testimony. Her husband was harassed mercilessly on his one visit to the U.S. to be at her trial. The harassment succeeded in causing their permanent separation, in part by denying him reentry rights.

When trial time came, an all white jury was chosen in two hours despite the extensive prejudicial publicity. Iva herself was grilled for eight days on the witness stand. Still, on the first ballot ten jurors and, on the second, eleven voted for acquittal. After nearly eighty hours of deliberation an exhausted jury compromised, acquitting her on seven and convicting her of one of the eight counts in the indictment. The press covering the most expensive federal trial up to that time was surprised, believing acquittal was nearly certain. The foreman and doubtless other jurors long regretted their decision. As her chief defense counsel said, it was "guilt without proof."

A terribly biased judge who gave an instruction that made acquittal difficult sentenced Iva to 10 years of imprisonment and a $10,000 fine.

Her father, who met the ship that brought his daughter home to face treason charges, attended her with perfect faith. He brought food, sat through the trial, even paid her fine by a provision in his will. This was a proud U.S. citizen whose wife died in an American concentration camp in 1942.

In all, Iva spent nearly 8½ years in prison. On release she said, "I am going into darkness." A business woman in Chicago now, she recently observed to the author, "There are those who think I started the war."

The defense lawyers were heroic. Wayne Collins, Theodore Tamba and George Olshausen served without pay in an extremely unpopular case. Lead counsel Wayne Collins had also defended Fred Korematsu in a famous constitutional decision. They struggled valiantly, imaginatively and effectively. One can only guess at the toll the verdict took on lawyers who believed so passionately in truth, justice and freedom.

Some years later, first in November 1968, Wayne Collins' son sought a Presidential pardon for Iva Toguri. This writer, Attorney General at the time, has no recollection of hearing about the petition. On January 18, 1977, some months after a courageous *Chicago Tribune* reporter, Richard Yates, wrote that the FBI had coerced perjured testimony, President Gerald Ford, on the recommendation of Attorney General Edward H. Levi, granted Iva Toguri a pardon. It was the first time in our history that a person convicted of treason was pardoned. Her contributions to the country she chose have never been acknowledged by tribute or compensation, however. They should be.

The proceedings against Iva Toguri, in addition to reflecting racist and wartime hatred, bearing false witness and creating a crime of innocent speech, thoroughly trashed the Constitution of the United States.

The hope that nationalist passions could be controlled by constitutional limitations on treason charges were dashed in a case involving popular music, "chit chat" and "small talk" further protected by the First Amendment. A person accused of crime was illegally detained and denied the Sixth Amendment right to counsel for over a year while in custody. The Eighth Amendment right to reasonable bail was ignored. The right to a speedy trial was flaunted for four years. Evidence was destroyed, perjured testimony introduced, the right to compulsory process for defense witnesses was rejected, due process of law was scorned.

The press which shared responsibility for her indictment failed miserably at even informing the public that the Office of War Information had said before Japan surrendered:

There is no Tokyo Rose; the name is strictly a GI invention. . . . Government monitors listening in twenty-four hours a day have never heard the words Tokyo Rose over a Japanese-controlled Far Eastern Radio.

A deadly myth survives to this day reflecting American racism, indifference to truth, fanatical commitment to might as right, tolerance of cruel injustice and utter contempt for freedom. We must read this story, think long about it, ask how it could happen, thank Russell Howe for his painful labors in presenting it to us, and resolve that it shall never be repeated.

Ramsey Clark
October 1989

I

Birth and Death of a Legend

1.

The Special Agent

OUTSIDE FRESNO, CALIFORNIA, the sandy, strangely flat vine-yards, quite unlike the hillside vineries of the rest of the grape-growing world, seem to stretch to infinity. Their dull green landscape, which resembles nothing so much as a sad painting by di Chirico, is broken only by the occasional citrus orchard, the rare house, the even rarer grocery store. A service road into one table-grape farm not far from Route 99 leads to a patch of high trees that hide a clapboard frame house which, as the tallness of the trees indicates, is over a century old. Here lives Fred Tillman, retired Special Agent of the FBI, the man who is proud of having arrested Baby Face Nelson, but who still reacts defensively when asked about how he later constructed the tenuous case against the young American woman who was convicted as "Tokyo Rose."

Nonetheless, he defends himself aggressively, chewing nervously on a buff cigar until one end is a sodden rag, and staring shortsightedly at his visitor like a chess-player trying to guess the next move of an adversary. Old generals in retirement are often sensitive and mellow; perhaps their consciences are pricked by the numbers of their own men they have seen killed or torn apart in the course of a career which, in the final analysis, makes no sense. If Frederick G. Tillman is anything to go by, old FBI agents have no regrets. The world might be better off if nobody had any soldiers; but things being the way they are, and people being the way they are—as General de Gaulle once said—the world will probably always need whores and cops. Yet it is obvious from his occasionally fractious demeanor that Tillman is still troubled by the Tokyo Rose affair and by its odd and tragic climax in a San Francisco courtroom in 1949.

That he should be troubled is not surprising, and it is indeed a tribute to his belated humanity; for if you probe the story and talk to Tillman's witnesses—the prosecution's witnesses—you find that it is like poking into a cankered boil. This was no ordinary investigation and no ordinary trial; it was, you find, not just another miscarriage of justice (inevitably, there are scores of these every month) so much as a disgraceful tragicomedy of ethics which reflects the power of the press to do harm as well as good, especially in such emotional areas as myth and legend, and the wartime and postwar cant that surrounds such a concept as "the enemy".

Tillman, Montana Irish but boastful of having forced the brogue from his speech, is still feisty at seventy-nine. Despite a stroke ten years before, he appears to be as healthy as he says he feels.

He has a "bad back" on the day the reporter calls, and like many people in discomfort, he prefers to stand or to walk around than to sit and fidget; yet he seems to have a need to respond to questions, however much he boxes with them, ducking and weaving. If he doesn't sense that need, why has he invited a reporter to cross the continent to question him? Surely it is to try to defend himself against future historians who may trample on his grave when they wander into the thicket of this cameo case from World War II.

Occasionally, he flashes hostile remarks like "What's your purpose?" or "You're not working for *her*, are you?" He frequently diverts the conversation into extraneous anecdotes, as might some gangster in the thirties who is trying to confuse the G-man he once was himself. The thought occurs, for a moment, that FBI agents are unused to being interrogated; but then one remembers the witness stand. At one point, he accuses the reporter of asking questions to which he knows the answers, to test if he is lying; then he grins mischievously and recalls that he has used that technique on a few rascals too.

He rebounds with a suspect anger against the notion that he coached and rehearsed his witnesses, saying that that would be illegal and that it is something which only a defense counsel would dare to do. The reporter tells Tillman that he has read his voluminous, thirty-seven-year-old investigative report, obtained under the Freedom of Information Act, a statute whose existence Tillman says is regrettable. The reporter does not tell him at first that he has found that two of the agent's Japanese witnesses are on record in the file as having given exactly the same replies to the same questions, in the same words, for over three pages, even in translation, so that one or both of these testimonies cannot possibly be genuine.

There were twenty-seven female disc jockeys on wartime Japanese radio in the Pacific; when the reporter asks Tillman if the idea of making Iva Ikuko Toguri d'Aquino the specific "Tokyo Rose" of legend was suggested to him by Lieutenant Colonel Shigetsugu Tsuneishi, who was in charge of Japanese propaganda broadcasting in English, the old G-man says weakly that he can't remember. Later, he does admit that Miss Toguri's Japanese radio colleagues had it in for her—the only Japanese-American they knew who was stranded in wartime Tokyo yet who had loyally refused to surrender her U.S. citizenship. (She had thus, ironically, made possible a charge of treason not always applicable to those with a dual loyalty.)

Tillman's lapse about his own interrogation of Colonel Tsuneishi, which is in the record, may be genuine; after all, we are talking of events four decades old; but, overall, what the former FBI agent appears to have is not so much the selective memory of most of us as a highly selective forgetfulness. Of all the anecdotes on the case which he cheerfully quotes, the majority involve remarks by Tsuneishi, for whom he expresses great respect.

What does Tsuneishi say? The gruff graduate of the Imperial Military Academy is almost the same age as Tillman; but the envelope of his Shinto soul is more worn out, and he is very deaf. Now the permanent vice president of the veterans' league branch on his island in the Inland Sea, he appears to have been an unusually cooperative witness for a career colonel faced with the bizarre demands of a kangaroo court, set up by the enemy to try one of its own. He seems to have understood the American demand: we have to sentence one, for political reasons; if we can do that, the rest can go free. Whether he ever understood why we pilloried a female subordinate, rather than her male commanders, is more dubious. Even *bushidō* Japan was more chivalrous.

A decade earlier, talking to Ronald Yates of *The Chicago Tribune,* Tsuneishi said of Iva Toguri: "She was never enthusiastic or eager about doing the Zero Hour program. I always had the impression that she was doing it just [to earn] money, not for Japan."

Tsuneishi, who was sixty-six when Yates saw him, went on: "It was meant to be demoralizing propaganda, but its main focus was entertainment. Ironically, we discovered that the show was so popular among American soldiers that it was having just the opposite effect. It was actually building the enemy's morale instead of destroying it."

In Chicago, about seven blocks west of the lake, in a quarter once predominantly "oriental" but invaded today by settlers from less well-scrubbed worlds, from cultures that are less dynamic, a tiny nisei woman of seventy runs a variety store as large as a small supermarket; it specializes in Asian goods, from Thai fish sauce to Japanese videocassettes. Her scratchy voice is almost as raspy as it was when Major Charles Cousens chose it to sabotage, as best he could, the Japanese radio program in the Pacific. Her family and marital life devastated, her hopes of motherhood ruined by enforced separation from her husband, this essentially lonely creature has come a long way from when she was the ultra-American teenybopper of 1941, sent to Japan to comfort a dying aunt in a foreign culture whose language she could not speak. She does not give trust easily. She says: "I swore once that I would never confide in a white person again." Being constrained to talk about the past only reminds her of a life destroyed, to nobody's gain, and she is not so much an enthusiastic collaborator of the writer as a dutiful citizen—the role her father taught her to play.

It was on January 18, 1977, his last full day in office, that President Gerald Ford signed a full and free pardon for the woman who had spent over eight years in prison for the minor count on which she was convicted; pronouncing a single sentence of which in fact there is no script or recorded evidence that she ever spoke, and which may never have been broadcast from Tokyo radio at all. [The jury dismissed the seven other charges.] The pardon was the belated work of the people who had let Iva Toguri down the most, in the past—the Japanese-American community.

A pardon, however, is not an acknowledgment of innocence, only forgiveness of guilt. It implies that the victim is culpable but has suffered too much, not that society owes her something for having made her suffer unjustly in the first place.

Franklin Delano Roosevelt said that December 7, 1941—December 8 in Japan—was a day that would live in infamy.

Wars—and not only wars—have produced many days of infamy, across the ages. The Japanese did more infamous things in China than they did against a purely military target that morning in Hawaii. And it was the United States which, without consulting its allies, would finally use the most infamous weapon of all time, and against a civil population. It may still be too early for most Americans to recognize that Oppenheimer and Truman were simply war criminals who won, but the next century will surely say so.

What happened to Iva Toguri was only a minor infamy: it affected only one family, and predominantly one person. But the victim is still among us, a silent reminder that it could happen again. This reporter's task was not only to find if she was in fact innocent or guilty, but ultimately to try to find the answers to more troubling questions.

Why did the United States belatedly decide that there was such a person as "Tokyo Rose," after the Office of War Information in occupied Tokyo had issued a statement accurately affirming that no such person had ever existed except in the GI imagination?

Tillman says: "You people."

"The press? Walter Winchell?" you ask.

"Winchell, and others."

If the case existed only because the press had invented it, or even if there were less dishonorable reasons for harassing Iva Toguri, why did the United States revive it two years after the attorney general had read the original investigation and decided that there was no case? Why were $700,000 of taxpayers' money, the equivalent of about $7 million today, then spent on this sidebar affair—even more than was spent on the Lindbergh kidnapping case, which led to another horrendous miscarriage of justice?

"You people," says Tillman sardonically, chewing his cigar.

If the FBI Special Agent in charge of the case believed that he was being manipulated by the press and by a prosecutor who was too far out on a limb to behave ethically, why did the United States prosecute a lowly typist and reluctant, part-time disc jockey, while absolving and promoting the delinquent officer POWs who wrote her scripts and even told her how to read them? Tillman's explanation, as the reader will see later, is frankly contradictory.

Why did the judge give her ten years after the jury had found her innocent of all except one minor count? Did he, as one respected journalist has suggested, improperly discuss the case outside of court and enter the trial with his mind made up—perhaps the gravest dereliction of duty a judge can commit?

2.

The Sandhurst Major

HE WALKED, TALL, emaciated, dignified, ragged, dirty, and unshaven, out of the unlighted fuselage of the transport plane and blinked at the flashlight which explored his face and commanded him to stop where he stood. He had been sitting or lying on the floor of the plane for two days, and now he was on a grass airfield of the sort that served most aviation until after World War II. From one constantly recurring word in the crew's conversation, which he could not otherwise understand, he knew he was at Haneda, which means Wing-place, or Airport. Today, expanded and paved, it remains the only airfield in the world to be called Airport Airport.

He was Major Charles Hughes Cousens and he had been given the rare and worrisome distinction, for a prisoner of war, of having been moved from Singapore by air. The journey had been through Japan's new imperium—Malaya, Thailand, French Indo-China, the Philippines, Hong Kong, and China— to Nagasaki and Tokyo. He had flown thousands of miles through Asia, and everywhere was now ruled by the Japanese. It would take years to reverse all those conquests, he thought, years before he could be released from captivity. He was homesick and despairing, and his situation was aggravated by dysentery.

Major Cousens was an Australian who had been the Walter

Cronkite of his country's radio in Sydney before the war. He was to become, both for better and worse, perhaps the single most determinant figure in Iva Toguri's life. A man of great bearing, even in dejection, Cousens was British-born and a graduate of Sandhurst, the ancestor of West Point. His actual birthplace was Poona, the cool hill station in India where the white memsahibs of the British raj went when they were pregnant to escape the heat and dust of the plain. It was to India, the proudest military nation in the Empire, that he had been posted after Sandhurst. But after a while he had resigned his commission there and emigrated to Australia, where he had been a sportswriter before joining the Sydney radio station 2GB, of which he became the chief announcer and finally the best-known voice of the Australian Broadcasting Corporation, the antipodean version of the BBC.

At the fall of France in 1940, with Britain poised for occupation and defeat, Cousens, like many British-born people in Australia, gave up his job and joined the Australian army, then being expanded to reinforce British troops in Asia. Now thirty-seven and the father of a family, the celebrity with the Sandhurst background at once became a captain.

Cousens had commanded an infantry battalion against the Japanese invasion of Malaya and had taken part in the jungle retreat to Singapore. Two days after his promotion to major, he had participated in that city's surrender ceremonies.

Prisoners of war are required to give only their name, rank, and serial number. When Cousens was nonetheless questioned on his prewar profession, he had said "journalist." He recounted later that he had deliberately avoided mentioning radio for fear that the Japanese were looking for people to broadcast POW messages and propaganda. However, when Australian prisoners were allowed to send messages to their families, Cousens' superior chose him to read them, noting that his easily recognizable voice would make it clear that the messages were authentic, thus relieving thousands of families from worry about their members "missing in action."

When the Japanese discovered Cousens' radio fame back home in Australia, he was ordered to Tokyo. He refused to go and was thrown into solitary confinement. When this failed to break him, he was briefly shipped north to join the labor battalions in Burma, whose tasks included the now well-known bridge on the Kwai River. He watched comrades beaten to death for minor infractions and learned the dream language of terror. Given his failing health, Cousens might well have ended his days in Burma had a fresh effort not been made by the Japanese to recruit him, this time with the support of his Australian superior officer.

Cousens was brought back to Singapore, where he watched a fellow-Australian beaten unconscious for stealing onions, and he finally agreed to do limited work; he would broadcast only POW messages to families and an appeal to the International Red Cross for food and other aid; but, as Cousens had warned his colonel would be the case, he was soon asked to do more.

It was in June 1942, four months after the fall of Singapore, that Cousens was flown to Tokyo, worriedly asking himself why he had not been packed into the hold of a ship in the normal way.

And now here he was, in the summer night, at Haneda, thirsty, hungry, diarrhetic, wanting sleep. But he was soon bustled into the back of a truck and driven to Japanese army staff headquarters. There, he was led to the office of Major Shigetsugu Tsuneishi, the head of all English-language propaganda—but who could talk to Cousens only through an interpreter.

The Australian had had dysentery since before leaving the great prison compound at Changi, and this emphasized his haggard appearance. His face and chin were covered in dirty stubble, burying the short bristle—the "toothbrush" moustache of a Sandhurst man; for fear that he would commit suicide to avoid working for the Japanese, he had been deprived of his razor. This gangling, hirsute figure in filthy uniform, stripped of all rank and other badges, found himself looking down on the small, trim, muscular Tsuneishi and the clerk who would translate for them.

At first, the Japanese officer's voice sounded terse but friendly. The interpreter spoke: "Major say he learn you famous man in Australia. Best man on radio. Very fine. He say now you write news and speak news in English on Nippon Hoso Kyokai, Japan Radio Corporation."

"Impossible, sir," Cousens said as firmly as he could. "Against my orders as an Australian officer."

The interpreter translated. Tsuneishi barked in a no-nonsense manner.

"Not impossible, major say. Not against orders *he* receive."

Cousens protested that he had agreed only to broadcast prisoners' messages and an appeal to the Red Cross. Tsuneishi said he couldn't answer for the consequences if Cousens resisted orders. Cousens asked for a revolver and a cartridge. Tsuneishi, noting inwardly that Cousens had the same rank as himself, offered the Australian his personal sword, laying it across the lacquered desk between them.

Even today, it is hard to persuade Tsuneishi to remember what his intentions were. It seems unlikely that he expected the skinny English-born officer to know how to perform *seppuku*, or to have the moral and physical strength for such an exotic task. Tsuneishi clearly had no authority to allow Cousens to commit suicide and thus avoid the duties prescribed for him, so intimidation seems to have been Tsuneishi's logical objective.

Cousens decided he would have to try to sabotage Japan's overseas radio program from within; he agreed to do as Tsuneishi asked. As a reward, he was taken to the Dai-ichi Hotel, given a room, and allowed to shave. Much was to be made later of the "luxury" in which "cooperating" officers lived, with American prosecutors and other desk-bound warriors harping on the fact that *dai-ichi* means "first." Actually, there are as many "first" hotels in Japanese cities—including several in Tokyo—as there are "first" or "premier" banks in American cities and towns. Nevertheless, his new accommodation, with clean futons on the *tatami,* was a signal improvement on the barracoons of Singapore.

The next morning, however, he was taken to the NHK studios and handed a script. It was a blatant attack on Roosevelt. Cousens protested that, as a prisoner of war, he could be made to do menial work, but that he could not be forced to participate in the war effort of his country's foes. However, the concept of a POW was foreign to the Japanese, who believed that a soldier, and even more an officer, should have taken his own life rather than allow himself to be taken captive.

Tsuneishi recalls that he was at staff headquarters when he learned of Cousens' intransigence. He came down to the radio building bearing an order in the name of the army chief of staff, General Jen Sugiyama. Under the order, Sugiyama "attached" Cousens to the NHK Overseas Broadcasting Bureau—a clear breach of the Geneva Convention. Tsuneishi called in all the senior members of the English division and explained the problem they were having with the Australian major. He announced that if Cousens remained obdurate, he, Tsuneishi, would execute him then and there. Tsuneishi was now committed and could not draw back.

Cousens was brought in, and it must have been a dramatic scene. Once more, Tsuneishi unsheathed his sword and laid it on the table from which he spoke, but this time there was no suggestion that Cousens could use it himself to satisfy his honor in the sole presence of a fellow major and an interpreter,

Tsuneishi then screamed a volley of words of warning and began hectoring Cousens at the top of the scale. In Japan, the gentry, including the officer class, was allowed to speak to others in a screech that was exclusive to them and which has no real equivalent in other cultures; even marine boot camp style at its most absurd lacks the emphasis. When the Japanese broadcaster, Akira Namikawa, who was to interpret Tsuneishi, did not raise his voice enough in English, Tsuneishi brushed him aside and chose another man, ordering him to shriek. All Japanese syllables end either in a vowel or in -*n,* and English does not lend itself to high-pitched sounds as do sonorous tongues like Japanese or Italian, especially if the English is being spoken by a foreigner. Somehow from among the Japanese interpreters, an English screamer was found who could satisfy Tsuneishi's demands. This high-C abuse of language is impressive enough to the native culture; to Westerners, it is animal and devastating. Cousens, sick and lonely, decided he had no choice but to go through with his original plan to try to sabotage the program from within. But how did one do that when one was ordered to start by reading a denunciation of Roosevelt?

He apparently succeeded, in the measure that this was possible, because the Foreign Broadcast Information Service (U.S. radio intelligence) analysis of that broadcast says that "Cousens, formerly a Sydney announcer, gives the impression that he is reading a script written for him, probably by a Japanese, as his phrasing rather resembles the style peculiar to Japanese speaking English."

The Japanese had not been entirely fooled, and Namikawa later testified that he had been angry with Cousens for his imitation of a Japanese announcer. For the next few weeks, however, Cousens took advantage of his physical state to read scripts like a man on a sickbed.

Tsuneishi noted that Cousens was demonstrating his acting ability in the way he transmitted a given personality just by a tone of voice. If Cousens remained a problem, Tsuneishi would get the blame, so the Japanese major had to think of other ways of turning the Australian major around. Namikawa was ordered to find female companionship for Cousens, but Cousens refused the offer of a trip to a nightclub. Finally, with Namikawa in trouble with Tsuneishi, Cousens did accept what he later described as a visit to a geisha house in Honmokugai, the pleasure quarter of Yokohama. There, he says he danced with a geisha (which sounds unlikely, since the activity seems too undignified for a geisha, and the girl was probably something less), then told Namikawa that he was not feeling well and wanted to go back to his hotel.

A bizarre and mannerly compromise was achieved whereby both majors, and everyone else, saved face. According to Cousens' testimony in Sydney, now in the FBI files, it was agreed that Cousens should not broadcast news, only essays on idealism, which he would write himself. For several weeks, he took advantage of the fact that one can talk almost indefinitely in English without saying anything that anyone would remember.

It is interesting to note that, despite his skills, Cousens' mellifluent voice was too "Sandhurst" for Japan's main propaganda target, the Americans. As a speaker, he could be used only on the Australians, and it was as a director, manager and coach that the Japanese wanted him the most. The strange persistence and drama involved in shanghaiing a Sydney radio announcer seems, on its face, inexplicable—except in terms of war's absurdities, and the relentless determination of a middle-echelon officer, in this case a Japanese major, to do whatever his general wanted.

Iva Toguri's connection with the NHK began on August 23, 1943, nearly two years after the start of her battle for survival in eve-of-war and wartime Tokyo, and fourteen months after Major Cousens' dramatic induction into Tokyo radio by sword. That day, Iva took up work in the business office of the English division. From then on, she would come to NHK daily after her main job at the news agency Domei Tsushin Sha. At the radio station, she would type for two or three hours in the late afternoon. She was working from hand-written English broadcasting scripts, correcting the grammar as she went along. Her salary—¥100 a month, or about ¥80 after deductions, was almost as much as the ¥110 for full-time employment at Domei.

Japan's army and navy jockeyed for control of the wartime overseas propaganda machine with each other and with Domei and NHK, as well as with various government information agencies and ministries, including the Great East Asia Ministry, a sort of prototype of Empire which managed a concept which had been given an almost Kennedyesque title: the Great East Asia Co-Prosperity Sphere. The army finally won the tussle, after losing its initial distaste for propaganda, originally seen as a shameful breach of the *bushidō* code and the chivalry of war.

Once propaganda had been made respectable, this form of warfare had been placed in the hands of Major Tsuneishi, a G-2 (intelligence) officer and military academy graduate. Like most of his colleagues in Germany and most of their counterparts in Western Europe and America, he was a total amateur on the subject, and his English was about at the level of American high-school French. Tsuneishi, who had earlier concentrated on producing leaflets to be dropped on American soldiers, and on a magazine, *Front,* inspired by *Life* and strong on American pinups, won the bureaucratic battle with the other armed services by securing an office at NHK itself.

Propaganda broadcasts, moderate in tone, had started before the war; but both then and after the fighting started, the effort had met with no success. The enemy, by definition, is a liar, and Japan found it just as difficult as every other country involved in the conflict to have even the truth believed by its adversaries. Moreover, just as Americans broadcasting in Japanese and other foreign languages mostly lacked radio experience, so the Japanese in the English-language services at Tokyo radio and the thirteen other Japanese stations soon spread across the Pacific, from Rangoon to Manila to Seoul, were equally underqualified. Most were nisei driven back to Japan by the difficulty of finding jobs in America, and possessing no particular broadcasting talents. Only the chief announcer of the English division, Yuichi Hirakawa, who had a degree in drama from the University of Washington, possessed some of the requisite skills.

The principal English-speaking women announcers on Japanese radio at the time included a husky Canadian contralto, June Yoshie Suyama, who had broadcast from the Chinese front in Japanese. According to the Japanese reporter-author, Masaya Umezawa Duus, Suyama had been known to Japanese soldiers as the "nightingale of Nanking." She was issei (first-generation) North American. Her two main colleagues were another issei, Ruth Sumi Hayakawa, who had the sort of light, pretty voice which distinguishes Japanese women from those of the rest of Asia, and Margaret Yaeko Kato, also born in Japan but raised and educated in London. Occasionally, English-speaking typists were drafted from the back office to help out. These included Katherine Kei Fujiwara, Katherine Kaora Morōka, and Miyeko Furuya, all Californian nisei, and Mary Ishii, whose father was a Japanese businessman and whose mother was English.

News items from Domei, from armed forces information bureaux, from ministries, and from German and Italian sources were grouped together, with the German and Italian material being translated into Japanese. A Japanese script was distilled from all this, then translated into the languages of propaganda, The scripts were mostly poor and peppered with grammatical faults. When nisei with fluent English tried to correct them, Japanese officials often preferred their own version. As Duus notes, all that Japanese propaganda services had going for them at the onset of the war was the fact that the victories which they were proclaiming were true. As the fortunes of war turned, the programs became even less effective, because the problems were more genuine. Tsuneishi's superior at the Eighth Division directorate, Colonel Yoshiaki Nishi, then hit on a solution which was internationally illegal. Nishi decided to seek out professional broadcasters among the hundreds of thousands of Allied prisoners of war who were currently idle and unproductive, while costing Japan the price of their food and accommodation and the wages of military guards.

On her second afternoon at Tokyo radio, Iva Toguri saw three skeletal and disheveled enemy officers arrive at the studio. They were in dusty tropical gear and wore rubber plimsolls with no socks. Two were of European stock, the other Eurasian. Ruth Hayakawa told Iva who they were. The most impressive was the senior of the three, Cousens, then thirty-nine. He was obviously sick, but the first thing that she recalls about him today is that he still had the demeanor of an officer.

Iva said she wanted to meet them, and when Ruth asked why, she said: "I feel sorry for them." Ruth warned against her expressing these sentiments openly because, she said, NHK offices were full of *kempeitai*—thought police—informers; but she agreed to help bring Iva together with the men. Iva's desire to do something for the Allied prisoners was to be a horrendous karma-turn of destiny, on top of the one that had brought her to Japan at the worst possible time.

The other two officers whom Iva Toguri was to meet over a year after they had joined the station were Captain Wallace Ellwell Ince of the U.S. Army and Third Lieutenant Normando Reyes of the Filipino Army, then a colonial affiliate of the U.S.

Army. Both had a brief background in radio and had been captured in the Philippines. It is noteworthy that, after a year in Tokyo, where conditions were obviously better than in Changi or Burma, what had attracted Iva's attention was the emaciation and wretchedness of the three men, compared to the also underfed staff of NHK, with their occasional attacks of scurvy and beri-beri.

Ince, who had used the professional name of Ted Wallace, was a former enlisted man who had rejoined the army as an officer just after Pearl Harbor. He had been a thirty-year-old information officer, broadcasting "Voice of Freedom" propaganda for the U.S. forces in the Philippines, at the time of his capture. Reyes, who was nineteen, had briefly been one of Ince's assistants on Corregidor.

Both, but especially Ince, had initially opposed the demand that they do radio work for the Japanese; but Ince had given way after being allowed out of Manila's Sant Iago prison to spend an hour with his Filipina wife, and Reyes had stopped resisting when his captain did.

The two men had been shipped to Tokyo. When faced with the same shrill blandishments from Tsuneishi that Cousens had endured, they had agreed to do as the general staff demanded. The handsome Reyes, who had a Filipino father and an American mother, and who had been "hooked" on radio work since high school, was soon a favorite with the nisei girls and seemed fairly contented in his work. Sometime after Tokyo proclaimed a puppet government in Manila, he ceased to be considered a prisoner of war and became, in effect, a second-class Japanese on the same lines as a Korean or a Taiwanese.

Ince soon had his own program, called "From One American to Another," while Reyes broadcast popular music on a show called "Life in the East." Like Cousens, they were initially lodged in the Dai-ichi and paid the allowances to which the Geneva Convention entitled them; eventually, in 1944, when their uniforms began to fall off their bones, they were supplied with civilian clothing. Cousens and Ince did not walk around town very much, but they now had freedom to do so with a Japanese interpreter. Soon, however, German and other visitors from countries friendly to Japan were complaining about the presence of the prisoners in the Dai-ichi, which the Japanese government used as a "foreigners' hotel." Tsuneishi moved them to the Sanno, which was actually a better hotel for *kempeitai* and Imperial Army officers; but they were soon moved again to a new local prisoner-of-war camp in a former girls' school, Suragadai.

Although the goodlooking Amerasian Reyes—especially when, as a Filipino, he ceased to be an "enemy"—was the most lionized by some of the girls at NHK, the two "Europeans" also attracted their share of attention. There was some sympathy for Ince, because he was known to have an Asian wife, but he had developed a Filipino distaste for all things Japanese. Cousens, the senior and the most professional of the three officers, had the charisma of a gentlemanly British film star. Thirty years later, Masaya Duus found that some of the now matronly "radio girls" could remember it. However, testimony from both sides of what later became a trial—and sometimes a contest of disloyalties—suggests that only the youthful Reyes took advantage of the situation.

As his health had improved over the year, Cousens had begun to assert himself. He artfully complained that the scripts written by the Japanese were so crippled with mistakes that he, Ince, and Reyes were wasting more time correcting them than being creative. The Japanese then conceded that all three men should write their own scripts—a great victory for Cousens. The three later testified that they used this prerogative to parody their programs, with Cousens teaching Ince and Reyes how to achieve this with subtlety. In reality, many of their double meanings probably went over the heads of the GIs who were listening in, and the sabotage was probably more important for the three prisoners' morale than for the Allied war effort. Moreover, had their subtleties become more apparent to their listeners, this might have led to a news story in the American press and to Tsuneishi getting out his long sword again. What is clear is that Cousens and his subordinates undoubtedly did ensure that the programs—as the later investigations by the Counter Intelligence Corps and the FBI showed—had virtually no value to the Japanese.

Equally obviously, however, Tsuneishi and his subordinates were not just sitting back and letting the sallow prisoners run everything. On March 1, 1943, Tsuneishi launched a new show, "Zero Hour." The title, with its suggestion to American ears of impending battle (for hearts and minds)—and which possibly also reminded listeners of Japan's best weapon, its highly maneuverable fighter plane—must have been a response to the General Staff's complaints that most of Tokyo radio's overseas programs were too vapid.

Reyes launched "Zero Hour" as a fifteen-minute program of jazz recordings, interspersing his deejay patter with news spots, mainly concerning true disasters—storms, plane crashes, forest fires, and the like—in the United States. Since U.S. armed forces radio usually left out such dispiriting news and concentrated on "happy talk," it made good sense for the Japanese to override this censorship. A *New York Times* dispatch on June 25 that year said that the GIs on Guadalcanal and in the Russell Islands liked the show and got a laugh out of the announcer (Reyes) reporting that civilian workers back home were stealing the GIs' jobs and girls. The available evidence suggests that Reyes, although as anti-Japanese as nearly all Filipinos, and as Cousens and Ince, was still very immature; he was the weak link in the chain of resistance—a point on which Japanese like fellow-announcer Ken Ishii, who was the same age, and FBI Special Agent Fred Tillman now agree. Years later, he was to be the one who most changed his testimony under threat, and helped support an artificial case against Iva Toguri.

Despite the supercilious tone of the *New York Times* report, Tsuneishi was flattered that one of his programs had created so much attention that the *Times* had chosen to write about it, and in fairly sympathetic words. He had finally pricked the skin of the enemy! "Zero Hour" was increased from fifteen to twenty minutes, then, shortly after, to forty and, later, forty-five minutes. Cousens and Ince were ordered to work on its development. So were Kenkiichi Oki and George Mitsushio, both nisei. Duus, who talked to many NHK veterans, says that Oki and Mitsushio "furnished material" and occasionally "wrote scripts themselves" but that "the three POWs [still] controlled the tone."

Reyes now deejayed exclusively jazz, and read light commentary. Ince was reading the news about catastrophes in America. Cousens relayed messages from prisoners to their families when these were incorporated for a while into "Zero Hour." As it became evident that the program was achieving a regular audience among American troops, thus giving Cousens the power to insist on his independence from his Japanese supervisors, the temptation to turn it into a private joke between Allied soldiers and Allied POWs became enormous. Because of the program's audience-creating ability, which Tsuneishi and his colleagues hoped would lure listeners to other Japanese radio programs from Tokyo and elsewhere in the Pacific, there appears to have been even more of a tendency to give Cousens his head; so that there remains a genuine question as to who was fooling whom.

Says Duus: "Some bureau staff criticized the program because it was pure entertainment and because the POWs were given so much latitude with it, but everyone recognized its quality. It was the only Radio Tokyo program [in English] that approached the standards of Allied overseas broadcasts."

In November 1943, Mitsushio was made the overall boss of "Zero Hour," and the show was expanded to sixty minutes. He was the obvious choice—a thoroughly Americanized, intelligent, capable Japanese-American who, revolted by discrimination in America, had chosen his grandfather's country over his own, and who had just that year become a Japanese national. Cousens and the other two POWs naturally objected to his appointment. They feared it would be vastly more difficult to burlesque the program if Mitsushio, a San Francisco-educated Japanese patriot with fluent English, was in charge. As Cousens later testified in court: "We protested because we had the thing, as we thought, fairly well under our control. It was comparatively useless to the Japanese." Further change might force them to think out a whole new strategy, Cousens felt.

Cousens feared an increase in staff, and more pressure to include propaganda. Handling the latter would have to be played by ear; the first he would try to control at once. He persuaded Mitsushio to let him decide on the expansion formula, including the staff expansion. His basic aim was to keep "Zero Hour" predominantly as entertainment. It was, he decided, time for a woman disc jockey, but it could not be one of those nisei who complained that the POWs had too much power: it must be someone whose loyalty to the Allies he could implicitly trust; and she had to have a voice which was unsuitable for radio and unappealing, so that if he was forced to include some propaganda in her scripts he could try to use her vocal limitations to make the information unconvincing. He had someone in mind: despite the treatment accorded to the Japanese-American community on the West Coast of the United States (she did not yet know that it had killed her mother), Iva Toguri was as loyally American as Cousens was loyally British and Australian.

Cousens knew that the best way to keep a secret is to keep it secret. Tell one more person, and the chances of it being divulged go up by one hundred percent. There was no particular need to tell Ince and Reyes at once why he wanted Iva; but both men objected to her raspy voice. Cousens responded lightly that he had his reasons for wanting that voice. Mitsushio recalls today that he thought at first that Cousens must be joking when he asked for Toguri-*san*.

"You can't use a voice like that," he remembers saying. But he gave in: Cousens was, after all, the only real radio talent the English division had.

Iva Toguri was far from convinced of the value of her choice, either. She was awed by Cousens, his style, his maturity, his avuncular concern, his professionalism in a world of American beginners and Japanese rank amateurs. She was tempted to work for Cousens but unprepared to work for anyone else. She asked him how long he could stay with Japan's overseas broadcasting services, and was reassured by his reply.

"Until we've defeated Japan," he said.

"Me too," she told him.

3.

The Stranger in Japan

IVA'S FATHER, JUN TOGURI, had come to the United States from Yamanashi prefecture in 1899, at the age of seventeen. He had arrived, fresh from high school, to establish himself, as other issei (first-generation) Japanese-Americans had done before him, in the farm fields of California.

He discovered a nation of opportunity, but one as reluctant as his own to give citizenship—or, willingly, opportunity—to people of different "race." By the age of twenty-five, when he returned to Japan for a bride, he still carried a Japanese passport; ever resourceful, however, he had managed to obtain Canadian nationality as well, thus ensuring that he could always reenter North America.

On June 8, 1907, according to the biography traced a decade ago by Masaya Umezawa Duus, he returned to Japan and married Fumi Iimuro, aged nineteen. It was, however, only six years later that he could afford to bring his wife to America, just ahead of a law prohibiting the immigration of "picture brides." In the meantime, he had paid visits to Japan, and a son had been born in 1910 and baptized in a Japanese Christian church as Fred. Neither Jun nor Fred Toguri was able to become naturalized until after the passage of the McCarran-Walter Act in 1952, when Jun was seventy. By then, his wife was dead and his daughter in prison.

The U.N. Charter, a largely American-drafted document, had stipulated that no member country should create stateless citizens; but since the issei remained Japanese, the United States had technically not broken the rule by still refusing to absorb them on racial grounds in 1945. The family's first American citizen, Iva (pronounced Aiva)—in whose case the United States did later breach the Charter—was born, appropriately enough, on the Fouth of July, 1916. Her mother gave birth in the family home at 947 Denver Avenue, in Los Angeles. Her birth certificate was signed by the midwife, Toune Ausai. Iva was entered on the family registry in Yamanashi, in accordance with custom, and she thus had dual citizenship until her father requested that her name be removed from the registry in 1932, following America's hostile reaction to Japan's first incursion into Manchuria.

Jun Toguri tried various jobs, moving in 1921 to Calexico, on the Mexican border, to grow cotton. But by then the Alien Land Law had made it illegal for noncitizens to own or lease agricultural land—an act directed against the over-industrious issei, who could not obtain citizenship. A third child, June, was born in Calexico. The next move was to San Diego, where another daughter, Inez, was born. He thus had one child, Fred, with an almost exaggeratedly English name; another, June, with an English name pronounced the same as his own; another, Inez, with a Mexican name; and an elder daughter with that most American name of all—an invented one. (She herself says, however, that it is not original. She told the author she knows of two other women of the same name.) Iva was sent to school in Calexico at the age of five, moving at seven to the Logan Street Grammar School in San Diego.

Despite the institutionalized racial rebuffs and the series of business failures, Jun Toguri obstinately still believed in the country which tolerated his presence but refused to adopt him. When he moved his family once more, back to Los Angeles in 1927, he opened a small import business that finally prospered. In 1930, the Toguris found a house in a non-Japanese area, 11630 Bandera Avenue, and Jun Toguri set about Americanizing his children further. He was now forty-eight and undeterred by the fact that all further Japanese immigration into the United States had been banned in 1924.

Fred was seventeen, Iva fourteen. They and the two younger girls were now discouraged from speaking Japanese— which, in any event, all of them except Fred had learned only pidgin fashion, to speak to their mother until she learned enough English to communicate with her family.

Iva's bitter experience later was to force Toguri to turn back to his ethnic roots, much as Arab-Americans, in recent years, have been forced to "discover" themselves, ethnically; before he died, Toguri was decorated by the Japanese government for his services to the Japanese-American community, the last thing he would have wanted two generations earlier. Iva, however, grew up in that sort of ultra-American atmosphere which is created by many immigrant parents, partly out of a need to confirm their own wisdom in emigrating, partly from a belief that total Americanization was the basic requirement for real opportunity.

The Toguri family observed Christian rites and holidays and ate a mixed Western and Japanese diet. The children's American preferences were manifest, and Iva even developed an aversion to rice. Although the family's finances now depended on selling imports from Japan, Toguri rarely attended Japanese-American events. The neighborhood in which he chose to live, Watts, was at the time one where Fred and Iva would have no choice but to make white friends, and he broke a time-honored issei custom by not sending Fred, the only son, back to Japan to finish his schooling, thus virtually forcing the youth to begin to forget his mother tongue. This was principally so as not to allow him to question his real identity as an American.

The American-born Iva had no problem fitting in with her father's all-American dream. Despite her diminutive size, she played every available school sport, and played as aggressively and undecorously as Americans, as though winning were the

29

reason for sport. She was, needless to say, a Girl Scout. In 1933, she became a zoology student at a junior college, Compton, transferring after one semester to the University of California at Los Angeles. After an appendectomy, she dropped out, helping her father at the Wilmington Avenue Market, at 11631 Wilmington Avenue, a block from their home in what is now a black slum but which was then a white working-class neighborhood. She returned to UCLA in 1936 and completed her degree in zoology. Her ambition was to enter medical school, and when she left for Japan in 1941 she gave her occupation to the Tokyo authorities as "pre-med student." She had by then registered as a Republican and had voted for Wendell Willkie in 1940.

Duus quotes an American professor who, as a graduate student, had accompanied Iva on paleontological trips, as saying she was humorous and extrovertive, "a hundred percent Yankee." He added a statement surprising enough to be significant: "I never got the feeling that there was anything Japanese in her." He was one of many who knew her and who had difficulty believing the government's later claim that she had switched sides in World War II. Later, after her arrest, she was to recall that she had "never" suffered from racial prejudice in her childhood. Although this is hard to believe—especially in California, where the work ethic of the Japanese was seen as a threat to the native American way of life—it explained how anxious Iva Toguri had been to accept America wholeheartedly, a fact which would have encouraged her to ignore racism when it appeared.

Fumi Iimuro (until recently, women in Japan did not change their names at marriage, but kept their father's patronymic) had been diagnosed as a diabetic. Her high blood pressure was inevitably worsened by childbearing. As it happened, her sister Shizuko Hattori in Japan had identical health problems, a fact that was to be the first major turning point in Iva Toguri's life.

In 1941, the family learned that Aunt Shizu was seriously ill and very much wanted to see Fumi before she died. By then, Fumi was bedridden herself, and she and her husband decided to send Iva to Tokyo in her place. Iva had had difficulty gaining admittance to a medical school and had once more been helping her father at the store. As in a Priestley time play, this natural and logical decision—to send Senior Daughter to Shizuko's bedside—was to entrain a whole karma-suite of circumstances for the family, and especially for Iva, who did not want to go to Japan and did so only out of filial obedience and charity toward her aunt.

If Aunt Shizu made it through the winter, and if he could afford it, Jun Toguri planned a visit to the old country himself the following year and, if Fumi's health was better, to take his wife. They and Iva would all travel home to California together.

In the summer of 1941, relations between Japan and the United States were deteriorating rapidly, as Washington moved closer to its ethnic cousin, London, in Britain's beleaguered conflict with Japan's friend (but not yet ally), Germany. All requests by Japanese-Americans to travel to Japan were now seen as suspect, and Jun Toguri's application for a passport for his daughter was handled extremely slowly, even by bureaucratic standards. By the time she left on July 1 on the Osaka Shipping Company vessel *Arabia Maru,* she had only a certificate of identity and instructions from the Immigration and Naturalization Service in Los Angeles to collect her passport from the American consulate general in Yokohama. She was now twenty-five—indeed, she spent that birthday in mid-Pacific.

Iva and an eighteen-year-old traveling companion whom she had been asked to look after, Chieko Ito—another nisei (second-generation) girl without a passport—were obliged to spend the night on board the ship when it arrived at Yokohama on July 24; neither girl had a visa, and getting one on arrival, and without a passport, wasn't easy. They finally disembarked the following day, with permission to remain for six months.

Apart from having neither a U.S. passport nor a Japanese visa, the reluctant visitor to Japan from Los Angeles was otherwise well provided with the wherewithal to weather an unwanted season in Japan; exotic Western gifts for relatives, from chocolates to a sewing machine; medicines for Aunt Shizu; and a massive supply of Western food provided by Jun to ensure that his all-American daughter could survive spending a year in a Japanese family. There were, for instance, impressive quantities of sugar, coffee, cocoa, jam, canned meat, and tomato paste. Since she disliked rice, she brought with her a whole steamer trunk of flour to make bread (her father had forgotten that the Japanese had virtually no ovens). She brought thread to repair her clothes, American soap, even a typewriter.

Of her twenty-eight pieces of luggage, nine were for Aunt Shizu—a typical bid by an immigrant couple in America to impress the folks back home with their success and affluence. The prosecution would later allege, however, that the huge personal cargo implied that Iva had come to Japan to stay. What was true was that, given the reluctance of Californian medical schools to accept "colored" students, she had given at least passing consideration to doing her medical studies in Tokyo, if she could master the tongue.

Her uncle, Hajime Hattori, and other relatives met her on the Yokohama quayside and took her to a local hotel for a Western meal, then to Tokyo by train. Already, except for the Western food, she felt thoroughly disculturated, bothered by all the Japanese passengers on the train stealing glances at her Western dress and talking about her in a language of which she understood only a few words. But her aunt turned out to be the spitting image of her mother, and there was a first cousin,

Rinko—Shizuko's daughter—who closely resembled Iva and was only a year younger.

Otherwise, life in Japan, with no family car, no familiar sights, and, for Iva, almost no knowledge of the Japanese language—was a shock. Her American clothes continually attracted attention, especially since she *looked* like a Japanese. She was no sooner over being stifled by Tokyo's humid summer heat than she began to fear for her survival in winter, when the limited traditional heating of the wood and paper houses would be worsened by the shortage of fuel caused by a Western oil embargo.

She was not really comfortable at 825 Unane-michi, which was in Tokyo's Setagaya ward, not far from Mr. Hattori's tailoring shop, a fairly ambitious affair with over thirty employees; but Iva had forced herself, like any foreign visitor, to learn how to squat to eat, and how to handle chopsticks, which her father had banned at home; and she was attending language school so that she could at least go shopping without taking Rinko along as an intepreter.

Duus quotes her as writing to her family: "I have finally gotten around to eating rice three times a day. It's killing me, but what can I do?" She was delighted when her uncle managed to get her rice ration card changed to one for bread. (Japan had been at war with China for nine years, off and on, and food, like fuel, was scarce.)

If the Americans were suspicious of all things Japanese, the feeling was mutual. Her letters from Tokyo arrived in California later or not at all, and the only sure way of communicating with her family was to find a traveler to take them. She advised everyone back home not to come to Japan but to "remain in the country you learn to appreciate more after you leave it. . . . Settle down and get married and plan to live and die in the country which can give you so much." Jun Toguri had specifically asked Iva to comment on the situation in the old country, and what she was saying bore out his own sacrosanct beliefs.

Writing thirty-five years later, John Leggett, director of the Writers' Workshop of the University of Iowa, had this to say in a magazine article:

> Although the Hattoris treated her as one of their own children, Iva found the diet and language strange and the customs awkward. Most of all, she missed the freedom to come and go as she pleased. Wherever she turned, there were new restraints. In a letter carried home by an acquaintance, she told of censorship and the destruction of previous letters by postal authorities, of police surveillance, of government restrictions on everything, of how different her cousins and their friends were in their humor and idea of a good time. The food was expensive, the clothing shoddy and the people discourteous. . . .
>
> "No mattter how hard life is, and how much [misfortune] you have to take," she wrote, "it is better to remain where you are and be thankful you can do as you please."

Unable to read the Japanese papers or to understand much of the news on the radio, Iva was slow in realizing how bad relations had become between Washington and Tokyo. By November, however, she was sufficiently frightened by the crisis to take the unusual and expensive step of telephoning her father to say she wanted to come home right away. Four days later, he cabled her to take a third-class passage on the *Tatsuta Maru,* which would leave Yokohama on December 2. The telegram took two days to arrive, leaving her only one day to make arrangements.

Somehow, she and her uncle got the two papers that she was told were necessary: a letter of identity (but still no passport) from the United States consulate general, and a certificate from her language school to say that she had been a student and had not been in salaried employment (this was required by the Japanese revenue service). At the last minute, however, she was also told to obtain a ministry of finance certificate confirming that she was not leaving the country with more money than she had imported. This, she was told, would take three or four days.

The *Tatsuta Maru* thus left without her, but this was to make no difference. Six days later, Japan bombed Pearl Harbor, war began, and the ship turned back.

4.

The English Typist

IVA IKUKO TOGURI HEARD the announcement of war on a radio news broadcast, but she had difficulty believing that it was true. She could understand the Japanese word *sensō,* war, but not the whole sentences. Was war being threatened? Was it just a possibility? Had it already started? The Hattoris seemed unsure, perhaps out of politeness.

"It was early in the morning," she was to recall later, "and the family was running around screaming. I didn't know what was going on."

Finally, one of her cousins said that it seemed that their respective countries were at war.

"I couldn't believe it," she says today. An uncle who lived in the house was a pacifist, as all Buddhists must logically be, "so that meant two subversives under the same roof," she adds.

The only way to get the whole truth of what had led to war was, perhaps, to buy one of Tokyo's English-language papers; but for anyone with a Japanese face to ask for this at a newsstand was a passport to problems with the *Tōkkō Keisatsu,* Japan's Gestapo. Indeed, the day after war began, a Mr. Fujiwara of the *Tōkkō Keisatsu* called on her. He questioned her about her daily routine and her sources of finance, then advised her gently to solve her problems by entering her name on the *Koseki Tōhon,* the family registry—a sort of Doomsday Book of all Japanese. She responded that she wanted to be interned as an American. Fujiwara said that since she was of Japanese descent and a female, she would probably not be dangerous; so for the time being she would not be interned. Nevertheless, visiting her twice a week, on one occasion getting her out of bed at 3:00 A.M. for an interrogation, he continued his pleas for her to become Japanese. The atmosphere had become very frightening. Now an American enemy alien in a country she had never liked, scorned all the more because her parents had gone to live in the enemy country, thus betraying their Nippon heritage, she became more and more melancholy, afraid, and lonely.

In January, the English version of the *Mainichi Shimbun* reported that the Swiss consulate general, which represented American interests after the break in relations, was seeking applications for repatriation. A ship was to carry Ambassador Joseph Grew home, and others could sail with him. Most of Grew's fellow passengers were journalists and businessmen, whom the Japanese stretched rules to repatriate with more grace than did the Germans in similar circumstances, or for that matter the Americans and the British. Iva Toguri and Chieko Ito were not accepted aboard only because the State Department delayed confirmation of their citizenship—which was never in real doubt since both women had been born in the United States.

Consular records show that Iva had applied for a passport at the U.S. consulate general on September 8. Vice Consul Frederick J. Mann had made a notation that there appeared to be no reason why the document should not be issued. She had produced her birth certificate and the State Department's certificate of identity. Mann had checked that her name had been removed from the *Koseki Tohon* and had reported that she had "renounced Japanese citizenship."

But the State Department had let her down. The ship which should have taken her home (to confinement in a concentration camp, of course) left without her. The situation was becoming daily more difficult. Her aunt and uncle were bothered about having an American living in the house, especially after she had rebuffed the security man so often when he had told her to take Japanese nationality; she had been refused renewal of her food ration card; and the money saved for her return trip was getting low. For the time being, however, she continued with Japanese-language lessons.

She has been quoted as saying that, at the time, she had about $300, over and above her fare. Since she was paying the Hattoris for her food and had daily travel and language-tuition expenses, the money needed for her liner fare would soon be spent as well. At the advent of the Tokyo winter, she sold some of her American woollens to raise cash.

Kazuya Matsuniya, the friendly director of her language school, agreed to reduce his ¥30 a month tuition fee if she would type up his latest Japanese grammar, written in English. She also got ¥5 an hour for teaching piano to the Matsuniyas' two children and to some of their friends, Duus records, but Matsuniya deducted ¥2.50 an hour for the use of his instrument.

To survive, and to preserve her return fare for when another ship would be commissioned by the Swiss authorities, she needed a real salary. By now, she could do some elementary interpreting work, but she could not translate because, although she could speak enough Japanese to be understood, she remained illiterate in the language.

The security police were still making calls. The Hattoris were becoming more and more nervous. The neighbors didn't want an "American spy" next door. Children jeered at her when she left the house. Once, she was stoned. Aunt Shizu, a very sick woman to begin with, began to reproach herself for having brought her beloved sister's daughter into this sordid political mess; as a result of her anxiety, her illness became worse. Iva herself took the decision to leave the house. "They never actually asked me to go," she says today. "In Japan, things are not said openly. But you could take a hint. It would obviously be a relief to them to get the police off their back." Now, she was entirely alone in an alien culture, with little knowledge of the language and no family to turn to.

In June 1942, she moved into a boardinghouse where a fellow tenant found her a job with the Domei Tsushin Sha, the national news agency. She would monitor English-language broadcasts from Hawaii, India, China, and Australia, and type them up in English. After a full day at language school, she went to Domei until late into the night for a wage of ¥110, or about $20 a month—¥82 after tax. This barely covered the ¥65 a month she paid to the boardinghouse.

She was reluctant to believe the Japanese reports that Japanese-Americans were being herded into internment camps. Her English-speaking radio sources in Hawaii and elsewhere carefully did not mention the matter. Only when she saw, later, on Red Cross reports, that her own family was listed as being in a camp called the Gila Bend "Relocation Center" in Arizona did she realize the extent of the tragedy. (The family had first been sent to the equally euphemistically named Tulare Assembly Center, where Iva's ailing mother had soon died.) But when the Swiss consulate general advised her in late August that another repatriation ship was to leave in September, she and Chieko Ito tried at once to get aboard. For both of them, returning home to a prison camp was better than staying in Japan.

The ship was to go via Goa. The first part of the trip would be free; but traveling to the United States from India, all across the Indian Ocean and the Atlantic on the neutral Swedish liner *Gripshölm*, was naturally more expensive than crossing the Pacific: $425 instead of $300. By then, she had gone through most of her "evacuation" money, and her family, which might have been able to raise the funds somehow, was in the desert and behind barbed wire. Her hopes of escape were gone. The Swiss consulate general listed her, slightly inaccurately, as having "renounced repatriation."

If the fact that she remained behind was later to be held against her by the United States, it also raised the suspicions of the Japanese. The *kempeitai,* or thought police, who were even more feared than the *tokkō keisatsu,* came to her room while she was out and took everything apart in search of evidence of her anti-Japanese perfidy. When she arrived home while this operation was going on, the goons said they were looking for English-language books. They, too, urged her to become a Nippon subject so that they would not be instructed to bother her again. She once more asked to be interned. The *kempeitai* officer, Toguri recalls, said that interning hostile foreigners was expensive enough already; the Japanese were not about to feed Japanese traitors at Japanese expense. There must, of course, have been another reason for Tokyo's reluctance to intern nisei: it would have made Japan's image as bad as America's on that score.

The *kempeitai* and the *tokkō keisatsu* continued to harass her. She was still deprived of a ration card. But moral support was at hand; her work at Domei had brought her into contact with another English-language monitor, a gentle draft-dodger called Felippe d'Aquino, five years younger than she, the son of a Portuguese Eurasian, Joseph d'Aquino, and a Japanese mother, Toki Susiyaka. His language skill came from his having been educated at the American Catholic mission school run by the Maryknoll Fathers in Yokohama, where all instruction was in English.

Although he spoke no Portuguese, Phil—as Iva called him—had dual citizenship, Japanese and Portuguese; and he shared her embarrassing hostility to Japan in the war. He was a pacifist, Duus notes, opposed to all military influence on the emperor and, like Iva, convinced that Japan was sure to lose the conflict. His Japanese police records, later obtained by the FBI, called him "mild and taciturn" and, despite his political views, "well-behaved."

Both monitors, Felippe and Iva, knew from their work that the enormous Japanese successes with which the Pacific war had begun had been reversed, and that the awesome weight of the American industrial machine was now avenging itself on the Japanese. The Japanese General Staff still announced victories, but Felippe and Iva knew, from the broadcasts they were paid by Japan to listen to, about the Japanese defeats at Midway and in the Solomons. In addition, unbeknownst to Iva, her passport question had been settled. On October 22, 1942, a State Department memo to the Swiss consulate general had ruled that she was entitled to a passport and to return to the United States. There is no record that the Swiss mission ever informed her at her new address.

Although surviving, Iva was ill—scurvy, beri-beri, and malnutrition. Her distaste for Japanese food meant that she ate even less than her half-starved neighbors, and she felt guilty because, without a card, she had to share the rations of her fellow boarders. Fortunately, when too sick to work for a while, she fell into the hands of a Dr. Amano, who had graduated from an American medical school and had been Ambassador Grew's physician.

Amano later told Duus: "She was definitely pro-American. She brought me the Allied news. She said before anyone else I knew that Japan would lose the war." She had, of course, no skills with which to make this judgment: it was jingoistic, all-American wishful thinking.

Six weeks in the hospital left her in debt to d'Aquino and her landlady. Since her Domei job barely covered her board and lodging expenses, and she now owed money, she had to moonlight. She answered an advertisement in *The Nippon Times*, offering part-time employment for an English typist at Tokyo radio. She got the job. It was to be another tragic turn in her karma-suite.

5.

Orphan Ann

RADIO THEN WAS WHAT television is now—the glamour medium. You could sit in a booth and talk to the world, projecting yourself onto firesides and dinner tables. Even today, radio still has a larger audience than newspapers, magazines, and television put together, but it has become something one takes for granted. During World War II, "wireless" was still a charismatic miracle. Putting a typist at a microphone with her own show was akin to putting her into the anchor slot of a TV program today. The prospect had terrified Iva Toguri.

It was sometime in mid-November 1943, she later said in numerous testimonies in the record, that stocky George Mitsushio ambled up to her in the typing pool and said an army order had been received that she was to work on a radio project being put on by the prisoners of war. That working for the prisoners might one day be held against her in America was understandably not her first concern. Mitsushio had talked of her being an announcer, and her reply, as she recalled in her trial testimony, had been: "I was taken on as a typist. I don't know the first thing about radio or radio announcing or anything about scripts or records. I don't want to be an announcer."

Mitsushio had answered: "It's not what you want. Army orders are army orders. If you want details, go and see your boss."

Her supervisor, Shigeshika Takano, had told her that he had heard of Major Tsuneishi's orders but had forgotten to pass them on when she had arrived for work. Upset with stage fright already, she had objected, but Takano had said: "You'd better not forget that you got a job at NHK even though you're a foreigner." He reminded her that the entire country was under the control of the armed forces, and added: "I don't think there's any need to tell you what will happen if you don't do it."

Later that afternoon, she had been taken to meet Cousens, and when she had told him it was a waste of time for her to take a voice test which she was sure to flunk, the sickly but still confident Australian had told her: "Don't worry about that. I chose you for a specific reason. Just go out there and take the test. It's a formality." Indeed, after a minute or two of reading a script, she was "passed."

Cousens had assured her that "Zero Hour" would be a "straight entertainment program." According to her testimony, which Cousens corroborated, he had told her: "I have written it and I know what I'm doing. All you've got to do is look upon yourself as a soldier under my orders. Do exactly what you're told. Don't try to do anything on your own, and you'll do nothing you don't want to do. You'll do nothing against your own people. I will guarantee that personally, because it's my script."

Iva had still doubted that she could do broadcasting, but already she trusted Cousens.

The job began at once. At 6:00 P.M. that day, she found herself in front of a mike, disc-jockeying her first program, playing records chosen by Cousens and reading his script.

Those who later believed that Iva Toguri somehow went from innocence to iniquity in the course of her fifteen-month, on-and-off career as a disc jockey, believe that Cousens, dragging Iva in his demented wake, became a bridge-on-the-Kwai case, determined to do professionally and well what he had risked his life to refuse to do in the first place. But everything in his own testimony and in the testimony of those with whom he worked suggests that Cousens' pride in his skills was directed toward making the program as much of a burlesque show as he could get away with. Toguri, trusting Cousens more than anyone else she had met in her two and a half years of exile from home, followed his instructions implicitly.

Predictably, the selection of the raspy-toned typist caused jealousy among the broadcasting staff, especially the other nisei girls, many of whom were furious that their fellow nisei Mitsushio had endorsed Cousens' choice. Mitsushio told Duus he recalled one of them asking him: "Why did you go and choose a peasant like Iva?" It was understandable that there should be at least curiosity that Cousens had passed over experienced announcers like June Suyama and Ruth Hayakawa—Japanese North Americans whose sympathies were not ones he trusted. Cousens still didn't confide in Reyes, who he feared might begin to change sides now that he had ceased to be seen as an enemy, a prisoner, and had officially become a "friendly alien." It was safer, he said later, not to tell the sometimes emotional and often irascible "Ted" Ince either, at least at first.

Ince and Reyes were dubious about Iva's American sympathies—as Cousens had been himself, when they had first met her, back in August—because her sentiments were so extreme. Was she a plant? John Leggett, of the University of Iowa, has quoted Cousens as saying: "She was very friendly—so much so that we were very suspicious. But by October we knew that we were on safe ground." The three officer prisoners, says Leggett, had decided that she was the "only available woman they could trust not to betray their efforts at subversion to the Japanese authorities."

In the atmosphere of suspicion that went with the predicament in which the quartet—the three officer prisoners and the female civilian exile—found itself, little could be said openly. Indeed, Cousens had told Iva only the main half of the truth of why he had chosen her, when he had assured her that she would not have to do anything "against your country." He had not told her that Ince had said she sounded "like a crow"—a judgment with which Cousens had pretended at first to disagree, although he himself was to say later that Iva's voice was "like a hacksaw."

Questioned later in the San Francisco court, and in her presence, about her voice, he was more genteel: "With the idea that I had in mind of making a complete burlesque of the program, it was just what I wanted—rough. I hope I can say this without giving offense—it was a voice that I have described as a gin-fog voice. It was rough, almost masculine, nothing of a femininely seductive voice. It was the comedy voice that I needed for this particular job."

Iva herself testified: "Major Cousens said my voice is not what you would call a sweet and gentle voice." He said he had told her that he wanted a voice that sounded like a woman army officer *ordering* her troops to be cheerful. He had told her that he would coach her to achieve this effect.

Duus quotes former staff members as having seen Cousens coach her daily, directing the delivery of almost every word, as though his script—his private war on Japan—was a work of art. He had had to slow down her delivery and make her sound more "jolly."

Cousens was too much of a gentleman to tell the frightened typist that her voice was a joke, from a radio producer's point of view; he had said only that it was "not sweet and gentle." She was aware that the other women thought her voice was bad, so she concentrated on following Cousens' elocution directions implicitly. What Cousens wanted and got was a voice that would not be so absurd as to be ordered off the air by Japanese radio supervisors, but one that was clearly not intended to be taken seriously as that of a romantic deejay by the GIs in the Pacific islands. Ince said once that it reminded him of the metallic voice of Gracie Allen.

Cousens' burlesque approach to a record show was to become popular, which pleased Tsuneishi and the army; but the American soldiers who enjoyed listening to it ran no risk of being demoralized or propagandized. In his starved and deprived state, the resourceful Cousens had managed to please his Japanese overlords while signaling derision to the audience—his fellow Allied soldiers. One easy trick was to have Iva mispronounce words or sound overly Japanese. She recalls that he would script her to call her listeners "honorable boneheads" and to pronounce the adjective "onable." He would script her to refer to herself sometimes as "your favorite enemy, Ann."

Ann? A radio personality needs a name. In her scripts, her lines were preceded by "Ann," for "announcer." So she became Ann on the air. The Australian forces, cut off from their Allies in many places, had called themselves the "orphans of the Pacific" and Cousens imagined that the GIs used the same expression; so he suggested that she signal her identification with them by varying "Ann" sometimes to "Orphan Ann." Ince then told his Aussie comrade about the American comic strip character Orphan Annie, and Cousens was delighted that "Orphan Ann" therefore had a ridiculous connotation. He scripted her to use it more.

"Zero Hour" now ran for an entire hour. The theme music with which it opened was "Strike Up The Band," played by Arthur Fiedler's Boston Pops Orchestra. It was Iva who had made this selection; it was the fight song of the football team of her alma mater, UCLA. The format varied, but initially Cousens read POW messages for five minutes, followed by the Orphan Ann sequence for twenty minutes—four seventy-eight–RPM records introduced by Iva. Then came Ince reading "American Home Front News"—all the stateside catastrophes that Domei could find. Cousens then scripted Iva to do a "wipe" of what Ince had just read by saying not just "thank you" but "thankyou thankyou thankyou . . . " about five times, so as to erase all trace of Ince's segment from the listeners' memory. Reyes then deejayed a twenty-minute jazz program called "Juke Box." Then there was five minutes of "Ted's News Highlights Tonight," written by Japanese script-writers, then edited and read by Ince. Again, Iva was scripted to do a "wipe" of this. Sometimes, there was also a commentary read by a renegade nisei, Charles Yoshii. There was a final piece of music, often military, and a sign-off by Ince.

The "Orphan Ann" segment was an eclectic mixture of light classics and dance music of the era, with many of the bands and orchestras being British. Some theorized later that this was because the Tokyo radio library had more British than American records, but it was mostly because Cousens and Iva felt sure British records would be less popular with their audience than American ones. Considering the audience, some of the choices were hilariously English—piano accordion pieces, for instance—and even possessed a pre-World War I flavor, such as Ketelbey's "In a Persian Garden."

The only parts of "Zero Hour" which involved a U.S. citizen being put at real risk for treason appear to have been Ince's two news broadcasts and Yoshii's commentary; but Yoshii had dual nationality—because he was not as loyal to America as Iva was, it was harder to accuse him of disloyalty.

On Sundays, when Cousens and Iva were both off duty, "Zero Hour" was replaced by a music program introduced by Ruth Hayakawa, and sometimes by Mary Ishii; Mary often replaced Iva on Saturdays, and for most of the final months before VJ day she shared the task of replacing her altogether with Miyeko Furuya. By then, Cousens had left the program, and some of the "Zero Hour" scripts would be written by the pro-Japanese Kenkiichi Oki (who had married Miyeko) and others.

By the time Iva met them, Cousens and Ince had been moved from their futons at the Sanno Hotel to the new Suragadai camp—called Bunka by the prisoners—in the Kanda quarter of Tokyo. This was a facility exclusively for POWs working for the Japanese government—mostly in radio. Suragadai initially had a civilian commandant, Nobuo Fujimara, but oversight was in the control of an army officer, Captain Koinai, who would "induct" each new group of arrivals with a stirring speech, warning them that he would not guarantee their survival if they disobeyed orders. By allowing themselves to be taken prisoner, instead of taking their own lives while they had had the chance, they had shown themselves to be less than men, he said, and had no right to exert opinions of their own anymore. Tsuneishi or a colleague would also give each new group a pep talk of his own, rhetorically asking if any of them were unprepared to do as they were told. When George Williams, a Briton captured in the Gilbert Islands, had raised his hand and declared that he would refuse instructions, a fellow officer of Tsuneishi's had raged and screeched impressively and ordered Williams taken away. This dramatic scene was to be narrated in testimony to the FBI and to the court, and appears later in this book; it made an indelible impression on Williams' comrades at Suragadai. The other prisoners assumed that he had been executed—as they were supposed to do. But Williams' stoic, lonely dissent had won Tsuneishi's approval; here was someone he could understand. Although sentenced to the hardships due to a "difficult" prisoner, Williams was allowed to survive the war, and later became the British Colonial Service's administrator of the Gilbert and Ellice Islands, thus returning to the scene of his capture.

The Japanese officers at Suragadai changed often; life in the camp will be described in the second part of this book, through the testimony of survivors. Cousens was the senior POW officer, and he used his rank to try to help the morale of the dispirited inmates, many of whom were soon ordered to work on radio. But since all scripts for shows other than "Zero Hour" were more strictly vetted, often by a nisei camp officer, Kazumaro (Buddy) Uno—denounced in numerous testimonies as a brutal guard—it was hard to try to emulate Cousens' sophisticated private war. (To his credit, Uno is said by some former prisoners to have obtained the transfers of two particularly vicious guards, using his role as a camp bully to impress his superiors with his pro-Japanese credentials. One of those transferred at Uno's suggestion was a lieutenant called Hamamoto who had particularly brutalized Ince.)

Normando Reyes (Norman to the others) remained established in a hotel. As a semifree man, and half Asian, Reyes was torn between two worlds. Advised by Cousens and Ince to "get everything you can out of the Japs," he asked for a raise—and saw his pay go from a "Geneva" ¥60 to a male-Japanese ¥500.

Three of the new American prisoners who were brought to Suragadai, Lieutenant Edwin Kalbfleisch, Ensign George Henshaw, and Sergeant John David Provoo, were put to work on an afternoon news program, initially called "Hinomaru Hour" and later rebaptized "Humanity Calls." Provoo, an army regular, whom Tillman scorns today as "that homosexual," had studied in a Japanese Buddhist monastery before enlisting, and in Bunka he converted to the Japanese cause. He was later convicted of treason, then acquitted on appeal, on a technicality. Kalbfleisch, who was from an old German brewing family, was refractory and emotional, and later braved execution in a similar way to George Williams.

In 1944, there was a vast growth in Japanese radio programs, directed toward both American and Australian soldiers.

With the war on the battlefield going sour, the Japanese were turning in desperation toward the least effective weapon of all for a losing side—psychological warfare. The quality of the new shows, as one might expect, was in inverse proportion to their quantity, and no doubt some of the poverty of perform- ance could be traced to the wretched prisoners' diet—mostly barley tea, radish soup and tiny rations of rice. When skinny pets from neighboring houses strayed into the Bunka com- pound, they were hastily flayed and grilled in secret.

The Japanese themselves did not live much better. Iva Toguri was to tell Rex Gunn of the Associated Press: "I some- times had nothing but water for two or three days. I was so skinny that I looked like a thirteen-year-old. I would braid my hair like a high-school girl and sneak off to the countryside to get citrus fruit for the POWs."

Several of the lower-level Japanese guards at Suragadai were also sympathetic to the plight of the prisoners and occasionally shared their own thin rations; in particular, the elderly civilian caretakers did what they could for the POWs. Most of Suraga- dai's prisoners have mixed memories of the camp. The condi- tions in all Japanese POW facilities were fairly uniformly dis- graceful, and as evidence was to show there was the usual quotient of beatings and other punishments. If the conditions were slightly less harsh than, say, at Singapore, there was a different tension at Suragadai: virtually all the prisoners were worried that, when the war was over, the well-fed civilians back home might arrest them all for treason.

In the NHK studios, the guard on the prisoners was relaxed, but they were under close scrutiny when they came to work and when they were taken back to camp. It was hard for even those members of the poorly fed radio staff who wished to do so to smuggle much to the POWs, or for the prisoners to take it away; but all the POW witnesses at Iva Toguri's trial testified that she was a frequent purveyor of contraband food and basic medicines (aspirin, yeast pills, or quinine for malaria) to Suragadai. They said she used her free Sundays to do what her colleagues did—go out of the city to buy fruit and vegetables—and that she brought some of these to Bunka. Sometimes she was accompanied to the camp by Ken Ishii, the Eurasian announcer, whose father had stocked up food against the fear of war. Ishii was working at the radio to dodge the draft. However poor the camp conditions, that the commandant often closed his eyes to the prisoners' receiving visitors is in striking contrast with most POW regimes anywhere else.

Another source of Iva's food for Suragadai was Felippe's grandmother in Atsugi, who ran a boardinghouse. Some of her pensioners were students whose farmer parents sent vegetables from their holdings. As well as to Bunka, Iva brought food to the station itself for Cousens and Ince to eat covertly on the spot, or to smuggle back to the camp themselves and share with their comrades. Once, in the freeze of March 1944, she gave her only spare blanket to a sick prisoner with a bad chill. Ince smuggled it into the camp, wrapped around his body.

Iva's radio job became more important when she was forced out of Domei in December 1943, because of her pro-Allied views. As the only nisei on the staff there who had refused to become a Japanese citizen, she had been a marked person from the start. She was to say at her trial: "For about three or four months previously to my quitting the Domei job, I had reasons for becoming involved in a lot of discussion with the other employees at Domei." She said she had expressed her belief in the "truthfulness of the news that came through the shortwave [i.e., American] reports." She had pointed out that although Japanese reports claimed ship sinkings, "they never announced the names," whereas the Americans could always name the ships they sank. She told them that America was winning the war. This in itself would have been heresy enough: what was even more unforgivable was that she obviously relished the news that brought her the promise of being able to go back home.

Her young admirer, Felippe, was in almost equal trouble. Recalling those days for a San Francisco reporter, Linda Witt of the *Chronicle,* Iva said in 1976: "The thing that drew me to Phil was that he was so anti-Japan. When we'd receive a communiqué about an Allied victory, we'd react in the same way. I couldn't share my joy with anyone until then. I couldn't trust anyone else. He was under the same police surveillance as I, and when I met him it was the first time I was able to express myself without the fear of being turned in."

After "mild and taciturn" Felippe got into a fight defending her one day, it was time for at least one of them to go. An advertisement in an English-language paper, asking for a typist at the Danish legation, made her departure less difficult. The Danish minister, Lars Pedersen Tillitse, gave her the job of being his clerk for ¥160 a month—a good salary for the limited work, especially considering her fractured Japanese. Now, except for the twenty-minute deejay program, she was no longer working for Japan at all.

Tillitse testified at her trial that she had told him and his wife that "she had had great difficulty adjusting to Japanese life. She also said repeatedly that she wanted to go back to America. . . . She was very sorry that she had been stranded in Japan. . . . She said America would win the war." From the way she spoke, "I always took it for granted that she wanted America to win the war," Tillitse said.

She had thought it wise, however, not to tell Tillitse that she was moonlighting at NHK. Likewise, her superiors, such as Oki and Mitsushio, say today that they had no idea that she had a full-time job at the Danish legation.

Ending her daily job at four o'clock, when the legation closed, she would get to the studio at about five, do her program an hour or so later, then go home. If Tillitse kept her

late, she would often arrive at the studio with barely enough
time to read through her script before going on. Mitsushio
often upbraided her about this. With her ¥160 from the Danes
and ¥100 from the radio, Iva Toguri was now quite well off,
considering the limited ways in which to spend money in Tokyo
under the blockade. Duus tells us that even the Canadian June
Suyama, regarded as the best of the women announcers, got
only ¥150 and some bonuses, although she worked at NHK
all day. Iva could now afford the little extras she bought for the
prisoners. She also got gifts from the Tillitses—luxuries like
soap and sugar—some of which she could pass on to Bunka.
Another reason she stayed on at the studio, she said later, was
Cousens; he was the "strong" figure she trusted in Tokyo, and
he was teaching her a skill which she was seriously considering
using in California after the war—radio announcing.

More news that a Tokyo radio program had found a willing
American audience came in the spring of 1944. The sketchy
report, passed to the Japanese by the neutral Swedes, referred to
a Sunday program and to GIs nicknaming a Japanese woman
disc jockey "Tokyo Rose." It was not clear to which Sunday
program they were referring. Was it the Sunday replacement
for "Zero Hour"? Was it the deejay Ruth Hayakawa or Mary
Ishii—or was it simply a program from another Japanese radio
station in the Pacific? Both Cousens and Mitsushio, the two
men most concerned with "Orphan Ann", concluded that it
was the latter, because the program described contained political elements in the woman's script, and a reading of the monu-
mental FBI investigative file and the scripts submitted at the
trial would suggest that they were right—that "Orphan Ann"
was never political. Moreover, since the deejay was described as
sexy, a plausible candidate could have been Myrtle Lipton, a
former Miss Manila who had just begun to broadcast for the

Japanese from that city. A beautiful Eurasian, she had the honeyed voice of the true romantic disc jockey.

Ruth Hayakawa was to testify later that Oki had told her that he thought "Tokyo Rose" must be she, because the report referred to a Sunday program. When Hayakawa suggested Iva Toguri as a possible candidate, despite the Sunday report, "Ken also pointed our that my voice was soft and appealing, as in the report, whereas Iva's was not." In other words, all seemed agreed that even if the voice of "Tokyo Rose" was by chance that of a female deejay on "Zero Hour," it would not be Iva Toguri but one of her replacements. At the trial, however, Oki, under threat of a treason trial himself if he did not cooperate with the prosecution, contradicted Miss Hayakawa's deposition and said he had identified "Tokyo Rose" as being "Orphan Ann". When the present writer interviewed Oki shortly before his death in 1987, he found him the most reluctant to talk of all of Iva's surviving colleagues. Even FBI Special Agent Frederick Tillman was more forthcoming.

By the spring of 1944, the fact that the war was going badly for Japan was now well known to the Allied prisoners. Ince began to take heart, and got into a fight with a Suragadai camp officer, Lieutenant Hishikari, whose proudest boast was that he had once slapped General A. E. Percival, the British commander who had surrendered at Singapore. Ince was taken off "Zero Hour." Duus says rumors circulated that he would be executed, and the FBI files reveal that he himself shared those fears; but he was later restored to a POW message program, "The Postman Calls."

On "Zero Hour," Ince was replaced by Keniichi Ishii, the Anglo-Japanese whose voice so resembled Cousens' that Cousens' wife in Australia—a fervent listener to the scratchy short-wave broadcast—got them mixed. Miyeko Furuya, a new typist who later married Oki, began to replace Iva when she was more and more frequently sick or absent, and she was also sometimes a substitute for Hayakawa on Sundays. Eventually, Miss Furuya took over the Orphan Ann segment completely, but without the name.

In June, Cousens, who had been conducting his private radio war for about two years, while being the avuncular father-confessor of the sick and tormented prisoners at Suragadai, finally knuckled under to the tension, the starvation, and the frequent bouts with illness: he had a heart attack and left the program for good. Iva, who had accepted the Australian major as her commander in their obscure resistance battle against Japan, now had no heart to continue with the program. She took two weeks off in July, hoping at first that Cousens would return. The next month, she was again absent for two weeks when the Danish minister went to his summer residence at Karuizawa. As she feared, with Cousens gone, Mitsushio and Oki, the two fellow Californians who were both unquestionably pro-Japanese, and the ambivalent, malleable Reyes began to take over Cousens' program. More writers and performers, many of them American or Canadian nisei, joined "Zero Hour."

Asked today if she began staying away from NHK after Cousens fell ill because attempts were being made to turn her scripts into something less innocuous, she says that, by and large, by reusing old Cousens material, and writing her own with some assistance from Reyes, she was able to resist all attempts to politicize her broadcasts. The recordings made by the FBIS seem to bear this out.

The only persons interested in propagandizing the programs, she says, were the Japanese and the dual citizens. "Everyone else [among the Japanese-Americans] sheltered behind their Japanese citizenship," she says today. "I don't understand that at all. But I was the only one who didn't."

Iva recalls asking Mitsushio to release her from broadcasting altogether. He said that Tsuneishi would surely refuse such a request. She tried to get herself fired by asking for a raise. To her surprise, her salary jumped from ¥100 to ¥180—more than June Suyama earned. The "Orphan Ann" whom Cousens had created had become important to Tsuneishi, who—as he later testified to the FBI and in court—was hoping to hold an audience with Iva's "pure entertainment" until such time as there would be some Japanese victories to trumpet proudly on the air.

More zealous efforts to get fired were clearly needed. She took a week off at Christmas 1944, and three weeks at the end of January 1945, pleading an "ear infection." In May 1944, she had moved from Tokyo to Felippe's family house at Atsugi. The five-hour round-trip commute provided excuses for being late or absent. NHK and Tsuneishi had of course no notion that she rose at 5:00 A.M. each weekday, in order to be at the Danish legation at nine; she did not get home until 10:00 P.M., after completing the radio show.

Duus quotes colleagues as saying that during this period she would leave the studio as soon as her portion of the show was over, and would now usually play truant on Saturdays, when the Danish legation was not open. She visited Cousens in hospital and told him her problems. He advised her that if Mitsushio and Oki were pressing Reyes to politicize her scripts, she should use his old ones. She did this "as best I could," she said at her trial; Reyes, by then terrified of the FBI, and often ambiguous and contradictory in testimony, was nevertheless among witnesses who corroborated this point.

In late 1944, Mitsushio had been promoted and Oki had asumed direct responsibility for "Zero Hour," with "friendly alien" Reyes as his assistant. More and more propaganda segments were introduced but, judging from the FBIS collection, the Orphan Ann music sequence remained untouched. Iva was reading old Cousens scripts and using them to introduce new recordings. By now, with her refusal to be "political" on the program, her frequent absences, and her "favorite's" pay from Tsuneishi, she appears to have been more unpopular than ever with her colleagues. She was to say later that, after Cousens left, she did not have a single friend at the station, and that she was quite sincere in the contempt she showed for those fellow nisei who had "swallowed the Japanese line."

In November 1944, Reyes had married Katherine Morōka. The following March, Oki married Miyeko Furuya. Iva, exhausted by the long daily commuting from the house of her own faithful swain, moved back to Tokyo; but she and Felippe d'Aquino were now thinking of marriage. She took a room at the house of a relative of Chieko Ito, her fellow *Arabia Maru* victim of the procrastinations of the State Department's passport office.

In January 1945, d'Aquino had introduced Iva to his priest, Father Heinrich Dumoulin, of the Sophia University church. She had told him that she wanted to study Catholicism with a view to marrying Felippe. She was passed on to a Father Kraus, who spoke good English, since Dumoulin, an Alsatian, could have instructed her only in Japanese, German, or French. From the end of February, she went AWOL from the station, attending Catholic catechismal classes after work at the legation instead, and telling Mitsushio that American bombing raids were preventing her from coming to work.

Iva and Felippe were married on April 19, 1945, by Father Kraus, who had baptized her and given her first communion the previous day. Among the wedding guests was the Portuguese minister to Tokyo. An American raid sent them all to a shelter for a while.

She had now boldly asked to be allowed to leave her job at NHK, and in fact she did not turn up for work for over three months. Her broadcasting career had thus lasted little more than a year, broken by long absences, and had been limited to twenty minutes of air time on the days she worked. Now,

Felippe wanted a "home wife" as other Japanese men did, and since home had temporarily become, once more, exurban Atsugi, she had procured a culturally acceptable pretext for limiting her work to that of being the Danish minister's typist. This had now become her most long-lasting job and her principal single source of income during the wartime years.

During most of the last six months of the war, the Orphan Ann segment of "Zero Hour" was handled by Miyeko Furuya, but without the sobriquet or the burlesque chatter. Miyeko's husband and supervisor, Oki, testified at the "Tokyo Rose" trial that his wife stopped working at the station in September 1944, "in preparation for our wedding"; but the wedding took place six months later, and the attendance records at NHK, checked by Masaya Duus, show that she was there until May 23, 1945. In 1986, Oki would neither confirm nor deny to this writer that the records were true; it would seem that Miyeko left only when Iva came back, briefly, at the end of the war, and that, on this, as on other matters, Oki perjured himself in San Francisco. Duus quotes staff members as saying that Miyeko's scripts were thick with propaganda, some of it written by her husband. When Miyeko was absent, with Iva still away, the stand-in was Mary Ishii, whose accent was unmistakably English—okay for the Australians, but not for the GIs.

When Tsuneishi sent messengers to persuade Toguri-*san* to return, it was improbable that she could have resisted a direct army order. In any event, however, in May, with Miyeko resigning and NHK needing Iva urgently, Denmark (which had been at war with Germany but not with Japan) broke relations with Tokyo. The Tillitses returned home, and Iva was out of a job. She went back to "Zero Hour" for approximately six weeks, until near the end of the war, but still took time off whenever there was an American bombing raid—several days each week. As defeat approached, she deserted the station completely again; but this time, she said later, it was because she had been warned by Oki and Reyes that out-and-out loyalists at the studio might now wreak revenge on the pro-American announcer before the American troops marched into Tokyo.

On August 15, the Japanese people heard their emperor's voice for the first time, on radio—his surrender speech. Listening, Iva and Felippe held hands and wept with joy, even though Felippe, like most of his fellow citizens, could not completely understand all of the emperor's classical Japanese. When the speech was over, they collapsed in a welter of tears and giggles of relief. They had been vindicated! He, a skinny, timid Eurasian youth, had challenged the veracity of the Japanese information machine and the threats of the *kempeitai*, the thought police. She, an enemy alien, had refused to copy the other nisei and take Japanese nationality; she too had scorned the imperial propaganda, she had worked for the POWs—her people—and now in their new home, a room in northern Tokyo, Iva and Felippe had finally won. She had no doubt that, in a few weeks' time, she would be introducing her husband to her family in America.

6.

"I Think She'll Do"

ALMOST ALL AMERICAN reporters arriving in Japan at the end of August 1945 had orders from their editors to try to interview Emperor Hirohito, Prime Minister Tojo, and General Douglas MacArthur. The first was impossible, the second nearly so, and the third only slightly less difficult. Fourth-best for many newshounds was "Tokyo Rose". Her story was sexy and human; and since she did not exist (although of course most reporters did not know this when they arrived) all that was needed was to find some woman broadcaster who was prepared to fit the image.

Among those on the search were two employees of the Hearst empire, Clark Lee of International News Service and Harry Brundidge of *Cosmopolitan* magazine. In the event, they became the first to identify Iva Toguri in print as Tokyo Rose. Both had reported from Japan before the war, in the dilatory style of the day, and Lee had contacts of sorts in the city, one of whom could surely find a woman who would accept to match the legend.

Lee later told the court that he had first heard the GI nickname "Tokyo Rose" on Bataan in April 1942, a year and a half before Iva Toguri's brief relationship with radio began. This makes much of his other testimony questionable, to say the least. Most of the people quoted by Tillman and others in the FBI also place "Tokyo Rose" as someone who was on the air well before Toguri's first broadcast in November 1943. Mae Hagedorn, a radio ham, told the court that she had noted the name "Tokyo Rose" in her log for the first time on July 25, 1943.

Since the name was clearly given to more than one (or two, or ten) women broadcasters, "Tokyo Rose" had taken on the dimension of myth. Like the false legend of Mata Hari (who at least was a single, identifiable person), "Tokyo Rose" was a fount of Allied secrets and an irresistible sex object, with the exception that in "Rose's" case the seduction was by voice alone, and the deluded soldiers never saw or touched her erotic form. GIs would testify as to what she said in broadcasts that were never made—broadcasts which, nevertheless, were said to have decided the outcome of battles. She was the mermaid of World War II, luring those who listened to her song (even if it was Victor Sylvester playing) to certain destruction on the Pacific rocks. When she was not teasing and alluring, she could be downright evil, like the image of Vietnam's Madame Nhu designed by *The New York Times'* David Halberstam. (At least there was some substance there.)

Amusingly, it was the sedate *Times,* which had given Normando Reyes brief fame in 1942, that appears to have created the "Rose" legend in print, but without discovering who had been the inventor of the *nom de théâtre.* (No one, not even a signal corpsman, has ever claimed to have said it first.) The paper had reported, once more, in March 1944, that some Japanese Pacific radio programs were favorites with American soldiers, and that two of the most popular entertainers were "Madame Tojo," who could be heard all over the Pacific, and "Tokyo Rose," who could—the *Times* informed its readers—be picked up only in Alaska and the Aleutians, and who was therefore presumably broadcasting from Manchuria, which the Japanese occupants called Manchukuo. The mess into which the FBI stumbled, when Tillman and others interviewed literally hundreds of former GI fans or critics of Tokyo Rose, was made considerably more absurd by the fact that nearly all the GIs could not distinguish between Japanese voices. Worse, they could not differentiate between Japanese and other Asian women's accents, even though a Japanese sounds about as much like a Filipina as a Swiss sounds like a Sicilian.

To be sure, not everyone was a victim of Rose-mania or insensitive to its absurdities. The U.S. Navy, on August 7, 1945, issued a citation to Tokyo Rose, in her round-the-clock, round-the-ocean multiplicity of voices, for her morale-building efforts. The citation said that "Tokyo Rose, ever solicitous of [U.S. armed forces] morale, has persistently entertained them during those long nights in fox-holes and on board ship, by bringing them excellent States-side music, laughter and news about home. These broadcasts . . . have inspired them to a greater determination than ever to get the war over quickly . . . so that soon they will be able to thank Tokyo Rose in person."

The Office of War Information had already done an investigation of the phenomenon, and shortly before the Japanese surrender had come to a conclusion. The OWI said:

> There is no Tokyo Rose; the name is strictly a GI invention. The name has been applied to at least two lilting Japanese voices on the Japanese radio. . . . Government monitors listening in twenty-four hours a day have never heard the words Tokyo Rose over a Japanese-controlled Far Eastern radio.

The reference to "at least two" is conservative, and the mention of "lilting voices" rules out Iva Toguri. On September 1, American papers carried an Associated Press story about the "frustration" of U.S. troops in Japan at finding that Tokyo Rose was a figment of their own imaginations and did not exist. There, the story should have ended.

Unfortunately, some less serious reporters than AP's man were still searching, fired by learning that Japanese radio staff had themselves, in 1944, wondered which of them was the "Tokyo Rose" mentioned in the Swedish reports. Asako Satō, a nisei working for Domei, was quoted as telling some correspondents that if "Rose" was an announcer on Tokyo radio, she was probably June Suyama, Ruth Hayakawa, or Iva Toguri.

The two Hearst reporters, Lee and Brundidge, went after the Tokyo Rose story only when they were at a loose end, Lee said later. Driving an elderly Plymouth which they had bought in Tokyo, Lee took Brundidge to Domei to meet Leslie Nakashima, a Hawaiian nisei who had been on the staff of United Press in Tokyo when war had trapped him there.

Nakashima had no idea who the GIs' Tokyo Rose could be, but he took the Americans to the Overseas Broadcasting Bureau of NHK. No one there could identify Tokyo Rose, so the reporters promised Nakashima $500 if he could find her. That was ¥3,750 and would be the equivalent, in purchasing terms, of at least $5,000 today. Making the offer to Nakashima was hardly resourceful investigative reporting, but the Hearst duo presumably felt that it was almost sure to produce results, even if Nakashima had to share the windfall with some Japanese radio starlet who would volunteer for the role.

Nakashima went back to NHK the following day and spoke to Oki, who was evasive. Oki had, according to Ruth Hayakawa, identified Hayakawa as Tokyo Rose earlier; but now he had to worry that his pretty bride Miyeko was an equally plausible candidate. He finally suggested to Nakashima one name—that of the outsider on the staff, Iva Toguri. Nakashima called Lee with the news. According to Nakashima's testimony, Lee told the Japanese-American reporter that if he could trace where Iva Toguri lived, Hearst would pay her $2,000 for an exclusive interview. This was the equivalent of more than

$20,000 now—or over seven years' salary for the Danish minister's nisei typist. Lee testified later that it was Brundidge, not he, who had offered the sum, for an interview with *Cosmopolitan,* but it seems to have been agreed that both INS and the magazine would share the precious discussion; in the event, it was to be Lee who did the questioning.

With no other probable "scoop" in view, Lee decided to concentrate on the "Rose" story. On the strength of the off-the-cuff suggestion by Oki—whom neither Lee nor Brundidge had ever seen—Lee cabled a dispatch to INS identifying Iva Toguri d'Aquino (also sight unseen) as "Tokyo Rose," and describing her as Los Angeles–born. *The Los Angeles Examiner* traced the name and even came up with her severe UCLA graduation photograph, in which she looked nothing at all like the sultry siren of GI legend.

Nakashima called on the d'Aquinos and urged Iva to do the interview, saying its exclusivity would save her from being bothered by other reporters. She protested, he recalled later, that she wasn't Tokyo Rose, only one of dozens of announcers. But the $2,000 was tempting, and Felippe said that if it would keep the other reporters away, it was worth accepting. Both d'Aquinos agreed to meet Lee and Brundidge at the Imperial Hotel.

The two journalists were disappointed. Iva was twenty-nine but looked like an innocent schoolgirl, just over five feet tall, her hair in braids. She was physically unattractive, with a determined jaw and a rather unfeminine, tomboy style. So this was the Lorelei of Tokyo Bay?

Lee, who frequently contradicted himself, actually said at the trial that she had identified herself as the "one and only Tokyo Rose" from the start; but she and her husband and Nakashima all agreed that she had pointed out right away that there were several "girl" announcers on Tokyo radio, and that

she was only one of them. Iva, however, remembered Lee
saying: "I think she'll do."

The tall American reporters, wearing officers' uniforms
and pistols, as was the style for U.S. correspondents in World
War II, closed the bedroom door. Two army photographers
moonlighting for Hearst took a couple of quick pictures of Iva.
Lee got out his portable typewriter, doing the interview straight
on to the machine, while Brundidge, swilling bourbon, listened
fitfully. But first, Brundidge gave her a contract to approve; she
made the foolish mistake of signing it and identifying herself as
the "original" Rose. As Tillman says today, even though it
destroys his case against her, she acted from "greed," not truth.
Brundidge's document said:

> Tokyo, Japan
> September first, 1945
> This contract, entered into at the Imperial Hotel, in
> Tokyo, Japan, on the above date, between Cosmopol-
> itan Magazine, party of the first part, and Iva Ikuko
> Toguri, known as "Tokyo Rose," the party of the
> second part, sets forth and agrees [sic] to the following:
> That Iva Ikuko is the one and original "Tokyo
> Rose" who broadcasted [sic] from Radio Tokyo;
> That she had no feminine assistants or substitutes;
> That the story she had [sic] related for publication
> is to be exclusive for first publication in Cosmopoli-
> tan, with subsequent syndicate rights for King Fea-
> tures of International News Service, is her own true
> story, told for the first time, and not to be repeated to
> anyone for publication.
> Cosmopolitan Magazine, represented by Harry
> T. Brundidge, agrees to pay Iva Ikuko [sic] $2,000
> (American dollars) for the above described rights. It is

also agreed and understood that any additional monies which might accrue from motion picture rights, publication by Reader's Digest, or any other source, shall be turned over to Iva Ikuko Toguri.

Apart from the pidgin elements—such as the contract itself, rather than the contracting parties, "agreeing" to something—the document also contains contradictions. If *Cosmopolitan* was getting only first North American serial rights, which seems to be what Brundidge was trying to say, why could her story "not . . . be repeated to anyone for publication"?

Iva signed. She did not append d'Aquino to her name, which others have since suggested as a vitiation of the document; but (as noted earlier) Japanese women, at the time, always kept their father's patronymics. Brundidge signed for Hearst. Three persons signed as witnesses: Clark Lee, below whose name appears "INS"; Leslie Nakashima, who is said to sign for "Domei"; and Felippe d'Aquino, under whose name Brundidge typed "Radio Tokyo," for which d'Aquino had never worked, and which was the American name for NHK. This semiliterate "legal document" was, however, to prove to be a large part of Mrs. d'Aquino's undoing.

She apparently felt that if *Cosmopolitan* was prepared to pay her a small fortune for an interview, Tokyo Rose must be regarded as a GI sweetheart, rather than as just a nisei who had worked for enemy radio. She herself was to say that she signed the contract on Felippe's advice, so that she could do one "exclusive" interview and then not be bothered by other reporters. But she told Sergeant Dale Kramer of *Yank* magazine shortly afterward:

I heard that newspapermen had been to the radio station and that my name had been given out as Tokyo Rose. The station people didn't get in touch with me,

'though they knew where I was, and I figured they
were trying to fix it up for me to take the rap, clearing
themselves. Then, this fellow from Domei came
around offering money. I knew I would have to give
an interview sometime, and I thought I'd get it over
with. And I figured someone was going to get the
money and I might as well be her [sic].

In addition to this all-American reasoning, Iva may well have
thought, at the time, that there were enough bloopers in
Brundidge's contract to invalidate its more serious implica-
tions—that she had no "substitutes" on her program, for
instance. Brundidge had originally wanted her to agree to be
the "one and only" Rose. When she had said this clearly wasn't
so, he persuaded her to agree that she was the "original,"
presumably because she (and perhaps Brundidge) did not know
at the time that the legend had begun in 1942. What had
emerged had been the Brundidgism "one and original." Felippe
d'Aquino signing for "Radio Tokyo," where he had never been
employed, was surely meant only to satisfy the crazy American
reporters so that the d'Aquinos and Nakashima could take their
money and run. It was a competition in false pretenses between
the d'Aquinos and the reporters or, as Graham Greene would
say, "when Greek meets Greek." As virtually everyone who
knew the truth has repeated since, the young couple were
horribly naïve, and Iva was indeed to make a practice of signing
documents, such as reports of interrogations, after only a
cursory glance. The newly marrieds were, it is true, only
playing with a couple of hacks from a not very serious press;
but beyond that, unbeknownst to them, they were playing into
the hands of the civilian armchair generals back home in
America, a more sinister force.

Lee's interview lasted four hours and filled seventeen dou-
ble-spaced pages. Iva was to recall later that he often answered

his own questions, so that much that she would be quoted as saying came from Lee, nor from her—for instance, the "confessional" remark that she was "willing to take her medicine."

She signed the transcript "Iva Toguri, Tokyo Rose," the same way that she had been induced to sign the "contract." It was at this point, her husband said much later, that he began to get nervous, and to consider the possible consequences; but his giggling bride, convinced that Cousens' burlesque formula had so succeeded as to make Tokyo Rose the darling of the American soldiers, was on a roll. The naïve young woman would have been surprised to see the headline which appeared over Lee's interview in *The Los Angeles Examiner* the following day: "Traitor's Pay."

Because he had fixed the story in his mind in advance—the beckonsome "Rose" of legend spewing out propaganda in sultry tones—Lee had completely missed the real and much more fascinating story of survival in wartime Tokyo, and of how Iva Toguri and a captive major had conspired together to travesty a Japanese propaganda show. Finally it was to be, not a reporter, but a Broadway producer who got the "scoop" on this, as will be related in Chapter 8.

How the *Examiner,* a Hearst paper, got the interview through King Features before *Cosmopolitan,* against the terms of the Imperial Hotel arrangement, is unclear. In any event, *Cosmopolitan* chief editor Frances Whiting refused to pay the $2,000 that Brundidge had promised Iva; in a harsh telegram, she ordered him to supply an explanation of his offer. Once again, if Brundidge had got the true story, turning the Tokyo Rose legend upside down ("How Rose and the Aussie Tricked the Nips"), Whiting would probably have been happy to pay, to scoop her rivals royally.

Brundidge was saved from indignity, and from possibly having to pay the $2,000 himself, when Dale Kramer of *Yank* magazine, a U.S. armed forces publication, persuaded Iva to let him interview her also, explaining glibly that his was a government periodical and therefore not affected by any agreement she might have with a private institution like Hearst. Some writers have suggested that Brundidge put Kramer up to this, in order to inveigle her into breaking the contract, and the FBI was to conclude that this was the case. In any event, as a consequence of her scatterbrained breach of the "exclusivity" agreement which she had given Brundidge, he and Lee were able to pay her nothing at all. Although King Features had distributed the "exclusive" all over the United States, Lee also reneged on the more modest financial agreement with his "old friend" Nakashima, the latter said later.

Her interview with Kramer begins with the words "If I am Tokyo Rose, which it seems I am. . . ." The interview is a more professional job than Lee's, and at least paints a picture of someone who does not match the GI myth. An army photographer, Richard Henschel, who took the pictures for Kramer's article, recalled later that Toguri had convinced them that her role in "Zero Hour" was innocuous and that the "only untrue portions of it [Zero Hour] or the only part that could be construed as enemy propaganda were contained in the news items which were read by another announcer into the program from time to time."

Kramer, apprised of her fears of being pestered by reporters, suggested that she give a press conference and get it over with. This of course was an even greater breach of the "contract" with Hearst—which Hearst, or more specifically *Cosmopolitan,* was not prepared to honor anyway—but she agreed. It was arranged for the following day, at the Bund Hotel in Yokohama.

The d'Aquinos came to the Dai-ichi in Shimbashi, which had become the press hotel; from there, Kramer was to drive them to Yokohama. Felippe recounted in his testimony at his wife's trial that Kenkiichi Oki had arrived at the Dai-ichi while they were there and had remarked to Iva's husband: "I should have given my wife's name instead of your wife's." Oki apparently shared Iva's feeling that she was about to be promoted as the GI sweetheart of the Pacific.

Over a hundred reporters, all wearing officer's uniforms, came to the Bund for the conference, and Iva said later that she felt "no hostility at all." Several of the American and Australian reporters, when they heard her voice, wrote that she was not the broadcaster whom they had heard making questionable statements about the activities of wives and girlfriends back home, or other "political" remarks.

The New York Times quoted Iva as telling reporters that she was "one of four Tokyo Roses" and that "I didn't think I was doing anything disloyal to America." The paper noted that she had "merely announced record programs, from Bach to jive," and quoted her as saying that she had "never, never broadcast any propaganda" or "mentioned wayward wives or sweethearts." Asked who the other Tokyo Roses were, she had mentioned Ruth Hayakawa and June Suyama, the paper said, without apparently naming the other member of the quartet (Miyeko Furuya? Mary Ishii?).

After the press conference, Sergeant Merrit Page of the Counter Intelligence Corps asked the d'Aquinos to meet with Brigadier General Elliot R. Thorpe, head of Eighth Army CIC. The meeting was arranged for the following morning, with the d'Aquinos staying overnight at the Grand Hotel in Yokohama as the brigadier's guests. A military police guard was placed on the door, which was locked from the outside; but still the gullible Iva was not suspicious. It "all seemed to be a big joke," she would say later. After all, if there was no case, why worry? Like most people, she did not know that miscarriages of justice are as common as typos in the press.

The CIC had its local headquarters in the hotel. Under Brigadier General Thorpe, the other counterintelligence officers were a Lieutenant Colonel Turner, Major James T. Reitz, a Captain Pearson, a Second Lieutenant Hardesty, and Agents Charles Hettrick, Milton H. Belinkie, and John Murphy. Questioning the following day by Colonel Turner started at 8:00 A.M., but Turner soon decided that this minor case could be handed over to Sergeant Page. Page's interrogation went on until well into the afternoon. It was, however, a light and, to Iva, untroubling encounter. Officers and enlisted men continually entered the room for a glimpse of "Tokyo Rose", and Page would pause each time for snapshot shooters and autograph hunters. There was no indication that he saw his task as more than a formality, even a bit of a caper. At one point, Lieutenant General Robert Eichelberger, the Eighth Army commander, telephoned Iva and asked her to come to his office, where he had a photographer take a picture of them smiling together like old friends. Eichelberger thanked her for her music, which he said his soldiers had appreciated, and asked if she had received a package of wartime hits which he had had parachuted over the Japanese capital, addressed to Tokyo Rose. She had to point out that no one would have known where to deliver it, since the Japanese postal service did not read *The New York Times*. Later testimony revealed that the general's gift had in fact reached earth, if in less than playable condition.

At two-thirty, she was fingerprinted and released "into your husband's custody." Colonel Turner said that CIC was uncertain of her nationality. In spite of the friendly treatment so far, the implication was that if they became sure that she was American, not Portuguese, she would or could be rearrested. The army sent the d'Aquinos home to Tokyo in a jeep.

The *Times* report of September 6 on her press conference and subsequent arrest noted that it was "uncertain whether charges would be filed against her for broadcasting sweet music and sour propaganda on the enemy radio. First, it must be determined if she is still a United States citizen."

A week or so later, the question of bringing charges appeared to have been dropped; two soldiers cheerfully begged her to help them make an army instructional film about Tokyo radio during the war. Lieutenant Jack Kaduson of the Eighth Army's intelligence and education section devised the script. With him was Robert Cowan, an enlisted man and an army still photographer, who operated the 35mm camera. Much later— October 2, 1948—Cowan told FBI Special Agent Chester C. Orton that they had shot two thousand feet of sound film (about one hundred minutes). He said the date of the filming was the day after Prime Minister Tojo had tried to commit suicide (September 15). Kaduson, Cowan, and Toguri all went to the NHK studios and the soldiers filmed an interview with her there. In the prepared part of the script, she described herself as Iva Ikuko Toguri and said she was "known as Tokyo Rose." She had not, of course, seen the American press, and did not know that copy editors were still giving the sobriquet a sour and treasonous connotation.

Neither the film nor the script survives, but Cowan was to remember that, after the interview, and for the final part of the film, Iva sat before a dead microphone in the now deserted place which had once been Tsuneishi's and Mitsushio's and Oki's empire, the place where she and Cousens had fought their secret resistance war, and read one of her wartime scripts again. For the last time, with Felippe watching, she played the GIs' sweetheart.

Visiting soldiers watched the shooting and asked for autographs—as Tokyo Rose, of course. Kaduson and Cowan got her to autograph some of her original (Cousens) scripts. Afterward, Kaduson complained, as well he might, that Iva's voice did not resemble the voice or voices that had been at the heart of the Tokyo Rose legend. She and Felippe now knew, of course, that, despite Oki's tip to Nakashima, she was not the origin of the legend, if indeed any single person was.

Not to be outdone by the army, the navy also filmed an interview with Toguri around this time. In the course of the huge investigation that preceded her trial, former Ensign Vaughan Paul came forward to describe how he and Lieutenant Charles Potts had conceived a plan to find Tokyo Rose, and how an unnamed Japanese man (it later turned out that it was Ken Ishii) had led them to Iva and Felippe's home. Paul and Potts, both naval photographer-officers, had been stationed on Guam and had arrived in Tokyo to shoot the surrender ceremony aboard the U.S.S. *Missouri*.

Paul, interviewed by the FBI in North Hollywood in 1949, remembered that they had in fact been a party of four: himself, Charles Potts, and two enlisted men called Thomas and Hunter, who were also both photographers.

Paul recalled telling Iva that he did not want to show her in either a favorable or unfavorable light, but mostly to give a face and a body to the legend they had heard on shipboard radio. She agreed. They had used, he said later, "no force or duress."

Initially, they wanted to stage an introductory vignette involving an American sailor, a Japanese policeman, and Iva. The sailor would ask directions to somewhere of the policeman, who would have difficulty understanding the sailor's colloquial English. A passing Japanese American woman would stop to help; this would be Iva. This would lead to a flashback to her wartime experiences.

All the actors were wooden and the scene "didn't work," Paul recalled. The light became poor, and before it got worse, Paul and Potts decided that they would simply film an interview with Iva in the street. Paul said he told her what biographic and other questions he would ask, and there was a brief rehearsal.

Then the short interview was shot three times, from different camera positions.

Iva then posed for snaps with each of the officers and men, and signed the back of Paul's navy identification card, which already bore the signatures of officers who had been present at the *Missouri* surrender ceremony. She signed, as requested, "Iva I. Toguri," with "Tokyo Rose" beneath the words, then her name in Japanese ideographs.

Shortly after, and also in Los Angeles, Special Agent Gary W. Sawtelle interviewed Potts, who said they had started their search at Tokyo radio that day and had found that none of the English-speaking staff had any idea who Tokyo Rose could be.

They had given up their project and had been driving around "the northern area of Tokyo," Potts said, when they had stopped to ask directions of a man because he appeared to be Eurasian and they thought that he might speak some English. By coincidence, according to Potts, it was Ishii, who claimed that he knew who Tokyo Rose was and said he would try to set up an appointment with her later in the week. Two days later, he had guided them to the d'Aquino dwelling and had gone in alone to persuade Iva and Felippe to come out. (In those days, most Americans in Japan had not learned to remove their shoes when entering homes, so it was less damaging to the floor mats to talk to them in the street.)

Potts remembered the filmed interview as having been in a very friendly tone, with Iva explaining how she had been trapped in wartime Tokyo, and recounting her problems with finding work to support herself. Potts also got an autograph identical to the one she had given to Paul and the others, although in the interview she had identified herself not as Tokyo Rose but as Orphan Ann. Potts still had some photos of Iva, Felippe, Ishii, and the American party, but the film, which would have helped to disculpate her later, mysteriously disappeared during the later investigation.

Felippe, now getting all the more jittery about all this dubious publicity, advised her to stop hamming around as Tokyo Rose, and especially to cease signing autographs with that name appended. It was too late. On October 17, she was arrested at her tiny apartment by "two officers and I think it was a master sergeant," she recalled later.

Paul A. Horgan, by then of the FBI's Knoxville, Tennessee, bureau, testified much later that as a special agent of the Eightieth Metropolitan Unit of the CIC in Tokyo, he had been one of the officers. The other had been CIC Special Agent Charles Hettrick, who had been in charge of the case at the time and had interviewed Mrs. d'Aquino "more than twenty times."

On the drive to Yokohama, Horgan recalled in 1948,

She said that the first time she [had] heard herself called Tokyo Rose was when the American army entered Tokyo. She stated that she had on occasion introduced herself on some of her programs as "Little Orphan Annie." During this ride, Special Agent [John] Murphy was kidding Iva Toguri by telling her that she had not damaged the morale of the American forces and [that], in fact, the commanding officers had requisitioned more radios for the men to enable them to hear the program. She laughed and said, in effect, that . . . she didn't see how her broadcasts could have [had] any damaging effects.

She had been told to bring a toothbrush, as they might have to keep her in Yokohama overnight. In fact, she was to be held in prison for a year.

It began with the Eighth Army brig at Yokohama. Felippe was not permitted to visit for three months, and she was not allowed to consult a lawyer. Why this massive breach of law did not ensure her acquittal later, or the quashing of her conviction, is one of the many still unresolved questions in the case. At a time when the United States was proudly announcing that it was successfully imposing democracy on imperial Japan, it was ironically riding roughshod over the most basic democratic rights of an American in Tokyo itself.

The dramatic switch in policy from being photographed with the general to being held incommunicado, of going from release to arrest, was not the result of any new information. It was the result of southern Californian politics. An ambitious U.S. attorney, Charles C. Carr, who later became a judge, had held a press conference to call for Mrs. d'Aquino's arrest and trial in—where else?—Los Angeles.

In what is oddly reminiscent of the fantasy woven around Mata Hari at her trial by an unscrupulous French prosecutor, Carr was quoted in the *Examiner* as saying: "This infamous woman, born and educated here, used myriad artifices and devices to spread discontent and dissension among American troops."

The Yokohama brig became a zoo for the first few days, with soldiers—some, according to Duus, accompanied by Japanese girlfriends—coming day and night to peer into the cell where Iva Toguri was held, and preventing her from sleeping. Resistant at first, but still too intimidated by the uniforms and guns to say no for long, she began again to give autographs, only half realizing that she was reinforcing her image as the "true Tokyo Rose." Eventually, the commandant, Colonel Hardy, sympathized with her complaint and ordered that only officers of the rank of major and above could, in future, peek at the diminutive American prisoner in her cell.

Her interrogators now took a new and ugly tack, trying to associate the little typist with espionage and intelligence. She was asked what her reactions had been to American leaflet dropping and whether she had advised the Japanese government on propaganda warfare. Perhaps the most bizarre question was "Is it true that you had dinner with General Tojo [the prime minister]?" There was questioning about the "real" reason for her visit to Japan in 1941 and about her nationality. The latter was for a bureaucratic reason: whether she was a suspected Japanese war criminal or a suspected American traitor would determine her prison diet and whether she should use a mattress or a futon.

Illegally deprived of a lawyer, and similarly forbidden spousal visits, letters, or even a change of clothes, she became depressed. It was not until ten days later that a Red Cross worker managed to smuggle in a pair of her pajamas and some other personal belongings from her apartment.

The only other woman in the brig was Dr. Lili Abegg, a Swiss Japanophile accused of "war crimes" for having made German-language propaganda broadcasts. The investigation tried to establish a link between the German-speaking Abegg and the English-speaking Toguri, questioning both women to find out if Abegg had done Cousens' job—writing Iva's scripts. These, of course, were thought to be something far different from Orphan Ann's chitchat about records and "onable bone-heads." Both women were moved in November to Sugamo prison in Tokyo, used at the time almost exclusively for alleged Japanese war criminals. Still, the American authorities would not tell Mrs. d'Aquino the reason for her arrest or grant her access to a lawyer or to her husband; nor was she allowed to write to her family.

There were, however, signs that her persecutors were running out of steam. Over the next two months, she was interrogated only four times, Felippe was finally allowed in for a Christmas visit. Distraught for three months, he was appalled to discover the conditions in which his wife was living. None of the sufferings of the war years had been like this. Her tiny cell, six feet by nine, was in a block reserved for women and diplomats but did not even contain a table. Mrs. d'Aquino later told Duus that she spent her time studying Japanese and reading books of piety. She was allowed a shower only twice a week and was frightened out of her wits one day to see a bevy of men's faces pressed, childlike, against the window when she emerged from the stall: it was a gaggle of U.S. congressmen, on a junket, who had been tipped off by a guard that Tokyo Rose could be viewed in the buff at that hour.

It was in the misery of Sugamo that she learned that her mother had died in 1942. The sick woman had been unable to tolerate the forced removal from her house to a barracks, where even the toilets were not private. She had actually died in a former cavalry stable. After Fumi died, Jun, Fred, and the two remaining daughters had been shifted to a concentration camp in Arizona, the "Gila Bend Relocation Center."

Jun Toguri was relatively lucky because he was used as a camp officer and traveled the country to buy supplies. In this way, he discovered Chicago; when the victims of the hysteria were told in 1943 that they could resume their normal lives as U.S. citizens so long as they did not return to the West Coast, Jun moved his family to the lakeside city. He was sixty-two, and now forced to start life again from scratch. With Fred, he founded the Diamond Trading Company at 1012 North Clark Street, and eventually Toguri Mercantile on West Belmont, which prospered modestly and which Mrs. d'Aquino runs today.

Eventually, Felippe was allowed to visit Iva once a month— but for only twenty minutes. There were only two more interrogations. In December, Horgan and Second Lieutenant Hardesty of the CIC went to Sugamo to take Iva, Sergeant John David Provoo (a Bunka prisoner captured at Corregidor and accused of treason), and Mark Streeter (a civilian and former

POW under threat of a similar indictment) to NHK to record their voices. Streeter refused to go, and his awareness of his legal rights finally won his release on bail—and eventually his release altogether. Sergeant Provoo and Iva agreed to make recordings from scripts which they had used in the past, Horgan said in 1948. Afterward, Horgan and Hardesty took Iva and Provoo to dinner at the Hotel Kai Kosha; then, the quartet paid a last visit to Suragadai before returning to Sugamo.

On March 14, 1946, the CIC produced a report which detailed its failure to establish any grievance against Iva Toguri; but it was not until April 3 that this was sent to the Eighth Army's legal section for a decision. The legal section agreed in a memo that she had not violated the Articles of War, but they passed the buck for releasing her to the Justice Department in Washington. At this point, no one in Tokyo appears to have believed her guilty of anything, but there was a political fear of the reaction in the press and in Californian political circles if she was released, after all the hullabaloo in the media about the "capture" of Tokyo Rose. However, on April 27, G-2 (intelligence) did recommend her provisional release. The legal section had already concurred, as now did the international prosecution section; but General Eichelberger's deputy chief of staff, in a memo dated April 29, overruled the call for her liberation because "her immediate release would cause wide publicity, sure to be unfavorable." So much for bringing the rule of law to Japan!

The legal section memo of April 17 had said:

> There is no evidence, and subject denies, that she ever referred to herself, or was referred to, on the Zero Hour program, as "Tokyo Rose." There is no evidence that she ever broadcast greetings to units by name and location, or predicted military movements or attacks indicating access to secret military information and plans, etc., as the Tokyo Rose of rumor and legend is reported to have done.

Perhaps the most signficant element in this memo is that United States intelligence had once again concluded that Tokyo Rose was a creature "of rumor and legend." Shortly afterward, a report from Tokyo appeared in *The San Francisco Chronicle,* under the byline of Mark Gayn, which said:

> No charges have been preferred against her, and none ever will be if responsible officials can persuade themselves that they will not be universally condemned for releasing her.
>
> The Allied prosecutors here feel they would have a tough time making charges against her stick, because broadcasting prepared propaganda is not regarded as a war crime. If it were, hundreds of broadcasters in Tokyo would have to stand trial.

(One of the broadcasters referred to in Gayn's story was then working at Eighth Army headquarters, according to Duus.)

Gayn, who wrote for the Chicago *Sun* service, had interviewed Colonel H. I. T. Creswell, the new commander of the Eighth Army CIC, who had complained that Iva Toguri d'Aquino was in prison *because of the press.*

"We've had her in Sugamo prison for months, and now we find that we have no solid evidence against her," Gayn later, in a book, quoted him as saying. "She was just taking orders," the colonel went on. "Yet we don't dare release her, because we know that you boys will promptly jump on our necks."

Washington was in no more of a hurry than Eighth Army headquarters to release the mythical traitor-seductress simply because she was innocent. It was not until September that the file reached the desk of James M. Carter, U.S. attorney for Los Angeles, whom the Justice Department in Washington had asked for an opinion. In short, the buck for releasing the little

American prisoner had not just been passed upward; it had continent-trotted sideways as well. Carter recommended against prosecution. A week later, assistant attorney general Theron L. Caudle sent a memo to the Attorney General, Tom C. Clark, which said that "it appears that the identification of Toguri as 'Tokyo Rose' is erroneous, or, at least, that her activity consisted of doing nothing more than the announcing of music selections."

CIC in Tokyo and Justice in Washington had by then read many of her scripts, which will be cited later in this book, in connection with the subsequent FBI investigation, and it was clear that these did not correspond to those of the legendary "Rose." As a consequence, Caudle was able to continue:

> A few recording cylinders of her broadcasts and a large number of her scripts were located, and these, as well as the transcripts of the only two broadcasts which were monitored by the Federal Communications Commission, do not disclose that she did anything more than introduce musical records.
>
> In addition, it appears that "Tokyo Rose" was broadcasting prior to the date of Toguri's employment.
>
> It is my opinion that Toguri's activities, particularly in view of the innocuous nature of her broadcasts, are not sufficient to warrant her prosecution for treason. The United States Attorney at Los Angeles concurs in this opinion. I believe that the case should be closed, subject, of course, to be [sic] reopened in the event more information is received at a later date, and that the War Department should be advised we no longer desire her retention in custody.

Unaware that the CIC had found her innocent, FBI Special Agent Frederick G. Tillman, in charge of the Tokyo bureau, had begun his own investigation of Mrs. d'Aquino at the end of

April. Early in the war, Tillman told the author recently, he had written a study of the Japanese-American community for the Bureau, and he had taken advantage of being an administrative assistant to the FBI director, J. Edgar Hoover, to have himself appointed to the new Tokyo post.

Tillman, whom Mrs. d'Aquino remembers as asking questions in an arrogantly sarcastic way, later told the trial that Iva had answered him "willingly" and straightforwardly. She agrees, today, that she was indeed anxious to clear the matter up. Tillman said she spoke so articulately that he was able to take down her responses on the typewriter. She had read through his twelve pages and initialed them.

Once again, she was careless. At one point, Tillman had asked: "Did anyone hold a gun to your head? Were you beaten to make you broadcast?"

She answered in the negative.

Although FBI instructions call for agents to make an "accurate periphrasis", FBI and other police transcripts almost always deform interviews with arrested persons; unfortunately, sometimes this is done in a deceitful way. What Tillman typed down was: "I did not broadcast under duress."

She was, of course, answering Tillman's questions under duress—the frightened little prisoner confronted by the tall, tough, armed, and sarcastic G-man—although he did not hold a gun to her head or threaten to beat her. She was under duress to cooperate, or stay in jail. Tillman's misleading periphrasis implies that she had been broadcasting voluntarily. However, because she attached little importance to the questions and answers, she initialed the page along with the others. This was to cause her some difficult moments at her trial, at which she also contradicted Tillman's claim that he had asked her to point out double meanings in Cousens' and Ince's scripts, and that she had failed to do so. She said this was not true, and that he had never given her that opportunity.

Tillman told her she could expect a decision on whether she would be tried or released in about six weeks—meaning, in June. In fact, his brief probe appears to have been ignored, although he would reappear as her nemesis later. As we have seen, Tokyo's decision to release had already been made and only awaited the approval of Washington. On October 4, assistant attorney general Caudle told FBI Director Hoover, Caudle's subordinate and Tillman's superior at Justice, that there was no basis for prosecution. Two days later, the War (now Defense) Department cabled Tokyo to release the prisoner unconditionally; but MacArthur's headquarters, still nervous about adverse publicity in the press, sat on the order for an astonishing three weeks before she was finally let out on October 25.

She was freed in the evening, to try to avoid the press; but while the timorous MacArthur was prevaricating, the story of her innocence had already leaked in Washington; reporters and photographers were there at Sugamo as she emerged carrying a bouquet of flowers brought by Felippe. The couple were accompanied to their apartment by two MPs in an army jeep.

The nightmare created by some segments of the American press and by an insensitive and ambitious U.S. attorney in California (who reversed himself later), and fanned by her own foolish, rash and indiscreet behavior with reporters and autograph hunters, appeared to be over. Now, it seemed, after a year of pointless misery, on top of the agony of the war years and the death of her mother, she could at last take Felippe home to Dad and Fred and June and Inez and start life anew in Chicago.

Fred Tillman says today that he told her to "keep her big mouth shut and stop yapping about being Tokyo Rose." However, placed in an invidious situation by an unscrupulous man, and failing to seek legal or other advice, she was to make the same mistake all over again.

II

The Legend's Rebirth

7.

Why the Case Had Been Dropped

DROPPING THE CASE against Iva Toguri had been a political decision, made in Washington. The CIC report, now in the National Archives, had said on April 17: "She was stranded in Japan, tried vainly to return to the United States, had to work to survive, joined Tokyo radio, found her work there distasteful, but joined with Allied prisoners of war there to water down the propaganda content of the broadcasts."

In short, once an investigation had been conducted, her innocence was never seriously in question; it was the legend, and the hysteria it had generated, that made her release difficult. How do you explain that a witch is not a witch, and get that through to public opinion? If the nervousness displayed at MacArthur's headquarters and at the Justice Department in Washington seems unconscionable today, the subsequent revival of the case proves that the hesitations were grounded, if not in ethics, at least in political facts.

The initial investigation conducted by Major James T. Reitz and the CIC, and by Tillman and the FBI centered on those who knew what had happened—Colonel Tsuneishi, prisoners at Suragadai (usually called Bunka Camp by the inmates) and Iva's co-workers at NHK.

Tsuneishi arrived from his island, Kochi-ken, where he was now running a teahouse. Speaking through an interpreter, he said he had been called back to the capital shortly after Pearl Harbor. He described his Tokyo appointment as "general staff officer, Eighth Section, Second Bureau, General Headquarters."

The words "Second Bureau" have a ring that says "intelligence." France's *deuxième bureau* had started it, but even in most English-speaking armies the general or other senior officer who heads military intelligence is called G-2. Tsuneishi stressed that the Second Bureau was separate from the *Tokumu Kikan,* the official (civilian) Japanese intelligence agency, even though this had come under military direction in the course of a decade of war.

Japan's G-2, and Tsuneishi's overall commander, was Major General Seifuku Okamoto. It was Okamoto, Tsuneishi said, who had adopted Colonel Yoshiaki Nishi's idea to find radio professionals among the POWs. The colonel recalled how he had had Cousens flown into Tokyo in late June of 1942, and how Captain Ince and Lieutenant Reyes had arrived by ship from the Philippines about a month later. The three men, he confirmed, had initially shared a room at the Dai-ichi Hotel near Shimbashi station.

They had been reluctant to collaborate, but their physical weakness and abjection had weakened their resolve and "neither Ince nor Reyes raised as big an objection to participating in the work as Cousens did," Tsuneishi recalled.

There was some discussion about how the title "Zero Hour" was chosen, and what it meant. Tsuneishi said he had the impression that Cousens, Ince, and Reyes had chosen it between them, pointing to his own lack of English. He said he did not know how Miss Toguri was selected to join the program. There was vagueness as to whether the Imperial Japanese Army received transcripts of the broadcasts made, or translations of the scripts, or the scripts themselves. Five carbon copies were made of these, he said, for military and civilian distribution.

It was all moot, anyway, he contended, because "all documents were burned at the surrender."

Tillman remembers today being impressed with Tsuneishi's postwar adaptation to the unimaginable situation which the emperor's peace move had brought about. Instead of having to commit *seppuku,* Tsuneishi, a modern *samurai,* could retire to a seaside teahouse and could even answer questions from the enemy about his duties. He was, Tillman recalls, not afraid to use the shameful word "surrender". When Tillman spoke politely of "information services," Tsuneishi corrected him: his had been a propaganda department, he said frankly.

Tsuneishi must have found it curious and retrograde that the Americans would concentrate on a young woman under orders, rather than on Ince and the other men, especially the officers. Tillman, in his reports, quotes Tsuneishi as having said that he had "dined" Toguri on "three or four occasions," which suggests a cosy tête-à-tête between the propaganda master and his star player; in fact, what Tsuneishi actually said was that she had been among the group of NHK staffers for whom he had held a typical Japanese office dinner a few times, and that on one occasion he remembered having addressed a greeting to her, along with others. Tillman's report was a typical example of a policeman hyping a witness' or a prisoner's statement.

Tsuneishi had been pleased about the notoriety of his broadcasts, as evidenced by the American news stories, and amused by the sobriquet "Tokyo Rose". He had not, he said, read about the various Tokyo Roses who identified American units and individual officers and who accurately predicted bombing attacks. The one he had read about, in translations of the American news reports, was a sort of "GI sweetheart," so he had concluded that it must be his disc jockey, Iva. He said that because of the American reports, the name "Tokyo Rose" was good-humoredly bandied about among the NHK staff. He did not, as many others would, recall that Iva Toguri had always rejected the idea that "Rose" could be she, and he said mysteriously that he had not learned that she was an American citizen "until June 21, 1946" (meaning, just before his interview). From the report, it appears that Tillman did not press the point. How could Tsuneishi not have known her nationality—from her fractured Japanese, her "shocking" American manners and dress, her payroll records? Was he pretending that he had not knowingly suborned an enemy alien?

Izamu Yamazaki testified that on August 7, 1943, he had become the assistant head of the English division at NHK and thus the "supervisor of Zero Hour," which was directed by George Mitsushio. Yamazaki comes across as a nervous witness, claiming that the broadcasts were not checked at delivery, and that although he "saw" the program about seven times (out of several hundred broadcasts), he had never actually seen Iva Toguri.

Tillman had called in Yamazaki mainly to try to recover the station's files (Tillman says "records" but it is clear that he does not mean recordings); the FBI man concluded that the files and the station log had been destroyed—"probably burned."

Yukio Ikeda of the NHK personnel office testified at his interview that Iva was *rinji shokutaku*—a temporary employee—and that she had been carried on the rolls from August 23, 1943, to September 26, 1945.

On one point, everyone, American and Japanese, was agreed. The Japanese purpose behind "Zero Hour" had been to make listeners homesick for America. Fumi Saisho, a Japanese newspaperwoman who had joined NHK in 1935 and had stayed until the end of the war, and Sugiyama (Bucky) Harris, a Eurasian announcer who went on to a career with the Occupation forces, stressed this point in early interviews with Tillman. Saisho reported that Cousens would oppose including any news about the war in "Zero Hour," giving the Japanese the tongue-in-cheek excuse that that would "sound like propaganda." Asked, however, if she thought Ince and Reyes were "enthusiastic about the program," she is reported to have said they were. One has to wonder whether Tillman's question was not whether they were manifestly reluctant, and whether she had not simply responded "no."

The first person convoked by Tillman who faced possible problems on the same lines as Iva was George Mitsushio, who was sometimes called Nakamoto, the name of the stepfather who had raised him in California. Born on September 29, 1905, in San Francisco, and a graduate of the University of California at Berkeley, he had faced dim prospects for employment in the United States at the time and had gone to his parents' country in the 1930s. In 1938, he had joined Domei, the Japanese news agency, serving in Japan and Shanghai. He had acquired Japanese nationality by registering himself in the *Koseki Tohon* on April 2, 1943, sixteen months after Pearl Harbor. Until then, he had been registered with the Japanese police as a U.S. citizen.

Mitsushio was therefore technically guilty of treason for over a year—and since he had never renounced American nationality, his treason had probably continued all through the war. He could have argued that it was difficult to renounce his nationality at a time when relations were broken, but this is not strictly true, since the Swiss mission acted as a diplomatic mailbox to Washington. Mitsushio was clearly aware that he was vulnerable to blackmail by the FBI if he was not completely cooperative.

He said he had been with NHK since January 29, 1940, writing commentaries in English. He claimed that he had personally chosen the name "Zero Hour," because of its be-witching sound and because, for the listeners, the program time would vary from one part of the Pacific to another. He chose his answers carefully, but a reader has to make allowances for the fact that they are subsumed by Tillman, rather than quoted, and may therefore say more or less than Mitsushio intended.

Mitsushio told Tillman that he remembered Reyes arriving in Tokyo, with his background in the American "Voice of Freedom" program in the Philippines. Reyes was a "radio enthusiast who wanted to do radio work regardless of for whom," he said, and it had been easier for him to work for the Japanese after he had become a "friendly alien."

Asked how Iva Toguri had been chosen for the program, Mitsushio said Cousens had assured him that she had "the quality of voice needed." The portly nisei said he had told her that the objective of the program was to "arouse nostalgia and homesickness." Subsuming Mitsushio's responses, Tillman says she testified that "her part was languid music and chit-chat to accentuate the sentimental side of the program." Mitsushio said that, at the time, he believed that such music was banned from U.S. Army broadcasts, so it would be welcome fare to the GIs.

Tillman apparently asked whether Cousens, Ince, Reyes, and Toguri had tried to "nullify" the program. Mitsushio said he saw no indication of this, "although there were rumors." The FBI office chief sought to suggest that Cousens had curried favor with the Japanese. All Mitsushio would say was that after the major was moved from the hotel to the prison camp at Suragadai, he "could always walk around if he had a Japanese companion," and that Iva Toguri, although American, qualified as a suitable escort.

Kenkiichi Oki, who followed Mitsushio on Tillman's ros-ter, had become a Japanese subject in 1940, before Japan and the United States went to war, but it appears that he also never renounced his American citizenship; for this reason, he too was in a vulnerable position with the FBI, albeit less dangerous than Mitsushio's.

Mrs. d'Aquino today believes that both men were the victims of FBI bluffing—that the U.S. courts had accepted that any Japanese-American who registered in the *Koseki Tohon* was regarded as no longer being American, and that by choosing to be subjects of the emperor they had released themselves from allegiance to the United States. This would cover Oki's case, but not Mitsushio's. Questioned about "Meatball" Kawakita, the dual citizen who was tried and convicted, she says she thinks his was a special case that went beyond nationality, because brutality was involved.

Despite the Kawakita case, the courts do indeed seem to have taken the view that by taking foreign nationality, a person would lose both the privileges *and* the burdens of American citizenship, whether he or she wanted to, and thereby cease to be a candidate for treason in America. However, this appears to have been a racist interpretation, applied only to "orientals"; as recently as the 1970s, it was, for instance, still illegal for Americans to join the Foreign Legion, part of the armed forces of a NATO ally. Dual citizenship was finally tolerated only when thousands of Americans took Israeli passports and a few hundred actually fought in that foreign country's armed forces.

There seems, however, to be no dispute that both Mitsushio and Oki were intimidated by Tillman and others into believing that they risked being extradited from Japan to the United States by MacArthur's occupation regime, and tried for treason. Under interrogation, Oki minimized his role and kept his answers brief. His principal concern may not have been for himself but for his bride, Miyeko, who had been the "Zero Hour" disc jockey in the final months of the war; a nisei, she was an obvious candidate for prosecution as Tokyo Rose.

Oki's background was similar to Mitsushio's. He too had been born in California, although he had received his degree at

New York University. He agreed that he, Mitsushio, and the Hawaiian-born Motomu Nii were the "censors" on the "Zero Hour" program.

Ken Ishii, the teenager who had worked at the station only briefly before being conscripted, said that Iva Toguri's replacements, including his sister Mary, had never imitated the style Cousens had taught to Iva. He probably saw this as distancing Mary from the Tokyo Rose legend—but by then the main direction of the investigation was toward the content of certain broadcasts, rather than the style.

Tillman never interviewed Cousens, who was already back in Australia, where he had been through a magisterial inquiry, following which all potential charges had been withdrawn. An Australian officer, Lieutenant Colonel D. B. Goslett of the Second Australian War Crimes Section, had sent a copy of Cousens' deposition of October 25, 1945, to the CIC. This recorded his birth on August 26, 1903, in Poona, and gave his 1945 address as 3 Kirk Oswald Avenue, Mosman, Sydney. He had apparently been asked how "Zero Hour" had come about, and had said:

> About the middle of 1943, as nearly as I can remember, Norman Reyes was broadcasting a quarter-hour program, in the evening, of modern dance music. He had been ordered to do this by the Japanese, and the purpose of the program which the Japanese had in mind was to create a longing for home amongst Allied, and especially American, listeners in the Pacific. Reyes handled this quite well and, in my opinion, kept the nostalgic element down to a minimum.
>
> About this time, there was some talk in the English section at Tokyo radio about a program being broadcast by some station in the South—either Saigon, Singapore, or Batavia. I heard it said on a number

of occasions that there had been some reference to this program in American papers.

Except for Reyes' disc jockey program, Cousens said, Tokyo radio was not then broadcasting "psychologically" in English to the central Pacific.

He went on: "The only two girls speaking English from Tokyo radio were Miss Suyama and Miss Hayakawa, a *nisei* from California [who was] suspected of being a *kempei* agent in the broadcasting station. One evening, George Nakamoto, who at that time was in charge of the English section, came to the room in which Ince, Reyes, and I were working."

Nakamoto (Mitsushio) told the prisoners that "orders had come from Army headquarters to the effect that Reyes' quarter-hour program was to be expanded."

The new program would "include news," and the "general idea which the army had in mind was to break down morale of particularly American fighting men in the Pacific."

Cousens continued:

He told us that we were assigned to the job, and he apologized but said that as it was an Army order there was nothing that he, personally, could do about it. We protested that it was impossible for us to do the work, but he [insisted] that as it was an Army order there was no escape from it. We then asked if he proposed to put anybody else into the program. He said he would leave that to us. I then asked that we be left alone to discuss how best to tackle the job.

In facing this new situation, we realized that one thing was quite safe, and that was the fact that any news in the program would be under the control of Ince, and that, therefore, it could be rendered completely harmless. His methods were to give each item of news either a Japanese or a German dateline, thereby emphasizing that it was not to be believed, and then taking the news so fast that few people would even bother to try to listen. The problem then remained to defeat the Army's purpose of running a program which would make the fighting men in the Pacific homesick.

Reyes was already in the program with his quarter-hour of dance music; Ince, we agreed, would write and broadcast the news so that we retained control of that; the problem arose of a third person in the program.

None of the *nisei* who were then broadcasting were suitable, either because they were not available at that time of night [then as now, women had to be allowed to go home early] or because we could not depend upon them to sabotage the program, and not to betray what we were doing. Just prior to this incident, a new girl had come to the accounting section of the broadcasting station. She was a Californian *nisei,* and her name was Miss Iva Toguri. She had been introduced to us, and we had all noticed her peculiarly rough, deep voice and her very vigorous, almost masculine style.

I believe, 'though I cannot exactly recall the circumstances, that I was the first to suggest that Miss Toguri represented the answer to our problem. We ascertained that she knew nothing about broadcasting and had never been on the air. This, combined with her masculine style and deep, aggressive voice, we felt would definitely preclude any possibility of her creating the homesick feeling which the Japanese Army were trying to foster. I approached Miss Toguri, and after some demur she agreed to try the experiment.

Cousens confirmed that she received no training until just before the first broadcast. He went on:

To make quite sure that the program failed in its intended effect, I selected the music and wrote the continuity for Miss Toguri to announce. Over a period, we built up a small library of records, nearly all by English composers, which we felt would have minimal appeal to American forces in the Pacific. The program, therefore, consisted of a group of records introduced by Iva Toguri, who took the name of "Ann," as *Ann* was the abbreviation for Announcer in the script. This was followed by news which was written and broadcast by Ince, followed by music, followed by what was called "News from the Home Front."

This latter segment was written by nisei writers, because Cousens and Ince refused to do it, Cousens said; but Ince had "used his skill as an announcer to render [the items] as nearly ineffective as possible."

After some weeks, they had seen an American press story about Japanese broadcasting, for which a reporter had interviewed members of the American armed forces in the Pacific. Said Cousens:

In this news item, the girl referred to was credited with statements which quite definitely did not come from the "Zero Hour." This was in either March or April 1944. There was some discussion at the time between Ince, myself, Miss Toguri, and George Nakamoto, and I think one or two others, as to whom this news item was referring to, as four fifths of the statements credited to the girl by the reporter had not been broadcast by Miss Toguri nor to the best of my knowledge by anyone else from Tokyo radio.

I recall that we discussed this peculiar problem at Camp Bunka, and Major Cox of the U.S. Army Air

Force, who had been shot down over Rabaul, told us that he personally, while in New Guinea, had heard announcements of the sort referred to by the newspaper reporter—for example, announcements commiserating with the troops and warning them that Japanese planes would be over at such and such a time. Major Cox was shot down before the Zero Hour even started, so we had still further reason to believe that, in ordering the Zero Hour from Tokyo radio, the Army was trying to develop something which had already been operating from some station in the South.

Cousens said he left the program when he "collapsed" in June 1944. Ince, he noted, had left it earlier.

Ince and Reyes were questioned by the CIC, in Yokohama and Manila, respectively. Ince, on January 8, 1946, told the same history of "Zero Hour"—that it had been created as an expansion of Reyes' existing brief program. He confirmed how Iva had been brought on to read "prepared introductions to the musical numbers" and how the name Ann had been adopted. Indirectly, he confirms Cousens' initial unwillingness to confide in Ince the reasons for choosing Miss Toguri for the task.

"During discussions as to her ability," Ince said. "I stated that she had a harsh unpleasant voice unsuited to radio work, in addition to her lack of broadcasting experience. However, the Japanese decided that she would be used. . . ."

This is a new twist. Is it an accurate account of the interview with Ince? We know that one Japanese at least—Mitsushio—had to approve Iva, but we know that Mitsushio thought Cousens "must be joking" when he selected her. We know from Cousens that the idea of using Iva came from him, not the Japanese, and that he encountered some opposition from Mitsushio and Ince but that he finally convinced Ince and

Reyes because they needed someone they could trust to "guy" the program.

Ince went on:

> During this time, I heard her say nothing that could be considered as detrimental to the prosecution of the war by the Allied forces. . . . I have talked to American officers who were taken prisoner by the Japanese. These officers told me that a female announcer whom they dubbed "Tokyo Rose" had repeatedly taunted the American forces in the Pacific area with threats of specific bombing missions by Japanese planes, and other items of military import such as naming specific units or mentions of the movements of specific Allied units. I am certain that no such statements were made by Toguri on the Zero Hour prior to February 1944. To my knowledge, this was the only broadcast she was connected with.
>
> Toguri's position at Radio Tokyo was only a part-time job. She told me she had to take it, as her salary from Domei News Agency was not sufficient to support herself. During the winter of 1943, she quit her position at Domei to accept a better position with the Danish legation. She told me that she was subjected to much criticism at Domei for being so American in mannerism and thought. She also said that the [legation] hours would be easier for her and the strain of maintaining two positions would be lessened.
>
> During the time I was at Radio Tokyo, I saw Toguri do many things which were of help to the prisoners of war working there. She furnished us a constant supply of news items while employed at Domei, and after she left there this service was continued by her fiancé, Phil d'Aquino, a Portuguese also employed at Domei. On several occasions, she gave us food from her meager rations. During the several

months that Cousens was ill in a Tokyo hospital, she visited him on a number of occasions although she was warned by the Japanese not to do so. On each of these visits, she took him food, cooking utensils and cigarettes in a sincere effort to help him recover his health. At all times, she was most sympathetic, denouncing the Japanese for their conduct toward the prisoners of war.

Nearly two years later, on December 19, 1947, Ince was interviewed again, this time in America and by Special Agents William C. Hay and George W. Smith of the FBI. By then, he had been cleared of all accusations himself, and promoted to major. He was questioned only about Iva Toguri, and his story remained consistent with what he had said before.

Describing once more how he had first met her, he said:

Cousens was in favor of using her for voice introductions to a musical section of the program. I was not.

Cousens wrote these musical introductions with comments for her, with the exception of several occasions on which he was physically incapacitated. There were many times when I was called upon to write the record introductions, and I believe Reyes [did so] also, on occasion. . . . During these broadcasts, I was either at the control table, where I could hear her actual voice, or in the control booth, where I could hear her over the monitor speaker.

During this period, Toguri made no statements . . . which contained factual or implied information of an intelligence or operational nature. [But] upon occasion, certain phrases were injected into scripts to which I took exception.

Ince said he could not say "from positive knowledge" that such phrases were "actually inserted by Japanese in supervisory capacities," nor could he confirm that they were ever broadcast; nothing of an objectionable nature had been written by Cousens, he said.

Questioned further, he said that "examples of these certain phrases include such statements as 'the forgotten men of the Pacific.' " Ince said he was "not able to state definitely that Toguri read this material over the air. . . . I have never heard Toguri make any statement of a derogatory nature against the United States. . . . Her statements to me were definitely in favor of the war effort of the United States."

Although this testimony carries the stamp of FBI periphrasis (for instance, Ince would not have said "Toguri," but "Miss Toguri" or "Iva"), Hay and Smith seem to have avoided Tillman's probably misleading implication that Ince had said that she was chosen for the program by "the Japanese" instead of by Cousens.

In answer to the G-men's further questions about Japanese control, Ince related that scripts were mimeographed in eighteen copies, but he said that alterations by the nisei censors were fairly rare.

Hay and Smith wrote: "He said that occasionally the Japanese would hand him a script of a news release from the Imperial headquarters; these were not subject to any change. Cousens and he were both forced to read these on the air, and they were always prefaced with 'This is a release from the Japanese High Command' or some such identification, because they wanted the Allied soldiers to know the source." The aim had been to make the program sound like that which the Japanese wanted—one to create homesickness—but not in fact to hurt troop morale.

The special agents continued:

The informant was unable to recall any specific information regarding broadcast material which might

have been intended to break down the morale of the
U.S. troops by making them homesick. . . . He had
never heard Toguri read any such material on the air.
However, he said he did vaguely recall such a phrase
as "the forgotten men of the Pacific" but . . . he could
not recall that any such material had been on the Zero
Hour.

Major Ince advised that all the workers at Radio
Tokyo were under various degrees of control by the
Japs [sic]. He did not know whether Toguri would have
been free to quit her broadcasting if she so desired, as
there was some kind of employment control. The
broadcasters were unable to read anything on the air
which had not been approved by the Japs, and they
were not allowed to deviate from the prepared scripts.

Major Ince advised that one George Nakamoto,
who had at one time been employed by a Japanese
newspaper in Los Angeles, was a liaison man between
the Japanese authorities and the prisoners on the
broadcasts. Nakamoto brought them instructions
from the higher authorities, and the informant believed that Nakamoto might have "watered down"
some of the orders to make it easier on them, as he
seemed to be sympathetic.

Miss Toguri had brought them news obtained at the Danish
legation. Ince had told the agents that "she had come to them
with news of American advances and was happy about them
and always appeared to be in sympathy with the Allied war
effort, and appeared to believe in the ultimate success of the
Americans over the Japanese." He did not follow her activities
after he was removed from "Zero Hour," Ince said; but he
noted that she had married d'Aquino, who was well known for
his "pro-American sympathies."

Reyes had been interviewed by two CIC special agents, A. R. Martin and Milton H. Belinkie, in Manila, on December 31, 1945, by which time he had been promoted to second lieutenant. As he understood it, a woman disc jockey was brought on to "Zero Hour" because the Japanese wanted

> to initiate a soothing, relaxing touch to the program whereby the troops in the South Pacific might be lulled into a receptive mood for Japanese propaganda efforts which would be inserted in the latter part of the program. . . .
>
> [Iva] broadcast her introduction, the continuity between musical numbers, and miscellaneous information about the recording to be played, including the name of the author [sic] and the band, and the popularity which had been achieved by the tune.

Cousens had borne the "brunt" of writing the scripts, Reyes said. Ince and he had substituted for Cousens when the latter was "indisposed." In the end,

> Toguri wrote most of her own material, attempting at all times to imitate the style which had been set for her by Cousens. [She] frequently came to me for advice. . . . She often asked me to aid [her] in removing from her scripts propaganda items which the Japanese constantly inserted, such as suggestions to the GIs that it was a "hell of a life in a foxhole" or that they did not know why this war had been started or a query as to whether they "regretted having gone to war."

Reyes, in short, confirmed the general picture of an innocuous program for so long as Cousens and Ince were there, with the occasional comment of the "foxhole" nature added by Mitsu-shio and others when she was on her own. Given her sex, her youth, and her alien nationality, her resistance seems to have been exceptionally strong.

Reyes is quoted as saying:

Iva definitely did not relish her job. She did not wish to become a part of the things which the Japanese were constantly attempting to insert into the program. She was unpopular with the Japanese who inserted their ideological warfare into her scripts because she discouraged such attempts in every way possible. I have often heard her say that she wanted to quit. In addition, she was worried about the possible conse-quences.

It seems safe to assume that the last sentence was provoked by a question "Was she . . . ?"

None of the CIC or FBI questioners seems to have ques-tioned whether she would have stayed at NHK at all if three Allied prisoners, a major, a captain, and a lieutenant, were not there as well, making it appear that her concerns about postwar retribution were perhaps exaggerated. Perhaps she had been more worried after the American press gave currency to the sobriquet "Tokyo Rose."

Reyes is quoted as saying: "I recall that Major Tsuneishi once called Iva 'Tokyo Rose' and we in the office sometimes called her by that name, in a joking manner. . . . She did not take kindly to the nickname—she resented it."

He identified Miyeko Furuya as the most frequently used substitute for Iva, with Mary Ishii as the next most often heard. Ruth Hayakawa had never, he said, participated in "Zero Hour"; some others were to contradict this.

Before interviewing Iva Toguri herself, Tillman had colleagues in the United States interview Lee and Brundidge about their interview with her. Lee said she had referred to her problems when Cousens left the program because of illness; then, according to Lee, she had said that in October 1944, after the U.S. fleet had just won a great victory over the Japanese in the battle of Leyte Gulf, the Japanese government was pretending to have "sunk the American fleet off Formosa."

Lee is quoted as saying: "They sent a Japanese major from GHQ and directed her to say 'You fellows are all without ships. What are you going to do about getting [home] now? Orphans of the Pacific, you really are orphans now.' " Lee said he had asked if she had thought that she might get into trouble for being forced to read such material. The FBI periphrasis of Lee's periphrasis reads: "She had often given thought to the fact that Cousens, Reyes and herself were in the same situation. There were times when she thought she was doing wrong but she felt instead [sic] that she was providing as much fun as propaganda."

Brundidge had said that Toguri had given them a "signed statement" that she was "the one and only Tokyo Rose and that she was guilty of treason," but that "this statement was stolen from him in Tokyo." The interviewing agent was apparently as unimpressed by Brundidge as the CIC had been, because he added: "There appears to be some confusion as to how extensive this statement was, and it appears from the interview of Lee that the statement by Toguri was merely the fact that she was the one and only Tokyo Rose." Moreover, much of the published interview was not in the notes, the agent said, but appeared to have been written from memory.

James J. Keeney and Dale Kramer, both formerly of *Yank* magazine, testified about their interview, which the FBI report said was suggested by Lee and Brundidge to enable the Hearst duo to get out of their "exclusivity contract with Toguri." Keeney remembered that Miss Toguri had "denied anything treasonous, although she had admitted to him that she had used the phrase 'This is your little enemy.' " Kramer remembered the interview but could not identify her voice as being that of the "Tokyo Rose" he had listened to in the Pacific. There was similar testimony from former Ensign Vaughan Paul, a naval officer who had shot a film of her in Yokohama.

Tillman, who was eventually to take over the case, did not interview her until April 30, 1946. He took the imprisoned exile over the familiar ground of how she had become stranded in Japan, her wartime difficulties, her frustrated attempts to return home, and her stint with Domei. She told him that because her parents had been interned and were probably impoverished, her uncle Hajime Hattori had advised her not to try to get more money from them but to stay in Japan.

She related the pressures on her to become a Japanese citizen, her brush with beri-beri, how she had gone to work at NHK as a typist and become an announcer. Cousens and Ince, she said, had explained the nature of the program to her in the presence of a Canadian nisei announcer, George Noda. In his periphrasis of her words, Tillman has her saying:

> [Cousens] said he would write the script and that the music would be chosen. I would only have to read what was written, that is, the introduction to the music, and not news or commentaries. Cousens said he chose me because he thought I had a Yankee personality. I think he talked over my selection with Nakamoto. I was then taken to a studio and given a voice test by reading an old radio script. Cousens said I would do, and that he would coach me so I could send a cheerful voice over the radio. He told me to pretend that I was among the boys and to speak as if I were talking directly to them. . . . I accepted the job

because I thought I could entertain American soldiers that way. . . .

I do not recall the contents of that [first] broadcast, but I did not feel that I was trying to destroy the morale of Allied soldiers, because Major Cousens said it was entertainment.

There is more in this synopsized language. She confirmed that Cousens had written the scripts until falling ill; then she had done them herself with some help from Reyes. She recalled the final format of the show, when it went to seventy-five minutes (6:00 P.M. to 7:15 P.M., Tokyo time), as being five to ten minutes of prisoner of war messages; music introduced by "Ann" for about ten minutes; "American Home Front News" by Ince for about five minutes; another ten minutes of music introduced by "Ann"; news highlights, usually read by Ince; jazz music introduced by Reyes; prerecorded news commentaries by Charles Yoshii for seven to ten minutes; and a closing band number, which Toguri introduced.

She said:

At the beginning of the program, and throughout the program, I was introduced as Orphan Ann, Orphan Annie, Your Favorite Enemy Ann and Your Favorite Playmate and Enemy Ann. I had specific instructions from Cousens to laugh when I said the word "enemy." I was told to be as cheerful and entertaining as possible, and I tried to do so. About Christmas, 1943, Cousens and Ince took me into their confidence and said they were trying to make the program as entertaining as possible rather than propaganda. [Cousens] told me never to think of it as propaganda. . . . They told me they were trying to soften the news broadcasts and increase the number of POW messages. They also told me they were putting a double meaning in some of their scripts. . . .

In the summer of 1944, Miyeko Furuya took my place on Saturdays, staying until the spring of 1945. I was ill from March until May 1945, at which time Mary Ishii, a Eurasian, took my place. When I returned, she was a regular member of the Zero Hour program, and remained so until the program went off the air in August 1945. I never heard the broadcasts of these women, and was not familiar with the scripts they used.

(Actually, being "ill" was one of her excuses to NHK, the other being Allied air raids; she was really, as readers will recall, attending Catholic catechismal classes and getting married.)

She identified a number of scripts "typed by me from longhand scripts written by Major Cousens, with portions pertaining to the band music typed by Ted Ince. I broadcast . . . all the parts indicated for '*Ann:*' on the dates indicated. These are scripts given to the military authorities by my husband." All dates are from February, March, April, and May 1944.

Tillman's carelessness in transcribing her statement, and her own in reading the transcript, is evident from her appearing to say that she was married in December 1943—sixteen months before the event. There are other, similar kefuffles in Tillman's account, and Iva apparently did not spot them. But she did note that when she and Felippe registered their wedding at the Portuguese consulate general, she was informed that she now had dual Portuguese and American nationality.

She concluded, in Tillman's rather awkward periphrasis:

My purpose was to give the program a double meaning and thus reduce its effectiveness as a propaganda medium. I was convinced that I was defeating the purpose of the Japanese, as Major Cousens remarked that the set-up of Tokyo radio was such that he could write scripts which had a double meaning. The Japanese did not check the scripts every day or make us record the program before it was broadcast. I did not feel that I was working against the interests of the United States. I did not pay much attention . . . to the Japanese aims of the program, except that I knew that all of their programs were propaganda.

The sentences obviously subsume Tillman's questions rather than her "yes" and "no" answers.

In America, there had been interviews with Mark Louis Streeter of Ogden, Utah, a former civilian prisoner at Suragadai who said he had appeared in a couple of programs with Iva, and with a former neighbor in California, not initially identified in the records, who had recognized her voice. Streeter had protested at her arrest and said that if she was tried he would testify for the defense. Her former neighbor said that he had known that "Ann" was Iva Toguri because she "had a mannerism and a teasing tone in her voice that could be recognized." He does not say what the mannerism was, but one witness did later say that she sometimes lisped.

No one—not Oki or Nii or other nisei at the station—had been able to identify any particular script as having been read by Iva Toguri; this is an indication of how closely the Allied quartet—Cousens, Ince, Reyes, and Iva—had kept the program to themselves. But Tillman did possess the scripts which had been given to Major Reitz of the CIC by Felippe—a selection she had saved in the hope that they would help her get a radio job in California. Tillman reported at the time that there were no samples available in the United States; it transpired much later that the Foreign Broadcast Information Service (FBIS) had recorded all the "Zero Hour" broadcasts, although not all of the recordings were of usable quality.

"Some recordings of partial broadcasts have been obtained, but [they] are so very poor that her voice is not distinguishable and has no evidentiary value," Tillman reported at the time, before knowing of the FBIS trove. Actually, if they had in fact been broadcasts by Iva Toguri, they would have been easily identifiable by the sobriquets Ann and Orphan Ann; so these are presumably recordings of some of the various other "Tokyo Roses." The Office of Strategic Services also later unearthed some "Rose" recordings, although it is not clear whether Iva Toguri is on any of them.

Tillman inserted in the dossier the scripts Reitz got from Felippe. Here are some samples:

> *Ann:* Hello there, Enemies! How's tricks? This is Ann of Radio Tokyo, and we're just going to begin our regular program of music, news and the Zero Hour for our friends—I mean, our enemies!— in Australia and the South Pacific. So be on your guard, and mind the children don't hear! All set? O.K. Here's the first blow at your morale—the Boston Pops playing "Strike Up The Band!" (Music)
>
> *Ann:* How's that for a start? Well, now listen to me make subtle attack on the orphans of the South Pacific. Sergeant! Where the hell's that Orphan Choir? Oh, there you are, boys. This is Ann here! How about singing for me tonight? You won't? Alright, you thankless wretches, I will entertain myself and you go play with the mosquitos. Thank you, Mr. Payne. When you're ready—

On another night she calls herself "Playmate Orphan Annie at the microphone presenting our regular special programme [Cousens' standard-English spelling] for our friends, sure, I said friends, in the South Pacific."

There is a lot of the London Symphony under Sir Malcolm Sargeant, and music by Coleridge-Taylor and others not likely to have much appeal to GIs; there are several thankyou-thank-you-thankyou "wipes," and some self-abnegating humor, such as:

> *Ann:* And here it is! Punctual, alert and smiling, her radiant personality electrified all those in the studio as she addressed herself to her vast worldwide audience. What's that you say? Who is it? Aw shucks! It's me, of course! Can't a girl give herself a little build-up when there's nobody else to do it?

There would be jokes about army food and the absence of beer, Nipponisms like "you onable boneheads" and "you are liking, please?" The sign-offs might be: "This is Ann of Radio Tokyo saying goodnight, and don't forget to be good" or "Orphan to orphan—over!"

The theme which Cousens used both to satisfy his own purposes and beguile the Japanese authorities was to make fun of the "enemy propaganda" line. On March 27, 1944, for instance, she began:

> *Ann:* Greetings, everybody! This is your little playmate, I mean your bitter enemy, Ann, with a program of dangerous and wicked propaganda for my victims in Australia and the South Pacific.

On April 21, it was:

> *Ann:* Dangerous enemy propaganda, so beware! Our next propagandist is Arthur Fiedler with the Boston Pops Orchestra playing Ketelbey's "In a Persian Garden." . . . Please to listening!

The picture of what Cousens had tried to do was clear, as it had been to the CIC earlier. He could tell his Japanese controllers that he was making it hard for the Allies to say that the program was propaganda, because he was labeling it as such, in a humorous way. To keep this up, he could say, he must be allowed not to use propaganda. Thus, he could sabotage the program. To pull off this little, hidden victory, the cultural differences between the captors and the captives in Tokyo had to be exploited. Iva Toguri, with her "Yankee personality" and her loyalty to the United States, was an obvious choice for Cousens' gambit; and, since she was of Japanese extraction, and a woman with a voice that the Japanese presumably thought that Americans would find attractive, she could be used. One could see the Japanese, men like Tsuneishi, saying seriously that this incomprehensible stuff must be American humor. They had tampered with the program a little after Cousens and Ince had gone, but the worst that she might have been forced to say—if the Lee/Brundidge "interview" could be believed—was that the U.S. had lost, not won, the naval battle at Leyte.

However, it had taken a year of imprisonment for Iva before all this could be sufficiently proved for Washington to agree that there was no "Tokyo Rose"—or that if there was one (or two of three) who had made genuine propaganda broadcasts, Iva Toguri was not she.

U.S. attorney James M. Carter, who had helped initiate her problems as part of a political campaign, now said honestly: "The legendary seductress of Radio Tokyo was little more than a myth, concocted by daydreaming GIs." Tokyo Rose was a "composite [of] at least a dozen voices."

Rex Gunn, a war correspondent who became AP Radio bureau chief in Tokyo, was interviewed in retirement in Reno, Nevada, in 1976, by the *The San Francisco Chronicle,* and recalled that he had heard Toguri's broadcasts when he had been on Saipan.

"She was the complete lampoon of the oriental seductress," he told a reporter, Linda Witt. "She would say 'Beware, this is vicious propaganda. I'm going to sneak up on you GIs with my nail file and murder a whole battalion'."

However, convincing MacArthur's intelligence people, the FBI, the Justice Department, and the Tokyo press corps was one thing; convincing the likes of Walter Winchell and the commander of the American Legion was something else. The witch hunters were soon in full battle cry.

8.

Free Press Versus Fair Trial: Why The Case Was Revived

THE WAR HAD BEEN OVER for more than a year. Most of the stranded nisei had now gone back to America or were about to leave. Iva had not seen her family for over five years. She wanted very much to go home. Felippe, astonished and terrified by the razzmatazz in the American press about his wife, advised doing nothing for a while; she should, he said, let the excitement die down first. Iva's reaction was all-American; she had been vindicated; she had her rights. She went off to the U.S. consulate general to reestablish her American citizenship. There, a Kafka-like situation awaited. Despite the October 1942 memorandum, Vice Consul Harry F. Pfeiffer told her he thought she was stateless.

How could she be stateless? She had been born in California. She had never renounced her citizenship, nor, despite her right to a Japanese and now a Portuguese passport, had she ever taken the nationality of any country other than the United States. She had been arrested on suspicion of *treason,* so how could she not be American? But the American authorities had been ambiguous from the start. The prison commander, a Colonel Hardy, had treated her as a Japanese in regard to accommodation and food; unlike the other American prisoners, she had not been allowed to write to her family.

The family, however, could write to Felippe, and they were constantly begging her, through him, to come home. This would require a passport, which Pfeiffer said might take about six months. He and the other consular staff had had nearly ten thousand applications from nisei and other Japanese-Americans who had been stranded in Japan, most of whom had complicated their situation by taking Japanese nationality as well. Many cases were still being processed. The Portuguese consulate general confirmed that she had a right to Portuguese citizenship, because of her marriage. That could get her out of the miseries of postwar Tokyo, and in Lisbon she could always ask for a visa for the United States. She rebelled against the idea; she had put up with so much, for five years, to remain American; why should she become a phony Portuguese?

It was nearly a year later, on October 20, 1947, that the head of the passport office in the State Department asked Justice for a ruling. Four days later, assistant attorney general T. Vincent Quinn confirmed that prosecution was not warranted, "therefore this Department will have no objection at all to the issuance of a passport to Mrs. d'Aquino."

But the press had got wind of her application to come home, and there must have been a leaker at State or Justice who shared the wartime prejudices against the Tokyo Rose of legend; four days later, James F. O'Neill, commander of the American Legion, issued a press release asking that Iva Toguri be prosecuted to prevent her returning. The Legion organized a letter-writing campaign and other organizations joined in the hysteria, notably something called the "Native Sons of the Golden West." The attorney general, FBI director J. Edgar Hoover, the Immigration and Naturalization Service, and the State Department were all bombarded through the mails. Even the Los Angeles City Council passed a resolution opposing her homecoming.

Iva was pregnant. Neither her father nor her brother yet

had citizenship because they had been born abroad. She wrote to one of the former Bunka camp prisoners, Mark Streeter, who had written to her in sympathy, saying that she wanted her child to be American-born. The baby was due in January. Trying to be helpful, Streeter passed on her concern to the press. He had been in Tokyo during the war, sharing the miseries, and he understood. But one man who had spent the war in the nightclubs and restaurants of Beverly Hills and midtown Manhattan thought differently.

When Walter Winchell's name is mentioned in journalism schools today, it is as an example of all that a journalist should never be. He was known to his colleagues as Walter Windbag, and he was about to become Walter Witchhunt. A noted film was made about this wretched individual, and it would be tiresome to expatiate on his shortcomings. Suffice it to say that if most journalists were like Winchell the idea of a free press would have to be abandoned as impractical and counterproductive. At the time, however, he was extremely powerful and influential. His daily column and his Sunday night radio broadcast could create or destroy reputations. Even Roosevelt feared him sufficiently to pretend to solicit his advice.

Winchell was drawn into the Tokyo Rose "debate," he claimed, by a letter from the mother of a soldier killed in the Pacific. His adherence to the crusade against "Rose" came just as Justice, like Mrs. d'Aquino, was hoping that the silly issue would go away. It is a measure of governmental fear of Winchell's power that U.S. Attorney James H. Carter called on Winchell in the latter's Hollywood office rather than inviting Winchell to his. Carter was accompanied by former district attorney Charles Carr, who had been the first official to call for prosecution but who also had now accepted that there was no case against Mrs. d'Aquino. Both men knew that Winchell had a private grievance against Attorney General Tom Clark, who had once falsely denied to the columnist that he was to be appointed to the cabinet post, and that Clark was afraid of the columnist's "revenge."

Carter and Carr tried to convince Winchell that the Toguri broadcasts had been innocuous, and more entertainment than propaganda. Winchell was ambiguous. He and J. Edgar Hoover were good friends, with Hoover feeding the Winchell column with leaks and scoops and Winchell helping to create the legend of the "G-men," which assisted Hoover at budget time. Moreover, Winchell knew that the FBI was about to cave in to the American Legion campaign.

Indeed, Hoover issued a public call for help in associating Iva Toguri with the "Rose" of legend by identifying her broadcasts and her voice. Meanwhile, Hoover said, she would not be permitted to reenter the United States while prosecution was pending.

At the same time, the House Un-American Activities Committee was just hitting its stride, accusing President Truman of being "soft on traitors." Truman was about to face election. Winchell typically confused the issue by saying that those who had fought for the fascist regime of wartime Japan had been "communists".

To appease the wolves, the Justice Department finally brought treason charges against Thomas "Meatball" Kawakita, the nisei accused of being a brutal guard in a POW camp, Mildred Gillars ("Axis Sally"), and John David Provoo, the solitary military turncoat of Suragadai.

Attorney General Tom Clark could hardly be accused of being "soft on the Japs." He had been the coordinator of the Relocation Authority in 1942, and it was not until 1966 that he washed his hands of the policy of putting Japanese-Americans into "concentration camps," as he called them then. Moreover, Clark was under pressure from Congress, his headline-hunting subordinate Hoover, the spiteful Winchell and others in the press, and also from the election-conscious White House.

By then, Harry Brundidge had parted company with *Cosmopolitan* and was trying to revive his career in a less glamorous post—reporter on the Nashville *Tennessean*. Brundidge read the FBI release and wrote to Hoover, offering to go to Tokyo and find witnesses to prove that Iva Toguri was "Tokyo Rose". He was, he said, aware that, to prove treason, there must be "overt acts" and that there must be at least two witnesses to each.

Brundidge was really reacting as much to a Winchell column as to the FBI appeal. Winchell had found out, presumably from Clark Lee himself, that Lee had given the FBI his Imperial Hotel interview of two years before. Winchell called Iva's responses to Lee an admission of guilt. Surely the two witnesses to her overt acts could be Ince and Cousens, who had been "tried for treason in his country and mysteriously released without either conviction or acquittal." He quoted Lee as saying that another "twenty-five" witnesses could be rounded up in Tokyo, and concluded indignantly: "Yet the State Department says there are none, ignoring the fact that the Office of War Information made transcripts of her programs." Winchell, in praising Lee, had also mocked Brundidge, who he said had lost his own copy of the interview and the contract in which she had guaranteed that she was the "one and original" Tokyo Rose.

Brundidge went to see Attorney General Clark and made the unethical offer to go to Tokyo on behalf of Justice. What took place next, reported in the FBI file on Iva Toguri, makes high drama out of what looks, in retrospect, like a piece of unblushing hype by Harry Brundidge.

Special Agent Joseph T. Genco of the New York bureau reported that on February 11, 1948, one of his staff called the assistant bureau chief, Special Agent Alan H. Belmont,

to advise that Harry T. Brundidge would be in New York [that night]; that he left Washington on the 4:00

P.M. train and would arrive in New York about 7:45
P.M., after which he would go directly to his apartment at 17 East 54th Street.

He would make the alleged statement of Tokyo
Rose available to agents of this office immediately
upon his arrival. He was told that an agent of the New
York office would call him at 8:30 P.M. at his apartment and the agent would then go there to secure the
alleged confession. Brundidge advised the Bureau that
he would be expecting the call.

One can feel the excitement growing. After years of the FBI
wasting the taxpayers' money and their own time—which was
money, too—and getting nowhere, here was ol' Harry of
Cosmopolitan, now down on his luck and working for a little-
known daily paper, coming up with a confession! The breath-
less narrative, with the usual police pidgin of "advised" for
"told," "located" for "found," "stated" for "said," "requested" for "asked," and "proceed" for "go," continues:

> At precisely 8:30 P.M., the reporting agent phoned
> Brundidge at his apartment, phone number CIrcle 7-
> 6132. Mr. Brundidge answered the phone and advised
> the writer that he had just arrived from Washington
> and requested a little time to search for the statement.
> He requested that he be phoned again at 9:00 P.M. This
> was done, at which time Mr. Brundidge stated he had
> located the document and that the Agent should pro-
> ceed to his apartment.

Brundidge had now earned the prefix "Mr.," and the agents
proceeded. To wit:

> Thereupon, the writer and SA [Special Agent] Charles
> M. Curry went to Brundidge's apartment where he
> produced two documents, one of which purported to

be the unsigned statement of the subject, and the other a narrative expansion of the unsigned statement which had been prepared by Brundidge and Clark Lee at a later time in this country.

Uh-oh. Unsigned. Just reporters' notes. Indeed:

The document referred to as the statement of Tokyo Rose bore the caption 'tokyo rose' and was uncapitalized. The pages were numbered one through seventeen, but it was noted that the pages numbered eight and nine were missing. It was typed on different sheets of paper and was similar in appearance to a rough draft.

The jargon thickens. "Was similar in appearance to" is FBI-ese for "seemed to be", and it is hard to see how seventeen pages of typing could be on one sheet of paper, anyway.

It continues:

Brundidge advised this statement, which was taken from a narrative furnished by the subject, was given in his room at the Imperial Hotel, in Tokyo, during the latter part of August 1945. [Brundidge appears to have forgotten the date.] Present in the room when Tokyo Rose [sic] was interviewed were Clark Lee and the subject's husband. The second document, according to Mr. Brundidge, was merely an expansion of the statement of Tokyo Rose which was prepared by himself and Clark Lee at a later period of time. Both the aforementioned documents were forwarded to the Bureau and photostatic copies of the same were sent to the Los Angeles office. A receipt for the above two documents was requested by Mr. Brundidge although he alleged he was not interested in the return of the documents. A copy of this receipt was made and is being retained in the exhibit folder of this case.

123

Buried among the jargon—"later" has become "at a later period of time" and Brundidge's willingness to part with his scoop for ever is something whch he only "alleges"—the reader will notice that Iva Toguri has twice become "Tokyo Rose," the one and original.

Brundidge left for Japan on March 12, 1948, in a military plane chartered by Tom Clark. It would appear that only his living expenses in Tokyo were covered by *The Tennessean*. With Brundidge was John Hogan, a former FBI special agent now working for the internal security division of Justice, investigating Ince and Provoo for suspicion of treason, despite Ince's clearance by the army.

Brundidge's passport specifically stated that he was on a special mission for the Justice Department, and Occupation headquarters had been advised of his arrival. Armed with this— incidentally, a totally unethical involvement with the executive branch for a professional journalist—Hogan and Brundidge were able to stop off in Honolulu and relieve Lee of the autograph she had given him at the Imperial: "Iva Toguri 'Tokyo Rose.'" They continued their journey, and Hogan reported that CIC in Tokyo was hostile to Brundidge, whom they regarded as an unscrupulous scoop artist. Hogan also told his superiors in Washington that they had found Tokyo radio employees reluctant to testify against their long–suffering colleague and as "uncooperative" as CIC. But however much branded as a witch hunt in Tokyo, the "special mission" went ahead anyway.

On January 5, Iva had given birth to a boy who had died the next morning. Physically and emotionally exhausted, she had been bedridden ever since. Nonetheless, she foolishly rose from her sickbed on March 26, went to the Dai-ichi Hotel to meet Brundidge and Hogan, and proceeded to repeat all of her old mistakes. Indeed, it is hard to read what happened without at least partially agreeing with Tillman when he says harshly that "Toguri was sentenced because she was stupid."

Pale, drawn, and weak, she told the two Americans she could not stay long. Hogan, the Justice official with a law degree, left the talking to the unlettered hack, who told Mrs. d'Aquino that the decision she took that day might decide whether she could return home or not. He asked her to sign Lee's typescript of the famous interview, certifying that it was correct. She read it through quickly and told Hogan: "Most of this is made up." Brundidge produced what he said was a photocopy of Lee's original notes, and repeated that signing the "interview" would help her get back to the States.

She signed.

Hogan, the Justice Department official, had not advised her of her legal rights—that she could have legal counsel, that she could remain silent, that anything she said could be used against her in a court of law. She in turn never asked either of the men in what way signing the document could help her go home.

At Hogan's request, she wearily got into a taxi with them to show Hogan the studio from which she had broadcast on "Zero Hour," and it was there that Brundidge answered this unasked question.

"You'll probably be indicted for treason," he said, "but they'll never hang a woman and you'll probably get a short sentence. Anyway, you'll get back to the United States."

John Leggett wrote in 1976: "Of this March interview, Iva remembers that she came hoping that it would bring her closer to home. . . . Her citizenship was still in question, and she yearned to see her family again, so that, while Hogan [sic] warned her of the possibility of further prosecution, she was won over by Brundidge's assurance that her signature on the 1945 interview notes would accelerate her return. Without legal counsel, she signed them."

Hogan then took a decision which must have reflected house politics in the days of Hoover more than common sense: he recommended prosecution. At Justice, attorney Tom de Wolfe recommended against it. He pointed out that the principal witnesses, Cousens and Ince, had been investigated and disculpated by their respective armies, and that they would testify that Iva "lacked the necessary intent for treason." De Wolfe said it was doubtful if a judge would admit the so-called confession obtained by Brundidge and Lee. "The government's case must fall as a matter of law," the attorney concluded.

What was clearly now needed was for the serious press to get onto the issue and blow Winchell, Brundidge, and the FBI out of the water. Astonishingly, the "scoop" was to be discovered by a Broadway impresario.

Having foolishly trusted Brundidge again, Iva finally met an American journalist of sorts who was on her side. Earl Carroll, the entertainment columnist and sometime film and stage producer, came to Tokyo to investigate the possibility of making a movie about the wartime city, and, after stumbling onto the Cousens-Toguri charade, he was considering making Iva one of the heroines. He learned, from army intelligence, of the parody which Iva and the prisoners had managed to put over on the Japanese propaganda machine, and saw great theatrical possibilities in the story. He discussed her case with General Charles Willoughby, the current head (G-2) of army intelligence in Japan, who told him the case against her was closed, and who encouraged Carroll's project.

Carroll passed his conversation with Willoughby on to Iva. He told her that her application to return home was being delayed at the State Department by the campaign launched by Winchell who, he said, was "throwing mud" at her in his column. Carroll suggested she write to Winchell explaining everything, including how she had accepted orders from Cousens. He said he would pass the letter to Winchell, an acquaintance of long date, himself.

She had lunch with Carroll, UP bureau chief Ernest Hoberecht and the actress destined to play Iva on the silver screen, Yoshiko "Shirley" Yamaguchi. That night—April 14, 1948— she gave Carroll the letter for Winchell. On April 20, back in America, Carroll sent it to New York along with one of his own. Again, in response, Winchell was ambiguous, even duplicitous. He told Carroll he "might" run some of the letter in his column; then, contradictorily, he said he was sure she would get a "fair trial."

The Justice Department, anxious to put the whole affair behind it, was appalled that the columnist had not given up the campaign for a trial. Carroll decided he would have to talk to Winchell in person when he next went to New York. On June 17, the plane taking Carroll and other passengers from California crashed and burned. The charred remains of the burly Carroll himself were not recognizable, and he was identified only by his wallet. In May, Brundidge had run a ten-part series in *The Tennessean* about his "special mission." In it, he said he had handed Tom Clark a "signed confession" by Toguri. By now, the FBI appeal for witnesses who had heard "Tokyo Rose" broadcasts was drawing scores of responses. The famous G-men, recruited to destroy gangsterism, were wasting countless dollars and days interviewing veterans who had heard some female voice, somewhere, saying something, in the Pacific. Winchell and Brundidge, two of America's worst journalists, had won. The Justice Department, the Counter Intelligence Corps, truth—and Iva—had lost. There would be a trial.

9.

Suragadai—"Camp Bunka"

THE INVESTIGATION NOW turned its attention to Suragadai, the prison camp that was the human generating plant of Tokyo radio's English-language services.

The whole concept of prisoners of war was novel to the Japanese. Those captured in their military expeditions into China and Korea had been turned into virtual slaves. Those taken much earlier, in the 1905 defeat of Russia, had been few, and were soon returned after St. Petersburg surrendered. Tokyo's startling successes when it joined in World War II on the Axis side involved the seizure of literally hundreds of thousands of hapless members of their foes. Many were stranded on islands by the Japanese conquest and could not retreat. There were about a hundred thousand prisoners in the expanded Changi complex in Singapore alone. Yet the Imperial Japanese Army seems not to have studied the problem of how to hold prisoners, feed them, and give them some semblance of medical care, until it happened.

By any standards, Camp Suragadai was unusual. Siting a prisoner-of-war complex in the center of a capital city was curious. Nor were the prisoners put there as hostages; Jimmy Doolittle's bombers had not yet started their ruthless bid to burn the wood and paper houses of Tokyo's largely civilian population when the decision was taken to convert a girls' school into a prison camp. Suragadai was there to make possible the whole Japanese breach of the Geneva Convention—the breach which Tsuneishi was ordered to implement: it would be entirely filled with "radio slaves," who would justify being fed and lodged and—after a fashion—cared for by helping keep NHK's propaganda broadcasts on the ether.

By the time the dead horse of the Toguri inquiry had been flogged to its feet by Winchell and others, the alumni of Suragadai (usually called Bunka by them) were scattered across the world. Key figures who were familiar with the NHK English-language programming had to be tracked down. Indeed, the prosecution of Iva was managed not out of the Tokyo office of the FBI but out of its much larger bureau in Los Angeles, which put out a guideline statement to G-men everywhere, which said, among other things:

> The Department has ruled that a person who has not known Toguri prior to her broadcasts will not be capable of identifying her program. Cousens, Ince, and Reyes were all interviewed by CIC in Japan. The Bureau has requested the Australian authorities to re-interview Cousens. Ince has already been re-interviewed by the San Francisco office. Reyes is reportedly in the United States and efforts are being made at this time to locate him for interview. Efforts should be made to determine the degree of collaboration on the part of Cousens and Ince.

Actually, there is no record that the CIC ever interviewed Cousens, who naturally rejoined the Australian forces when he was liberated; but the notion that only people who knew Toguri would know her voice was sensible. Unfortunately, in a final wild effort to have a case to present in court, the idea was soon abandoned, as will be seen in chapter 11.

The U.S. Embassy in London got in on the act, with a message suggesting that the FBI interrogate Cousens. The dispatch breathlessly implies that he is someone whom the FBI must not have heard about before. He is described as having gone before a "trial" in Australia, and the dispatch adds: "During his trial, Tokio [sic] Rose herself was brought to Australia and she gave damaging evidence against him; however, this was not sufficient and the defense made capital of the fact that accepting the testimony of an enemy to the country in preference to that of a citizen was something unheard of."

The only Japanese subject who gave evidence at Cousens' investigation was a woman radio reporter who helped to clear him. The only woman broadcaster over whom Cousens had had any control was Iva Toguri, who was American and not an "enemy" of Australia, and who was not allowed to leave Japan.

The dispatch goes on: "It is believed that Cousens would more than welcome the opportunity of now giving evidence against Tokio Rose and certainly in view of his present employment by the broadcasting company [presumably a reference to the state-owned Australian Broadcasting Corporation] is not in a position to refuse."

The embassy also thought it was the first to discover what it called "Bunker or Banker Camp," and recommended interviewing former prisoners from there. It described Suragadai as a "luxury camp" as "all the inmates collaborated with the Japanese authorities by writing script [sic] for Tokio Rose and Radio Tokyo in general."

Finally, the embassy suggested that the FBI should interview Edwin Kalbfleisch, "a former U.S. Army lieutenant who is now connected with the Pabst Brewery in Milwaukee." An informer, whose name is blanked out in the FBI file given to this writer, is said to have reported that Kalbfleisch "worked openly and actively while a prisoner of war for Tokio Rose for approximately eighteen months. He wrote numerous scripts for her and for Radio Tokyo." The only American at Suragadai who finally refused to collaborate and who was sentenced to death for his pains (and who was then stationed at the Pentagon rather than at the Pabst Brewery) becomes the prime collaborator!

The dispatch reflects the tone of the time and the widening circle of ignorance and hysteria surrounding the case. The little typist has become a dragon lady, employing Lieutenant Kalbfleisch as a scriptwriter, flying off to Sydney to betray one of her other subordinates, a major—and of course a Japanese subject, which, if true, would have put her beyond the reach of U.S. courts, anyway.

Before concentrating its attention on former Bunka prisoners, the FBI in Los Angeles had found someone else, a Los Angeles neighbor who had known Toguri before the war. On January 31, 1948, Special Agent Chester C. Orton interviewed Gilbert Vasquez Velasquez, who had served in the army from 1942 to 1946 and had heard his grocer's daughter while in New Guinea and the Philippines.

"I first remember meeting Iva Ikuko Toguri in about 1927, and I saw her many times each week from 1927 until she left for Japan in the first part of July 1941," he related. "[She] resided with her family at 11630 Bandera Avenue, which is just one block from where I used to live."

He remembered the Wilmington Avenue Market on the block next to Bandera. Vasquez had been a frequent customer there and had often chatted with the Toguri girls. "For a time, I went to school with Inez Hisako Toguri at the Willowbrook Junior High School." After moving out to Downey, California, in 1938, he would "drop by" the store whenever he returned to Watts.

"I was always very friendly with Iva Toguri, her father, her brother and her two sisters. Her mother, Fumi Toguri, was an invalid," he said.

Vasquez had first heard Iva "on September 5, 1944, when I was at Finchafen, British New Guinea, and I listened to her every evening for a period of about three weeks until I was transferred." Later, he said, he heard her broadcasting between October 24, 1944, and the end of the war, while he was on Leyte in the Philippines. He said his army buddies thought he was kidding when he claimed to recognize her voice. For his comrades, she was just another Tokyo Rose."

He remembered that her program began with the Tokyo radio station identification; then a man would announce that this was the "Zero Hour." Next, "an announcer would introduce Iva Toguri. . . . Generally, she would refer to herself as Ann, Orphan Annie or 'Ann of Radio Tokyo'." Neither she nor anyone else on the program had ever used the pseudonym Tokyo Rose, he said.

Vasquez went on: "Iva Toguri . . . never read any news items and never gave any commentaries. The only thing that I ever heard her do was to announce the musical numbers . . . with chit-chat." The girls who replaced her at the weekend were different, and less friendly, he said. He also remembered one unusual broadcast by Iva in December 1944, after Cousens and Ince had left the program and Mitsushio was in direct charge.

"I do recall that in December 1944, while I was on Leyte, she stated that the Japanese were kicking the hell out of us in Palo [but] I knew [that] the Japanese were the ones who were having a bad time and not us."

Another neighbor of the Toguris and relative of Vasquez' said he had heard an "Orphan Annie" broadcast but had failed to recognize the voice.

Around the same time, the FBI in Los Angeles was interviewing the first of many Suragadai alumni, former Ensign
George Henshaw, who gave his address in 1948 as the Hollywood Athletic Club on Sunset Boulevard. The young officer
was described as a "member of the first group which opened
Bunka on December 1, 1943, and remained until the camp was
closed on August 23, 1945." Henshaw had testified for Cousens
at his inquiry in Sydney—indicating that the Australian's defense witnesses were able to go to Australia at government
expense much more freely than Iva Toguri's would be to come
to America. Henshaw's interview is subsumed by saying that
he confirmed that no prisoners except a name or names blanked
out—probably Sergeant Provoo, and possibly the civilian Streeter—had collaborated with the Japanese. Henshaw was suppor-
tive of Cousens and Ince, the synopsis says.

Although he said that he had never seen Toguri and that
there was no radio in Bunka to listen to her broadcasts (which
were on shortwave and could probably not be heard in Tokyo
itself), he had succeeded in keeping a diary; his testimony is
valuable for what it tells us about a camp which, perhaps more
than any of its contemporaries in World War II, deserved to be
put on film.

Born in Honolulu in 1918 and graduated from Stanford in
1940, Henshaw was commissioned as a naval officer in May of
the following year. In Hawaii at the time of Pearl Harbor, he
was transferred to Wake Island as communications officer and
taken prisoner there on December 23, two weeks into the war.
He was shipped to Yokohama for interrogation, spent some
time at Zentsuji Island prison camp, then the Ōmori prison in
a Tokyo suburb, then brought to Bunka. Since he had no
background in broadcasting, he was presumably sent to Suragadai for his radio engineering skills—which NHK did not
need. He was to be employed putting on records.

In his diary Henshaw listed every prisoner in the camp,

along with their duties. In a very few cases, he has details wrong, but his is a valuable document. Some arrivals at Suragadai had been found by the Japanese to have "fudged" radio skills in order to get a transfer to what sounded like a better camp than the ones they were in; these usually ended up as cooks and cleaners, after failing microphone, scriptwriting, and other tests. Those who had some function at NHK are listed in appendix 2, with Henshaw's descriptions of their duties.

The fourteen prisoners who "opened" the camp included such potential NHK "collaborators" as Henshaw; Kalbfleisch; Technical Sergeant Newton Light of Roanoke, Virginia; British army Lieutenant John McNaughton of London; Kenneth Parkyns of the Royal Australian Air Force; Provoo; Warrant Officer Nicolas Shenk of the Dutch army; Henry Charles Ralph Fulford (George) Williams of the British Colonial Service; and two Wake Island civilians, Stephen Shattles of New Orleans and Mark Streeter, the Utah native who settled after the war in Mesa, Arizona.

Henshaw told the FBI:

> On December 10, 1943, these fourteen prisoners were read an order under which they would agree to perform such duties assigned to them by the Japanese in connection with broadcasting programs over Radio Tokyo as directed by the Japanese authorities. Any person who did not desire to comply with the order was to advise the Japanese. Williams refused and was that day removed from the camp. The Japanese told the remaining thirteen that Williams had been executed. However, it was subsequently learned that this was not true.

Henshaw recounts the arrival of Cousens and Ince on December 18, relates their earlier sojourn in hotels, and says curiously that

Ince "had been doing work for the Japanese in the Philippines. When he got to Tokyo, he and Cousens did many programs together."

Japan's lack of familiarity with handling prisoners shows again in the unconventional mixing of officers and enlisted men—and even civilians—in the same camp; but the arrival of the officers—and the more senior the better—was probably initially welcomed by the enlisted men as giving them leadership and a measure of protection against abuse. (Later, however, there was to be class conflict of a sort.) By the time of their arrival at Suragadai, most of the POWs had been in harsh conditions of captivity for about a year, under which even officers had "broken." It is notable that Cousens, despite extreme physical weakness, tried to resist at first, but that Ince arrived by sea, in the hold of a ship, from the Philippines, and already substantially dispirited, which probably sapped Cousens' own will to resist forcefully.

Henshaw notes that the one American officer who was refractory to the Japanese, Kalbfleisch, was soon, like the brave British civilian Williams, dealt with:

"On March 28, 1944, Kalbfleisch was removed by order of the Imperial General Headquarters in Tokyo because, according to the order read to the prisoners, Kalbfleisch's work and attitude were unsatisfactory," says the FBI synopsis of Henshaw's testimony, adding: "According to Henshaw, Kalbfleisch was extremely antagonistic toward the Japanese and made no attempt whatsoever to conceal his concerted effort to sabotage the programs ordered by the Japanese. Henshaw claims that the others felt the same way as Kalbfleisch, but were more discreet." (Kalbfleisch was to give the FBI a more complete account of his own resistance, which is narrated later in this book.)

For the first eight months at Suragadai, Henshaw operated the turntables for the "Hinomaru Hour" records. This was a seven-days-a-week program, with the Sunday show prerecorded on Saturday, and was directed by a nisei prison guard, Kazumaro (Buddy) Uno.

The FBI report continues:

> Henshaw, in the first part of 1944, commenced writing the program called "Three Missing Men," which consisted of the story of POW life, acted and read by various POWs. From time to time, Henshaw himself would take one of those parts. This was the feature program of the "Hinomaru Hour" and ran from January 1944 until VJ Day. The actual program itself was started by Provoo. As far as Henshaw can recall, he is the only individual who continued on one program during the entire time he was in the camp. He did not participate in any other program. Most of the other prisoners worked on various programs at different times.

The FBI report related the existence of Henshaw's diary, which was then at the home of his parents in Honolulu and was being edited for publication as a book, *Calling America,* by Adela Rogers St. John for Curtiss-Brown. Neither the book (which the Library of Congress says never appeared) nor his FBI testimony deals more than incidentally with Iva Toguri, whom he never met, but he did tell his interrogators a little (but not much) about her colleagues.

"Henshaw appeared to be somewhat reluctant to discuss the activities of Cousens and Ince," the report says.

> He said . . . they would leave early in the morning and get home late at night, and spent all day at Radio Tokyo. Although they were in close contact with him and their fellow prisoners, they did not discuss their activities with him to any extent. He did ascertain that

they were both connected with the "Zero Hour" and had written, worked, participated and spoken on various other broadcasts. Cousens and Ince were the motivating forces behind the "Zero Hour."

Henshaw had had some contact with Reyes initially, but after the young third lieutenant became a "friendly alien" (when Tokyo set up a puppet Filipino government in Manila) he heard about him only through Cousens and Ince, who in turn saw him only at the station.

Henshaw testified that prisoner-writers went to NHK under guard, but that Cousens and Ince were allowed more liberty to move around between the station and the camp with an interpreter. "All the prisoners were allowed free access at Radio Tokyo and were not under guard while in the building," the report says, adding that conditions and food were better at Suragadai than in the other prison camps, and that "Cousens and Ince were given regular civilian suits to wear." The report goes on: "Henshaw claims that Cousens and Ince at first refused to accept these suits as a gift. Henshaw claims that all the prisoners in Bunka were of one thought—" Three lines of the paragraph are then blanked out, as are the first three lines of the next paragraph.

It seems reasonable to assume that Henshaw was referring to an exception—the allegedly treasonous activities of Provoo and the allegedly sycophantic attitude of Streeter, the Wake Island civilian—because the uncensored portion of the FBI file continues: "Henshaw cannot remember the exact time, but Streeter was subsequently removed from Bunka and given private quarters in Tokyo. He was assisted by two or three men whom the Japanese had brought up from the Philippines at Streeter's personal request. These men were quartered with Streeter, and Henshaw never saw them." Streeter's equivocal attitude was to be referred to by other witnesses.

Henshaw testified that Tamotsu Murayama, Major Tsune-ishi's interpreter, was assigned to "Bunka" and was "very favorable to the prisoners and smuggled food to them. As a result of this activity, he lost his job." Since the war, Murayama had gone to work for *The Nippon Times* (now *The Japan Times*) and he and Henshaw were corresponding on a monthly basis.

A sketch of what life was like at Suragadai begins to emerge. "Good food"—the actual term in the periphrasis—is obviously a piece of FBI misreporting, because all of the other reports confirm that the prisoners were starving, due to the shortage of food in blockaded Japan, whose own subjects were in dire straits. Henshaw must have said that food was "better" at Suragadai than in the camps at Singapore and on the occupied islands. In further testimony some time later, he described food as nearly nonexistent. Moreover, it becomes clear that all the Bunka prisoners, not just Cousens and Ince, were provided with civilian clothes, because the shirts and trousers (in the case of the Aussies, shorts) in which they had been captured had long ago worn out. There is clearly already an attempt in the various FBI periphrases to "hype" the evidence about the prisoners and thereby damage any support that they might give to their ally, Iva Toguri.

Otherwise, this second-hand version of Henshaw's responses forms a useful account of life at Suragadai, introducing into the story such Japanese officers as the intractable Ikeda, Hishikari, and Hamamoto and the more reasonable Tamotsu Murayama and Kaji Domoto. Overall day-to-day command of the camp, Henshaw said, was exercised by Major Tsuneishi from GHQ, and he in turn was answerable to the camp's official commandant, Lieutenant General Seizō Arisue (misspelled Arisne by the FBI).

Except for Cousens and Ince, the other prisoner-writers, announcers, and turntable spinners spent little time at NHK and had little opportunity to get to know the Japanese and the nisei there. What knowledge Henshaw had of Iva Toguri had come, he said, from conversations with Ince and Cousens, according to Special Agent "Blank" (the only case in the records of an FBI official not being identified). "Blank" quotes Henshaw as saying that Cousens and Ince "never discussed 'Zero Hour' or Iva Toguri with him or other prisoners at any length." As a consequence, Henshaw had presumed that Iva was chosen for "Zero Hour" among several applicants, rather than imposed by Cousens because of her "hacksaw" voice.

Special Agent Charles Hettrick, who had been with the Counter Intelligence Corps in Tokyo and who had conducted the initial inquiry which concluded at Iva's innocence, was later to say that Ince had testified to him that he and two others— presumably Cousens and Reyes—had auditioned "ten Japanese girls who spoke English for the purpose of selecting a female propaganda broadcaster." Ince, then "under confinement and investigation for collaboration," apparently told the CIC that all three had selected Iva Toguri because her voice would sabotage the program. Later, however, when Ince had been cleared of charges of collaboration and promoted, his testimonies made it clear that using Iva's scratchy voice to trivialize the program was Cousens' idea alone. If Henshaw's diary was accurate—and there would appear to be no reason for doubting that—it seems that Ince initially sought to protect Iva by seeking to share responsibility with Cousens for choosing her. No one else refers to the auditioning of "ten girls," but it must have been true that several existing announcers were considered by the officer-prisoners, at least in conversation.

Iva Toguri's work is described by Henshaw as being "light commentaries," but he

> got the opinion from Cousens and Ince that Toguri was very pro-USA, and that she did on several occasions help Cousens and Ince by getting food and

medicine to them. It was her desire to leave Japan and return to the United States. It was also Henshaw's opinion that Toguri was in the same position as the POWs, and that she had no alternative but to broadcast, as she had to live and eat and could not do it with only her job at Domei. He said Cousens and Ince thought a great deal of Toguri and were not of the opinion that she ever did or said anything which was in any way wrong, and certainly did not think that she was a traitor.

It is interesting to note that, because of the GI legend of "Tokyo Rose," it was only Toguri's radio work that was considered possibly treasonous, and not her work at Domei.

Henshaw said that Cousens' magisterial inquiry in Australia had lasted two months and that he himself had been in Sydney for three weeks, testifying for his former "Bunka" comrade. He reported that the inquiry had ended when the Attorney General of New South Wales had said there was no indication that Cousens had done anything "treasonable."

Like Ince, Henshaw won promotion back home while working for Tokyo radio. When interviewed in 1948, the ensign had jumped three ranks to lieutenant commander but had decided to retire from the navy.

The report, like all FBI documents of the type, is mutilated by periphrasis, and made heavy to read by classic police pidgin. Police periphrasis is often deceptive. For instance, a witness will say that he has never met Miss Toguri, but because the question is framed to begin "Insofar as you can recall," he is falsely made to say "Insofar as I can recall, I never . . ." as though he entertained some doubts. Henshaw can never assert, only "claim" (as in, "he claims he was born in 1918").

If the periphrasis is irritating, the pidgin is laid on with a palette knife. Iva Toguri is always "Subject" or "subject," with no article. A person is demeaned as "this individual." Nothing is ever learned, always ascertained, so that dichotomously what is certain is only "so far as I can recall," and what is obvious is "claimed," while what is merely learned is always made certain. Nothing is ever said, always "stated," "indicated," or, more bizarrely, "advised," but these verbs are almost always used ungrammatically, without the "that"; as in, "he stated he did not remember" or "he advised he had not met subject."

As a more florid example, at one point Henshaw must have said something like this: "After VJ day, we tried to get our old scripts back but were told at the station that they had been incinerated." This became: "Henshaw advised after VJ Day they were desirous of obtaining same and were advised by the authorities at Radio Tokyo that they had been destroyed by being burned."

Since this investigation was conducted out of the Los Angeles bureau of the FBI, it is not hard to understand why California saw the need to vote, in 1986, to make English the language of the state.

In February, Special Agent John A. Parker reported from the Knoxville, Tennessee, office on an interview with Major Williston Madison Cox, Jr., a thirty-year-old retired lieutenant colonel, who had been, after Cousens, the second-ranking officer at Suragadai. Cox, who was still recuperating from his prison-camp years on his father's farm, stressed that Cousens and Ince had been "forced to participate in Jap [sic] propaganda broadcasts," as the FBI periphrasis puts it.

Cox said he had joined the U.S. Army Air Corps in February 1941 and had been command pilot of a squadron of B-25 bombers at Port Moresby, and part of the Thirty-eighth Bombardment Group, when he was shot down in the water on a raid on Madang. A sergeant had been killed. Cox and four

other crewmen had managed to swim ashore. The four com-
panions later drowned when American forces sank the Japanese
ship in which they were being taken to internment in Japan.
Cox went through several different camps before arriving at
"Bunka," which was devised for "quartering POWs who were
to be used in radio broadcasts and other Japanese propaganda
activities," he said. He had since kept in touch with some of his
fellow prisoners.

Newton Light, for instance, had become a master sergeant.
He and his Filipina wife were living in Roanoke, Virginia.
Provoo, who was from San Francisco, had learned Japanese
while studying Buddhism for a year and a half in Japan before
the war; following his capture on Corregidor, he had been used
by the Japanese as an interpreter. Cox said that Provoo "is, I
understand, presently being held at Fort Sam Houston, San
Antonio, Texas, awaiting court-martial on charges of collaboration."

This led to his mentioning Mark Streeter, the Ogden,
Utah, native who had been a civilian captive on Wake and who
had been recently arrested in Arizona and charged with "treason because of his collaboration activities," Cox said. (Streeter
was later acquitted; Provoo's conviction was quashed on appeal.)

Of Iva Toguri, Cox says—in the FBI periphrasis—that he
has "no firsthand information whatsoever" (a favorite FBI
word) that would be of "evidentiary value in treason proceedings against her." He directed the FBI to Cousens and Ince,
who had also been "forced to participate in Zero Hour broadcasts."

Cox said that apart from participating in "Hinomaru
Hour" choruses, he had evaded broadcasting by "feigning
illness." He had not played in a dramatization of how his plane
was shot down, which had been performed before his arrival at
Suragadai, where he had shared a "small room" with Cousens,

Ince, Henshaw, Kalbfleisch, Jack Wisner, McNaughton (all officers), and Shenk, the Dutch warrant officer. He had returned home on September 4, 1945, been promoted half-colonel that month, and honorably discharged the following January; but malaria and malnutrition had left their effects, and he had spent a year in army hospitals; he was still convalescent, and not working.

On February 9, Special Agent John J. Henry reinterviewed Henshaw at his apartment in Beverly Hills. The former naval officer was shown a CIC interview from Tokyo with George Kazumaro (Buddy) Uno, the nisei camp guard and radio producer, who was reported to have said that his own program "competed with the popular Zero Hour which featured Ruth Hayakawa as Tokyo Rose." (If Uno actually made this untrue claim—that Ruth was the key female on "Zero Hour," and that she was "Tokyo Rose"—it may have reflected his emotions: he and Ruth had broken up as lovers.)

Henshaw said that Uno's program, on which he worked, had initially been called the "Hinomaru Hour" (*hi-no-ma-ru* was the name for the red sun on the old Japanese flag) and that this had been changed to "Humanity Calls." This show, and "The Postman Calls," did compete for popularity among the GI audience with "Zero Hour," Henshaw agreed. He thought Cousens and Ince had used Iva Toguri as their principal disc jockey and he thought she had been identified as the GIs' "Tokyo Rose"; but Ruth Hayakawa, he said (probably wrongly) had also taken part in the program.

Questioning followed to see if the GI "Tokyo Rose" figure could have been a part of "Hinomaru Hour" or "Humanity Calls." Henshaw said that "Humanity Calls" was composed of patter by a master of ceremonies, theme music, political commentary, and the "Three Missing Men" playlet series, which he had written. Sometimes a record was played; sometimes the commentary would be replaced by POW messages—seen as more likely to draw in the audience.

It was in the fall of 1944, Henshaw said, that the name of the "Hinomaru Hour" was changed to "Humanity Calls," and Ince started "The Postman Calls," which consisted of POW messages, some music (with Ince on the turntable), and, two or three times a week, a commentary. The POW messages were read by Corporal Frederick Hobblitt.

Women who had appeared on "Humanity Calls," Henshaw said, included Ruth Hayakawa, Miyeko Furuya, and "Mother" Topping—Genevieve Topping, an octogenarian American missionary. The CIC had quoted Iva Toguri as saying that Ruth Hayakawa had replaced her with a different program on Sundays, but that her most constant "Zero Hour" replacement when she was absent had been Miyeko Oki, née Furuya.

Henshaw pointed out that Ruth and Miyeko were full-time employees of NHK and therefore likely to be called on as replacements for *shokutaku* like Iva and others. Henshaw said Ruth Hayakawa was a friend of the intimidating guard-producer Uno and was rumored to be a member of the *kempeitai,* which Henshaw called the "Gestapo of Japan." Both Hayakawa and Topping, who Henshaw said had "become indoctrinated by the Japanese," had retained their American citizenships. Miyeko, like Ruth, was a dual American citizen–Japanese subject and had appeared in many programs. Henshaw also confirmed Iva's statement that Mary Ishii had often replaced her full time during the period of March to May 1945, when Iva was becoming a Catholic and getting married, and on Sundays thereafter until the end of the war.

Henshaw knew Mary because of her brother Kenneth, who, the FBI report relates, "visited Camp Bunka and on one occasion got Henshaw a pair of shoes." Ishii was well regarded by Cousens and Ince, and Henshaw had stayed in correspondence with him since the Eurasian had returned from the

Japanese army and gone to work for Reuters. Henshaw said he had last seen Mary a year before in Tokyo: she was then working in a canteen for American enlisted men. (She later married an American professor.)

Otherwise, Henshaw added little that was new. After recovering his health, Cousens had returned to NHK—but on the "Humanity Calls" program, not on "Zero Hour." Henshaw said that Uno, in his CIC testimony, had exaggerated the feeding schedule at Bunka, which was generally "rice and thin soup," and had generally made the place seem more relaxed than it was. But he confirmed that those prisoners who had been transferred to Suragadai on false pretenses—by pretending to have a radio background—had been allowed by the Japanese to stay on as camp servants, cooking and cleaning. Henshaw said again that he had never "seen or spoken to Toguri," and that the books which she procured for him were passed through Cousens and Ince.

Henshaw did clear up the mystery of the "Tokyo Rose" who, the U.S. Embassy in London had claimed, had testified against Cousens in Australia. He said Fumi Saisho had been convoked by the Australians and had brought with her scripts that Cousens had written, some of which it had been her duty to censor. This was apparently part of the evidence that led to charges against Cousens being lifted; but there is nothing in the FBI file that indicates whether the scripts which Miss Saisho brought to Sydney were from "Zero Hour," "Humanity Calls," or some other program.

In Detroit, on February 12, Special Agent Mahlon F. Coller interviewed Lieutenant Albert P. Rickert, the marine from Wake Island who, as a corporal, had spent time in a prison camp in Shanghai before joining the Wake Island civilians Shattles and Streeter at Suragadai and becoming Ince's script typist. Other civilians from Wake Island who also ended up at Suragadai were Darwin Dodds, Joseph Asterita, Larry Quille, and a "Los

Angeles cattle buyer" named Jack Taylor. All except Taylor
were to be interviewed by the FBI. Rickert said he had remained
in touch with all of them, and that Streeter had "been arrested
by his fellow prisoners, awaiting the arrival of the United States
troops following the fall of Japan, and charged with treason."
Soon, Edwin Kalbfleisch, the American George Williams of
Suragadai, was to explain what had got Streeter into trouble.
Anything done by Cousens, Ince, or Iva Toguri pales in com-
parison.

Kalbfleisch, the feisty German-American from a brewing
family who had elected to be sent away from Suragadai to more
spartan surroundings rather than collaborate, was interviewed
by Special Agent Stanley T. Blascek in Washington, D.C., on
February 27 and on four dates in early March. He said he had
been a prisoner in the Zentsuji Island camp when the camp
commandant had told him and five others that they were being
transferred to Suragadai. Chatting among themselves, they had
found that they all had radio or writing backgrounds.

Before they left Zentsuji, they were given Red Cross
parcels which had been formerly withheld, and better clothing.
On the way to Tokyo, they were detained for questioning at
Camp Ōmori, where Kalbfleisch let slip to his interrogator that
he had been an assistant news editor at radio station KWK in
St. Louis, Missouri.

The FBI periphrasis says: "From the line of their questioning, Kalbfleisch declared that it was apparent he would be part
of the Japanese war propaganda machine." Shortly after
Kalbfleisch arrived at Suragadai, Provoo, Henshaw, and
Kalbfleisch were taken to NHK to rehearse a program. They
were given scripts by a Eurasian from the Foreign Office, Count
Ikeda, who decided, after the test, to make Sergeant Provoo
master of ceremonies, Second Lieutenant Kalbfleisch the reader,
and Ensign Henshaw the turntable spinner. As Kalbfleisch saw

147

it, the prisoners were in the hands of the army—specifically, Tsuneishi, with Lieutenant Hamamoto involved in supervising the day-to-day running of the camp, but with the Foreign Office helping to shape the direction of propaganda.

The periphrasis reads: "Kalbfleisch recalls that their first broadcast, for which the script was prepared by the Japanese, started off with Provoo identifying the program as the Hino-maru Hour, the 'Voice of Greater East Asia, strong, determined and ever victorious'." Kalbfleisch had described his own script to the FBI as "a piece of tripe," but had claimed he could not remember the subject. The emphasis had been on the invinci-bility of the Japanese and the futility of continuing the war in the Pacific, and there had been some popular music as accom-paniment.

As Kalbfleisch recalled, four of the Bunka prisoners were cooks and cleaners, two were "engaged as artists," about three did the clerical work for the programs—typing, mimeograph-ing, and filing—and five did most of the writing, the others being essentially performers. He recalled that the British pris-oner George Williams had told his fellow inmates early that he would not accept to "do propaganda," and that Williams had taken the opportunity to rebel when a Major Hidota of the Imperial Japanese General Staff had addressed them on their "great work" of "helping to bring peace between two great alliances."

Kalbfleisch said Hidota had assured them that they would not have to do anything "traitorous," and that everything was voluntary; but, if they failed to follow instructions, "nothing can be guaranteed." The major asked if anyone in the group felt he could not cooperate. Williams was the only one who responded, Kalbfleisch recalled, and within an hour he had disappeared from Suragadai.

The periphrasis says: "Kalbfleisch declared that this episode made quite an impression on the group, and subsequent to

Major Hidota's talk they were constantly reminded to cooperate or they would go the way of Williams; that there were only two places to go from Bunka—to their homes at the end of the war or to their graves like Williams."

Initially, Kalbfleisch said, Uno wrote their scripts, but gradually they wrested this task from him and "took every opportunity to write meanings into the script which might be of help to our intelligence." Provoo wrote the "master of ceremonies introductions and remarks," and Henshaw wrote the "wisecracks and musical comments." Uno became convinced that they were cooperating and "allowed them more and more latitude." Kalbfleisch wrote on "current topics viewed through the eyes of a prisoner of war far from home," the periphrasis says, adding: "He stated that this field became his specialty and that he turned out thousands of words of dribble [*sic*—presumably Kalbfleisch said 'drivel'] on every conceivable subject."

Henshaw and Provoo had begun "Three Missing Men" together, but finally Henshaw had taken the series over. Another feature on the "Hinomaru Hour," Kalbfleisch said, was "The Voice of the People," which was mainly handled by Streeter, a firm opponent of Roosevelt. Kalbfleisch called Streeter "disgusting."

The periphrasis continues: "He said that Streeter began his broadcast by stating that the American people had been duped into the war by a wily, oily, double-dealing politician who would hesitate at nothing to further his personal ambition to become the Alexander or Napoleon of the Twentieth Century." Americans should wake up, not shore up the British empire and be left holding the bill, as after World War I, Streeter intoned.

Kalbfleisch said Streeter's calls, day after day, for Americans to lay down their arms finally got to the other prisoners, who threatened a strike if Uno did not take Streeter off the air.

149

Streeter was moved out of the camp and to a different NHK program. Kalbfleisch took over the "Voice of the People" segment of "Hinomaru," which led to regular clashes with Uno about Kalbfleisch's changes and the young lieutenant's habit of altering the script while he was reading it. Uno reported Kalbfleisch to his military superiors. The lieutenant was deprived of food for a day. But the spats with Uno continued, and he was called in by the camp commandant and told to be more cooperative.

When Major Tsuneishi gave a dinner for the hundredth edition of "Hinomaru Hour," he "complimented the prisoners of war on their cooperation," the FBI report says, and asked everyone present what could be done to improve conditions at Bunka. Each of them prepared a report. Kalbfleisch, then bedridden, urged improved medical and other conditions, better food rations, and the removal of Uno and Hamamoto from the camp; he asked that the Japanese stop stealing the Red Cross food parcels for themselves. Finally, he said, he recommended that the POWs' participation in radio be abandoned, "inasmuch as the American people would never believe what they heard," the periphrasis says.

On March 28, 1944, the prisoners were called together and told that everyone had cooperated except Kalbfleisch, who was removed from Suragadai to solitary confinement in a Japanese army hospital. During the second week there, he was called before the commandant, told that he had been accused of disobedience to a civilian employee of the Imperial Army— "Buddy" Uno—and that this was punishable by death. Kalbfleisch said he had been told he would have a formal trial and an execution. Two weeks later, he was moved to another camp, where he remained. He learned later that his life had been spared through the intercession of Murayama, Tsuneishi's gentle interpreter.

So much for the forced treasonous activities of Kalbfleisch

and the other prisoners. What of Iva Toguri, the typist with a twenty-minute record program? Kalbfleisch said that on one occasion someone had pointed out a girl in a control booth and had said that she was the girl whom the GIs called Tokyo Rose. Kalbfleisch was shown a photo of Iva Toguri and said that was not the girl in question. (It was probably the beautiful Ruth Hayakawa.)

Kalbfleisch also could tell little about Cousens and Ince, who, he confirmed, were the only two prisoners who remained at NHK all day long. The periphrasis concludes: "Kalbfleisch was of the opinion that both Cousens and Ince were in the same boat as other prisoners who were told to cooperate or else 'nothing would be guaranteed.'" The FBI investigation was still at the stage where it was letting the former prisoners respond spontaneously—not, as was often the case later, cajoling or even bullying them to say what had to be said to make a prosecution stick.

Darwin Halbert Dodds had been a bellhop and a radio announcer in his native Boise when he had decided to see the world by going to Wake Island, just before America's entry into World War II. Like the other Wake Island civilians at Suragadai, he had worked for the Morrison Knudsen construction company on the naval base. His title: head timekeeper. Like the others, he had been captured on December 23, 1941.

Interviewed by Special Agent Harvey D. Kutz of the FBI's Butte, Montana, office, he described how he had been in the Woo Sung prison camp in Shanghai, having arrived from Wake on the *Nitta Maru*. There, the prisoners had organized a dance band and he had been the announcer. There also, he had met "Buddy" Uno, the nisei prison guard. Dodds had been moved to the Kiang Wang camp in China the following June, then to Ōmori, near Tokyo. All the prisoners at Ōmori were "special" in some way. They received a little more food than before, having been selected for propaganda duties. At Ōmori, he had met Corporal Fred Hobblitt. After a couple of weeks of questioning at Ōmori, he and four others had arrived at what he called "Bunka Propaganda Prison Camp," where he had met Uno again.

The eighteen other prisoners who were already there had filled in the new arrivals on the radio work. Major Cox had told them to "play ball with the Japanese." According to the periphrasis, Cox "indicated it would be better for them to try to get along with the Japanese and broadcast as they were instructed, with the hope of getting a message over to the folks at home by inflection or otherwise in a way that would not be spotted by the Japanese, than to refuse to broadcast at all and literally to lose their heads." He talked about Williams and Kalbfleisch, who were "presumed to have been executed." Having survived thus far, Dodds told the FBI, he and the other new arrivals agreed with Cox. Three days later, he had been made a "master of ceremonies" on "Humanity Calls." He opened the program by singing "When You're A Long, Long Way From Home." Then another prisoner read POW messages, which had to imply that Red Cross parcels were being distributed and which had to contain nothing unfavorable to the Japanese. Dodds said he thought the messages from the prisoners were genuine. Records were played and the program was concluded by Dodds singing "Until Tomorrow." Dodds later was a part of "The Postman Calls."

How about Tokyo Rose? Dodds said Corporal Freddy Hobblitt, the announcer, had introduced him to her at the station after word of what the American press was saying reached Bunka. Shown six photographs of Iva Toguri, he said, as Kalbfleisch had, that this was definitely not "Rose," but he could not remember the name of the girl he had met. Says the periphrasis: "He said that for one thing the Tokyo Rose he had met was a good-looking girl and he did not consider this characteristic applied to the photographs shown him." Most people have said that Ruth Hayakawa was the best-looking woman in the NHK English division, but others, especially Miyeko Furuya, were also noted for their prettiness.

In counterpoint, another Wake Island civilian, Joseph John Asterita of Brooklyn, was to tell Special Agents Chester Orton and Thomas J. McShane much later that Cousens had pointed out "Tokyo Rose" at the station for him. Asterita identified Iva's photograph. Like Tsuneishi, Cousens was presumably making a proprietary claim. She was "their" Rose, their radio creation. After all, Iva clearly *was* one of the twenty-seven Tokyo Roses, indeed one of the half dozen better-known ones. The true question was whether she was the one who made broadcasts about troop movements.

Dodds said that when he arrived at Suragadai, Cousens had just had a nervous breakdown (actually, a heart attack) and "it was because of this that Major Cox had assumed leadership of the Bunka camp, Cousens normally holding this position." Cox was young and inexperienced at anything but flying a bomber, but the Australian major, Dodds said, "was the confidant of the other prisoners in the camp. . . . He and the other prisoners did everything to help America. He [Dodds] said he had absolutely no suspicion that Cousens was in any way sympathetic to the Japanese." Dodds had been "very much surprised" by Cousens' brush with the law in Australia after his liberation. He denied that Cousens and Ince had been better dressed than the other prisoners and said Ince was "loyal and beyond reproach and suspicion." There was "no indication" that he was sympathetic to Japan or had helped Japan, or had hindered the United States or its allies through the radio broadcasts.

Dodds said he had never been at NHK when "Zero Hour" was broadcast. He had never met Reyes or Major Tsuneishi, and "knew little" of Streeter and Provoo.

Special Agent Orton, who had taken on much of the task of interviewing the Suragadai alumni, traveled to the Richmond office, from where, on March 30, he interviewed Newton Light, the career sergeant, at Roanoke. Light had told Orton he had never seen or heard Iva Toguri; his responses were those of a typical career noncom anxious not to get involved in something that could do him no good. The former script clerk was unwilling to admit that he had even been that:

"According to Light, he was a staff sergeant at the time of his capture, and he was the general clean-up man or handyman around the camp at Bunka," the periphrasis reads. It continues:

> He stated that he had no clerical ability whatsoever [that FBI word again] and that he at no time typed or prepared any part of a program or script which was used on the program Zero Hour. He stated there was in the camp, however, a hand-operated mimeograph machine and on two or three occasions he [had been] ordered by his superiors to use the machine to run off copies of something, but that he did not know just exactly what was [the nature of the material that he mimeographed]. Light stated he had been forced to go to Tokyo radio on several occasions, but that he always went with the group and that, as far as he knows, none of the individuals in his camp participated in the program Zero Hour.

Phew! No names, no pack-drill. . . .

The day before, March 29, Orton had been in Laredo, Texas, filing a report through the San Antonio bureau on an interview with former Private First Class Ramon Perez Martinez. Orton must have been getting tired of all the rail travel (airlines were still a luxury) because he noted that Martinez had been born on May 21, 1941 (fewer than seven years before), and had joined the army three months earlier still, February 21, 1941.

At Suragadai, Martinez had been told by a "Japanese propaganda officer" that he would be doing broadcasts in Spanish, and "You will do as I tell you or else!"

Says the periphrasis: "Martinez stated he then became part of the radio program known as 'The Saturday Jamboree' which was broadcasted [*sic*] from Radio Tokyo every Saturday at 2:00 P.M. Tokyo time. This was thirty minutes of English and Spanish songs and personal messages from the prisoners to their families." Martinez said Henshaw and Harry Pearson, a British soldier, wrote the scripts for the program; the use of the Indian word jamboree probably came from Pearson, but one wonders whether the idea for the title did not come from Cousens, who had been born in Poona and who had served in the Indian Army before the war.

Martinez said it had been Uno who had caused his transfer to Bunka, but he had no feelings of gratitude to "Buddy" because of that. Says the periphrasis: "To his knowledge, Uno never afforded any assistance to the prisoners in any manner whatsoever." The prisoner had been "compelled to wear" civilian clothes, he complained.

On April 9, Orton was in Wells, Texas, interviewing Jack King Wisner, who had just ceased to be the town postmaster. The report, filed through the Dallas bureau, recounts a story that begins similarly to that of Major Cox.

Wisner had been a second lieutenant bombardier in a B-17 based in Port Moresby, and bombing Rabaul, when he had been shot down at 3 A.M. one tropical morning, June 13, 1943, by a Japanese night-fighter. Both pilots had been killed. Wisner and the navigator had bailed out, landing in thick jungle. He had been unable to find the navigator, and had walked south for about a week until he reached the Torrio plantation, owned by a Dutchman. The planter and his native workers had fed him and hidden him in thick brush on the plantation, but he had been discovered on June 21 and placed in a "Japanese garrison on the plantation."

After various camps, he and nine other prisoners, including Major Cox, had been led blindfolded onto a ship, arriving in southern Japan on December 6. They had been led ashore, blindfolded again, and put into a train with drawn blinds. He had been held in the Ōmori camp until December 27, being interrogated by Japanese officers, then had been led into "Bunka" by Uno on January 8, 1944, along with Cox, Rickert, and the British corporal, Harry Pearson. Uno had marshaled them in front of the intimidating Lieutenant Hamamoto, who had plunged a sword into the floor and "proceeded to indoctrinate them in the rules of the camp—Japanese supremacy and the weakness of the United States."

They were told they could prepare their own broadcasts, but that these would be censored. They learned about the presumed fates of Williams and Kalbfleisch for refusing to cooperate. Wisner had been assigned to read scripts on "Hinomaru Hour," which became "Humanity Calls," and on "The Postman Calls," of which he was the master of ceremonies.

What if you had refused? he was asked.

"I felt I would have been killed," the former officer said.

He remembered Provoo's introduction to "Hinomaru Hour"—". . . the voice of Greater East Asia; strong, determined, ever victorious." Wisner said they had had to boost Japanese victories. He had never heard of an "Orphan Annie" program, but he had heard of Iva Toguri, and knew that she worked for Cousens and Ince.

On April 17, Orton quizzed James Gutierrez Martinez in Waco, Texas, a Suragadai prisoner not related to Private Martinez. He identified a photograph of Iva as being "the girl I saw give a small sack of potatoes to Ince on two occasions in the hallway of the Radio Tokyo building."

In San Francisco, on April 29, Special Agents Eugene E. Bjorn and Edward Dornlas, Jr., caught up with Corporal Hobblitt. Freddy related his work on "The Postman Calls." He had "known" Iva and Felippe but had never spoken to them. He had seen her in the record library, where both were choosing selections for their respective programs. When in Tokyo in the fall of 1947, to testify at the War Crimes Trials, he had identified Iva Toguri but she had not recognized him. He knew Ruth Hayakawa and Miyeko Furuya Oki on the same basis.

Hobblitt said he was "not aware of any collaboration with the Japanese on the part of Ince or Cousens and he did not think they received any special consideration from the Japanese." He remembered Ince protesting, in Manila, at being taken to Japan. After that, at Bunka, "Ince was very outspoken and as a result was often in trouble with the Japanese guards."

On May 6, Orton interviewed Larry W. Quille, the night office manager of the Morrison Knudsen construction company, at the Pacific naval base on Wake. Quille's prison-camp work at NHK had led to his becoming a reporter on the Fullerton *News-Tribune*. Speaking at Fullerton, Quille, one of the "founder" inmates at Suragadai, said Cousens "did only what he was ordered to do and he played down the efforts of the Japanese as much as possible."

Quille said he thought Uno had proposed him for Suragadai and NHK because his papers showed he had been a copyboy on a newspaper. However, his writings had been ultimately rejected by the Japanese and he had been "detailed to the galley" and beaten up by Hamamoto. He had never seen Iva Toguri.

Another Wake Island civilian interviewed by Orton was Stephen Herman Shattles, of Hattiesburg, Mississippi, and New Orleans. Shattles, who was also questioned by Special Agent John J. Henry, had been a timekeeper at the Pacific Naval Air Base when captured.

According to the FBI report of the interview, Shattles said

that the Suragadai prisoners had the "intent and purpose to sabotage the program as best they could and to insert as many double meanings into the scripts [as they could] without inciting the Japanese or causing disciplinary action to be taken against them." He recalled receiving threats to be "taken out and shot," and confirmed the deep and abiding impression made on the Suragadai inmates by the presumed executions of Williams and Kalbfleisch.

Shattles said he did mimeographing, read some commentaries, and played in dramas. He had never heard of "Zero Hour" or Iva Toguri.

On May 10, Special Agent Leo E. Kuykenball of the Oklahoma City bureau had gone to El Reno, Oklahoma, to see Frank Fujita, another Suragadai prisoner. Fujita, an American soldier, said someone had once pointed out "Tokyo Rose" to him in a studio at NHK, but the girl had already passed him and he did not look back.

Kuykenball also did an interview with a second lieutenant who had taken part in the "capture" of Tokyo and whose name is blanked out in the file. The interview took place at Nash, Oklahoma. The lieutenant thought that Tokyo Rose was Ruth Hayakawa, who had, he said, escaped attention by going south to Kyushu and getting a job with the American occupation forces.

Kuykenball wrote: "He stated that Ruth Hiakawa [sic], of Japanese descent, was a very clever and good-looking woman and it was his understanding that both she and subject [Iva Toguri] had attended college at one of the Californian universities . . . [She] was engaged as an interpreter by the commanding general of the U.S. Army at Fukuoka . . . and this general was probably attached [sic] to either the 5th Amphibious Division or to the 32nd Division. He stated that Ruth Hiakawa had travel permits during early 1946 to Tokyo when travel among all Japanese was entirely restricted." In his opinion, Ruth Hayakawa was "the main 'Tokyo Rose.' "

10.

The Key American Witnesses: Ted Ince and Normando Reyes

THE CORE OF THE SO-CALLED Tokyo Rose case was at Suragadai. There, Iva Toguri's superiors and script-imposers, Cousens and Ince, had been interned. The rest of the former prisoners from there could report on Ince and Cousens and on what they knew, at least indirectly, of Iva. The feedback from the long and expensive FBI investigation was remarkably homogeneous. Cousens and Ince had done only what they had been compelled to do, and they had tried to sabotage the NHK programs discreetly. Kalbfleisch, who had been less discreet, had been driven from the walls, and risked death. No one, not even Kalbfleisch or Cox, who had successfully evaded doing much at NHK, blamed Cousens or Ince, who directly or indirectly controlled Iva Toguri for most of her effective time on "Zero Hour." She was clearly as innocent as they, if they were innocent, and she had a record of pro-American sentiments and of helping the prisoners. Left without the protection of Cousens and Ince at the end, and going absent without leave as often as possible, she had perhaps been forced by Mitsushio, Oki, Uno, and others to include a few untoward comments in her script; but no one could seriously expect a young woman, especially an enemy alien, to say no too often in the Japan of the times;

moroever, it was clear that, even at its worst, "Zero Hour" was innocuous. But the pressure was on—not to see if *someone* had broadcast things that were unacceptable; that was not in doubt; but to see if something of this could be tied to the hapless Iva Toguri.

The weak link among the officer-prisoners obliged to do really risky things had been Normando Reyes, the impressionable nineteen-year-old who enjoyed any form of radio work better than sitting in a prison camp, and who had been made a "friendly alien," instead of a hostile one, by a stroke of the imperial pen. Nonetheless, he had been a third lieutenant in the Filipino forces, which were part of the U.S. forces, and he had not exactly obeyed the rules for American officers taken prisoner. And he was now in the United States, and presumably still impressionable.

Special Agent Winfred E. Hopton of the Memphis bureau first went to see Reyes at his American mother's home in Nashville on April 17. His brother and two sisters were also there. Reyes had become a student at a local university, Vanderbilt, on a student visa issued in the Philippines, the American colony which had recently become independent. The synopsis at the head of the FBI report highlights the point that Reyes is unable to connect Iva Toguri to "the Tokyo Rose referred to in the American shortwave broadcasts."

Reyes recounted his capture on Corregidor, his imprisonment at Fort Sant Iago, and his interrogations there, which revealed that he had worked in radio, both as a civilian and on the American forces' "Freedom" station.

"While I was at Fort Sant Iago, I was informed by a member of the military police of the Japanese army, through an interpreter, that I was being given the choice of either going to Japan or being decapitated," the FBI report quotes him as saying. He confirmed that he had been nineteen at the time.

It was in Tokyo that he had learned the nature of his radio assignment and had met up again with Ince, who had introduced him to Cousens. He had not known Ince before the war, he said, but they had been captured on the same day on Corregidor, after working together there.

At NHK, Mitsushio had "told us they wanted [a program which would] sound unlike any other Japanese program, and that as much as possible they wanted it to sound like an American disc jockey program; that in the beginning they wanted it to sound innocuous, so that they could gradually work into it the news which the Japanese military wanted to get across." The purpose was "to demoralize American troops in the Pacific."

About Iva, he said much the same as he had said two years before: "I noticed that about a month or so after she was assigned to the program she seemed to register some disgust with it. It was about this time that the military began to have the say-so as to the type and nature of the program. She remarked to me that she disliked the program and said something to the effect that it was beginning to 'smell'."

There had been occasional calls from Major Tsuneishi, reminding them of the basic objective. Ince was by then reading "bad" news from the home front, about floods and other catastrophes.

How had Iva managed the pressures to include propaganda?

"I would say that Iva used Japanese propaganda in her program to a minimal extent," Reyes said. She had avoided "military or political propaganda" and had "concentrated on the good old life back in the States." This was, of course, something that reflected her own feelings of homesickness.

"The military propaganda," Reyes said, "was injected into other portions of the Zero Hour program." He thought it was "doubtful" that Iva had had any demoralizing effect; she herself

had expressed the hope that her show would not be demoralizing.

He summed it up: "The substance of her remarks was
[such] that . . . individuals with any degree of intelligence
would not believe what they heard on the program. . . . After
Iva [had been] on the program for a month or so, she [told] me
several times that she would like to get off [it]," Reyes said
again.

He said she had been offended when she was jokingly
referred to as "Tokyo Rose" by Tsuneishi, and had said that she
"could not possibly be the Tokyo Rose referred to in the
shortwave broadcasts from the United States."

Her first problem, it would seem from this, had already
appeared: she was Tsuneishi's candidate. Tsuneishi did not
speak English. He may have imagined that her rasping voice
sounded aristocratic, since that was patrician style—including
his own—in Japan.

Reyes said he also had never connected Iva Toguri with the
"Tokyo Rose referred to in American propaganda broadcasts,"
because the statements attributed to Tokyo Rose were never a
part of "Zero Hour." The worst that Iva had had to do was to
make soldiers "homesick and sick of the army," Reyes said. To
the inevitable question that followed, he said that he had "no
close personal friendship with her."

Reyes was re-reinterviewed by Hopton on May 8, 10, and
15, and there seems to have been a studied attempt to break him
down. He was interrogated, not in the reassuring comfort of
his mother's home, but in the office of the manager of the
apartment complex where they lived. Once again, we get a
rather unnatural periphrasis, which Reyes, the vulnerable student who wanted to stay in the United States and get his degree,
signed on May 15.

It began:

I was born on February 2, 1922, in Manila. While I was a sophomore in high school in 1937, I started to work as an announcer on radio station KZIB in Manila. I attended the University of the Philippines from 1940 to December 1941. I went to Corregidor in February 1942, as a civilian, for broadcasting equipment. Upon being unable to return to Manila, I joined the Philippine army and was automatically inducted into the United States armed forces for the Far East. I held the ranks of private through third lieutenant or warrant officer.

He had been promoted second lieutenant after the war, demobilized and made program director of the Manila Broadcasting Company, leaving Manila in August 1947 to come to Nashville as a student. Reyes also gave some information about his family. He said his mother, Grace, had been born in 1893 in Brooklyn, "of English parents." His father, Ildefonso Reyes, had been secretary to Manuel Quezon in 1920, when Quezon was Senate president. Reyes said the entire family, except for himself, had lived in exile during the war, and had settled in the United States in 1945; his father had since returned to the Philippines.

Reyes said he had been captured on Corregidor on May 7, 1942, interned in the former British Club in Manila, then in Sant Iago fort, a local jail, then in Bilibid prison. In September, he had been shipped to Taiwan and transferred to a troop ship for Japan, arriving in Tokyo in the first week of October. He and Ince had worked together on American forces radio from February to July 1942 and had been reunited on the prison ship for Formosa.

Reyes went on: "The Japanese apparently knew that I had been doing radio work and, while I was at Fort Sant Iago, I was informed by a member of the military police of the Japanese army, through a naval interpreter, that I was being given a choice of either going to Japan or being decapitated." The repetition suggests that Hopton was trying to get the youth to change his story.

In Tokyo, Reyes said, he and Ince had been assigned to NHK, where they had met Cousens. Working under Mitsushio, whom Reyes calls Nakamoto, he was initially given the task of correcting grammar in news broadcasts and commentaries, then of writing commentaries himself. Later, he said, he was "assigned exclusively to the Zero Hour program." The three prisoners, he noted, were at first the only non-Japanese at NHK.

He recounted living with Ince and Cousens at the hotel, and how his status had changed in November 1943, about a year after the Japanese had set up a puppet government in Manila. He had been photographed and fingerprinted by the police and told to stay away from the prisoners and the Suragadai camp in Kanda. Except on the program, he was not allowed to talk to them or to English-speaking Japanese; but he had met an American, Katherine Morōka, a typist in the business office of NHK, and had married her on September 29, 1944, at the Filipino Embassy. He said that he and Katherine were now separated and that she was working for the American Red Cross in Tokyo as one of the local director's secretaries. (In fact, she was already back in America.)

He dated the inception of "Zero Hour" to approximately March 31, 1943. Initially, it had been a fifteen-minute program, from 6:00 to 6:15 P.M., featuring only himself, under the direction of Mitsushio and Oki. Ince and Cousens joined him about a month later, he said. He thought Mitsushio had coined the program's name—a point with which Mitsushio strongly agrees today. After Iva Toguri was added to the show, it grew in length.

In its final format, Reyes said, "Zero Hour" consisted of a five-minute opening with band music, handled by a male announcer, Sali Nakamura, followed by five minutes of "News from the Home Front" read by Ince, fifteen minutes of records by Iva Toguri, five minutes of world news read by Ince, fifteen minutes of jazz records by Reyes, ten minutes of pro-Japanese commentary by Charles Yoshii, five minutes of fill-in music, ten minutes of an "Amos an' Andy"–type sketch handled by a single Japanese whose name Reyes said he could not recall, then a five-minute monologue "supposed to portray a GI marooned on an island, reminiscing and talking to himself," handled by a "Japanese called Moriyama"; the program was signed off by Nakamura.

This adds up to seventy-five minutes and therefore seems correct, although it is marginally different from Iva Toguri's earlier recollection—perhaps the format varied from time to time—and it is hard to believe that Reyes had forgotten that it was Mitsushio himself who did the Frank Watanabe sketch. Reyes did not say how Ince was replaced after he left the program.

Reyes had operated the turntables both for his own jazz and, after Ince left "Zero Hour," for Iva's music. Cousens' job was coaching: "I do not recall his ever having taken any actual part in the program itself," Reyes said, not quite accurately. He thought the decision to have a woman's voice on the program had come from Mitsushio, but that the choice of Iva had been mainly Cousens'. He did not remember there having been any other applicants for the job. "It was my impression," said Reyes, "that they were looking for a certain type." He confirmed again that Cousens had written Toguri's scripts and that, after he fell ill, she had written them herself in the Cousens style.

In explaining the aim of "Zero Hour," Tsuneishi had told Mitsushio in Reyes' presence that it should produce a feeling of homesickness among listeners. "He would occasionally use the [English] word 'homesick,' " Reyes said, adding: "Apparently, there is no word in Japanese to describe nostalgia." After Cousens fell ill, since Ince had already left the program, Toguri would seek advice from Reyes. Reyes had heard Mitsushio, apparently passing on instructions from Tsuneishi, ask Toguri to "lay it on a bit thicker."

He returned again to the theme of Iva's unwillingness to continue in the program, even before Cousens left.

"I recall that about a month or so after she was assigned to the Zero Hour, Toguri [told] me that she did not particularly care for the program because of its purpose," he said once more. He and his wife and Ken Ishii had occasionally visited her at her home, where she had confided in them. He identified some of her scripts, and added: "I have never heard Toguri make any mention of military operations or give any news on her program on the Zero Hour. I cannot recall her ever having made remarks in her broadcasts regarding the sweethearts and wives of the GIs associating with the 4Fs back home. I would say it is quite possible that such talk as this was probably included in the five-minute monologue portion of the program [by Hisashi Moriyama]. This was . . . straight-out raw propaganda. I do not know how it could be confused with Toguri's [sic] broadcast, except that it was on the same program." (He had, of course, reportedly made such remarks himself in the early days of "Zero Hour.")

He said Ruth Hayakawa, "a Japanese born in California," broadcast an hour of classical music between 6:00 and 7:00 P.M. on Sundays, in place of "Zero Hour"—on which he said Miss Hayakawa had never appeared. The only time he had heard a Japanese official praise Iva was when Tsuneishi had told her she was doing a very good job. He also confirmed that the first person at NHK to refer to her jokingly as Tokyo Rose had been Tsuneishi. Reyes said the nisei at the station were divided into "those who were trusted Japanese and those who were not."

Iva had told him that she had to watch her step more than the others.

The key American figure at Suragadai, as far as the Toguri investigation was concerned, was Ince. The army had investigated him and cleared him, and loyally managed to keep one of its own out of the clutches of the FBI. It was only much later, after Iva's rearrest, that Ince was obliged to come into the San Francisco office of the Bureau and face interrogation by Special Agents Tillman and John Eldon Dunn.

Most of his testimony on these occasions about Iva appears later (in chapter 14); but he began his three days of responding to questions by outlining his wartime experiences before and especially during captivity, and these give flavor and meaning to the testimony of Henshaw and the others at Suragadai.

Wallace Ellwell Ince had been born in 1912 in Spokane, Washington, and had joined the national guard as an enlisted man at the lowest point of the Depression, in 1932. He had joined the regular army four years later, had gone to the Philippines, where he had met his wife, and had taken his discharge there in 1939. The young former corporal had then become a part-time radio announcer with station KZRM and the full-time "public relations manager" of the Marco Polo Hotel. In 1940, he had joined station KZRH as a full-time announcer, staying there until December 23, 1941, just after Pearl Harbor, when he was commissioned as a first lieutenant and public relations officer in the army.

Ince, who by the time he testified had reached the rank of major and was awaiting promotion to half-colonel, recounted how he had taken part in the retreat from Manila to Corregidor, where he had set up a shortwave station, "The Voice of Freedom," with a transmitter and other equipment which he had taken from KZRH just before the fall of Manila. The "Voice" remained in action until May 6, 1942.

Those captured with Ince and Reyes at the Corregidor radio station included a Filipino lieutenant colonel, Carlos Romulo, later a long-serving foreign minister of his country, a Lieutenant Isidoro of the Filipino army, and two American privates. Ince said he had known Reyes earlier as an announcer's voice on KZRM after he (Ince) had left that station, and that he had been "acquainted" with Romulo before the war, as Romulo had been on the board of directors of the station. Reyes had just escaped through the Japanese lines when he reached the American forces.

At this point in his interrogation, Ince handed over a statement of his wartime activities which he had made for the Counter Intelligence Corps in Yokohama three years before. In this, he related that when the Japanese took Corregidor they were looking for "Ted Wallace"—his radio name. They had soon discovered his true identity and he was brought to a Japanese officer for questioning. Ince said he twice denied that he was Ted Wallace, insisting that Ted Wallace the local radio announcer was dead. The officer, however, did not believe him, and began to ask questions about the Voice of Freedom station. Interrogation resumed a few days later.

On May 24, 1942, Ince was among ten thousand prisoners marched to the docks and put on ships to be taken to Manila; just before sailing, however, Ince, Reyes, and Private Charles W. Boyle, a "Voice of Freedom" announcer, were taken off the ship and subjected to questioning again. Around midnight, the three were put on another ship filled with Filipino prisoners, including their fellow broadcaster Isidoro. In Manila, they were taken to the British club, to sleep on the floor, and made to broadcast lists of the names of prisoners on shortwave radio.

On May 28, the four radio men were incarcerated at Fort Sant Iago, where Boyle contracted dysentery. The Japanese were reluctant to give treatment until it was too late, and Boyle died in the infirmary of the Bilibid prison nearby. Isidoro, who had helped Ince carry Boyle into Bilibid, was released, but Ince was soon joined by Reyes, brought from Sant Iago. Both men were asked if they would do radio work for the Japanese and both replied that it would be a breach of their duty, Ince said. They were told they were being taken to Japan. The Japanese officer interrogating them, a Lieutenant Kano, allowed Ince to spend an hour with his wife and child, who were living not far from Bilibid. While at his home, Ince's confessor, a Father Turner, arrived and Ince told the priest that the Japanese were trying to force him to broadcast for them; he told Father Turner he was considering jumping off the ship on its voyage to Yokohama. Father Turner made the distraught prisoner promise he would not commit suicide, pointing out that he did not yet really know what would happen when he reached Tokyo. Reyes, Ince, and some other American prisoners were shipped out of Manila the next day.

Ince confirms the account given by Reyes of their initial days in Japan. When they first went on the air, Ince, an orphan, broadcast a message to his grandmother in America, while Reyes, he said, addressed a message to "someone in New York." Then they spent "several weeks" at Tokyo radio, doing no work. "Both of us were amazed at the disorganization and state of confusion that reigned," Ince told the CIC and, later, the FBI.

The Japanese, at that point, were going out of their way to be friendly, Ince recalled, until the two prisoners were asked to write a critique of NHK; they made their report as uncomplimentary as possible.

Around the end of the year, a Japanese called Watanabe, who broadcast a daily talk in English called "From One American to Another," was drafted into the forces, and Mitsushio ordered Ince to take his place. The scripts were written in Japanese and translated by Mitsushio. Ince complained of the "bad English," and from the start he was allowed to correct

169

mistakes. Gradually, he said, he changed the scripts more and more, putting in "a few comments of my own which were just the reverse of the idea that the original Japanese author had in mind." If the script arrived too late for translation, Ince would read stories from a local English-language paper, which he figured "could have no possible value to the Japanese nor be of any disservice to my own country."

On one occasion, in February, he wrote a ten-minute script about golf and the weather, saying that it was unusually fine in Japan just then. He told the CIC: "Not knowing if we were ready to bomb Japan or not, I was trying to put out the idea that the weather was right. Unfortunately, the censor cracked down on that one."

Reyes and Ince were mainly employed correcting grammatical mistakes in scripts, but often inserted new ones that they felt would sound funnier than those the Japanese had made unaided.

Cousens was already at the station, and he and Ince discussed what could be done to sabotage the program further without being discovered. Cousens had recounted his session with Tsuneishi, when he had asked for a pistol to kill himself and had been offered a sword instead. Ince said that they decided that they could "put on our own propaganda if we went at it slowly and carefully and [gained] their confidence. This Cousens did later with a series of commentaries."

Ince managed to end the "From One American to Another" series by saying the translated scripts were too poor and that he had no ideas of his own. By then, Reyes had started the fifteen-minute "Zero Hour," a purely musical program. When this was expanded, Ince was ordered to do a five-minute news roundup, using copy from Japanese wire services.

"It was quite easy to rephrase and condense the news in such a way that it told just the opposite story of the same broadcasts from the same station, or to set off by phrases the army communiques, so that anyone listening in would know it was a fake from beginning to end," Ince said. It is not clear if the CIC asked him to elaborate on this intriguing statement, but the FBI certainly never did. Later, Ince had to read "home front" news based on broadcasts picked up from American radio stations. Cousens was doing mostly coaching work, Ince said, but also reading Australian POW messages. When Ince fell sick in December 1943, he was replaced in his broadcasting duties by either Cousens or Reyes.

After Ince returned, he pleaded a sore throat and asked to be allowed to run the turntable. By then, he and Cousens had been moved from the Sanno Hotel to Suragadai on December 18. Four days later, they were already in trouble for bringing cigarettes and books from outside to their fellow prisoners.

Lieutenant Hamamoto, the effective camp commandant ("Hamomoto" throughout in the FBI files), told Cousens and Ince: "You will do what you are told. You will obey camp orders or else!" He then drew a finger across his throat to indicate beheading.

Ince recalled: "He said that he could take us out on the square in front of the barracks and execute us at any time and no questions would be asked. At this point, I might add in seriousness that anyone who had been a POW for a year was not going to argue the point with a mad Jap."

The weather became freezing. On January 5, the prisoners were doing calisthenics in the courtyard and Ince thrust his cold fingers into his trouser pockets. Hamamoto, who had been watching from a window, strode out, hit Ince with a kendo stick, then grabbed him with a jiujitsu hold and threw him to the ground.

A few days later, still sick from the previous month and unable to retain much of his food, Ince asked Shenk, the Dutch warrant officer who was the officers' cook, to overboil his rice.

Hamamoto, seeing some rice still on the fire, asked why Ince had ordered "soft rice."

"I said I had not ordered it," Ince recounted, "but had asked if it were possible. He said I lied and slapped me, then told me to go to bed without dinner. Yet on the following day he ordered soft rice for me [for] as long as I felt ill."

One of Hamamoto's subalterns, Hishikari, told Henshaw that Ince was arrogant and uncooperative and had even made irreverent remarks about the emperor—virtually, blasphemy at the time. Hishikari told Henshaw to talk to his friend and to urge him to repent, because otherwise, Tsuneishi had apparently warned, "it would be serious for all concerned." On April 28, Ince was told he would no longer be used at the station and would be sent to a punishment camp instead.

He was, however, given one more script to read and was then berated by "Buddy" Uno for putting the emphasis in the wrong places. From then until September 1944, he only acted in dramas but was allowed to continue to live at Suragadai. In August, at a meeting of all the prisoners which was addressed by Hishikari and Uno, Ince said he wanted to be transferred out of radio work and placed in an ordinary prison camp. Many others present at once asked the same thing. Nothing happened, so, two days later, all of the officers signed a letter of "resignation" from NHK. They were told by Tsuneishi that whether or not they stayed at the station was not for them or him to decide.

Tsuneishi, addressing the mutinous group, said: "If any man does not want to continue his work here, he can always go, but the sword may not feel so good."

Ince, conscious that Tsuneishi dared not lose all the broadcasters by executing them, found the spirit to respond. According to his own account, he said: "None of us are afraid to die. We are all soldiers who expect to die some day. Threats of decapitation do not frighten us."

Tsuneishi, instead of raging, told them bluntly that orders were orders and that they would continue to do what they were told. Ince and some other "Bunka" prisoners asked for the removal of the brutal nisei Uno and the disloyal Provoo. Actually, Ince told the CIC, their main grievance against Uno was not his occasional violence but that he spotted what was being done with the scripts and often derailed their attempts to burlesque the programs. Provoo, as well as being cooperative with the Japanese generally, was seen as the camp snitch.

Ince and others then began to ask Tsuneishi that more POW messages and less "commentary"—propaganda—be broadcast, arguing that this would create a good impression of the Japanese abroad. Tsuneishi asked what Ince would do if some POW messages were critical of the Roosevelt administration. Ince said he would "throw them out." What about a prisoner saying he is "sick and lonely," the major asked. Ince said that might be used, because it would sound true, whereas the other would sound like Japanese propaganda. Ince cites this as a good example of how the prisoners sought to achieve their own ends by appearing to advise the Japanese on their image and on how to make their broadcasting more effective.

Provoo's pro-Japanese attitude was essentially cultural and not likely to have much influence on listening GIs. Of more clear value to Tokyo were the commentaries of the Wake Island civilian Mark Streeter, an arch Republican in the Charles Lindbergh mold who blamed Roosevelt for his personal predicament and for the miseries of the American soldiers in the Pacific theater. Domoto told the officers they were not to interfere with Streeter's work or to harass him. "If harm comes to him, the results for you will be severe," Ince quotes him as saying. Domoto particularly upbraided Lieutenant McNaughton, a British officer, and told him to leave Streeter alone. The otherwise friendly Domoto insisted that his superiors were "reading double meanings into everything."

McNaughton related later that Domoto had complained of Ince's "tactlessness." Streeter, Ince recounted, was from then on given the "silent" treatment, but when B-29s bombed their area of Tokyo, and everyone had to flee to the basement of the former school, some prisoners started a rumor that the bombers were "looking" for Streeter, whose anti-Roosevelt polemics had thus put all their lives at risk. It was then that Streeter was moved for safety to different accommodation in the city, away from his fellow Americans.

Soon, the Japanese had discovered double meanings in Henshaw's "Three Missing Men" scripts. Word of this was passed to Henshaw by Provoo, who insisted unconvincingly that he himself had "seen the light" and was now an enemy of Japan; but when talking to the other enlisted men, Ince said, Provoo would try to stir up resentments against the officers. From time to time, Ince added, Japanese officers would take individual officer-prisoners aside, with an overt show of friendliness, and try to probe the secrets of how scripts were "doctored."

Ince claimed he told Domoto that conditions at Suragadai were intolerable under international convention, and that the radio work was an unlawful imposition. Domoto then made a bid to replace Hishikari in the general running of the camp, which led to a face-off between the two Japanese officers in front of Tsuneishi. Hishikari, who did not want to be sent back to combat duty, told Domoto he would report the argument to his father, who was a general; but the following March Hishikari and an unpopular army censor, Ozaki, were in fact transferred.

On April 25, with victory less than three months off—but with no one yet aware of the fact, of course—Cox, Ince, Wisner, McNaughton, Henshaw, Smith, a prisoner called Odlin, and Provoo sat up until one-thirty in the morning discussing the radio programs. Provoo insisted he had been deceiving the Japanese all along but charged that it was really Cousens and Henshaw who were collaborators. This naturally led to a shouting match, and the prisoners nearly came to blows.

"The following day, I called Provoo in," Ince related,

> and I told him that his record at Suragadai was the blackest. I accused him of stooling to the Japanese, lying to his fellow soldiers and cheating. I said he was a pervert and a thief. I told him he was unstable and preying on the minds of the other enlisted men. I then asked him why he didn't go out on the square in front of the barracks and commit *seppuku* . . . and thus benefit all humanity.

Even though Ince had typed all this months later, his rage and revulsion with Provoo that day come through bitterly; but an objective observer is obliged to note that by marking out Provoo and Streeter as traitors or collaborators—and eventually "arresting" them at the liberation of the camp—the other prisoners managed to lessen any charge of treason against themselves. Ince claims Provoo "shed tears" after the tongue-lashing.

On August 14, just before the surrender, Domoto "leaked" to Henshaw and McNaughton that "all the officers were very nearly lined up and shot on the strength of Provoo's written reports to Major Hifumi, who relieved Major Tsuneishi in June," Ince wrote to the CIC. He added:

> Provoo charged Cousens, Ince and Henshaw with sabotage of the program. Domoto said he and Hitoshi [had] staked their lives for us with the major, and [Hifumi] chose to wait before taking any action to see which side was right.
>
> At 9:00 P.M. that evening, Major Cox, Major Cousens and myself called Provoo in and told him

175

that he was under arrest in quarters and that he would be accompanied wherever he went. . . . We told him that this was for his own protection as well as ours. This order was maintained until the 24th when we were moved to Ōmori, and immediately upon arriving there this information was passed on to Commander Maher, U.S. Navy.

He was also given a report on Streeter, who had rejoined the group that morning. On the arrival of the American landing party, this information was passed on to Commodore Simpson, U.S. Navy, who placed Provoo and Streeter under personal arrest to me.

The collaboration activities of Provoo and Streeter had provided a touchstone against which the conduct of Cousens, Ince, and the others could be understandingly judged. Domoto was there to prove that Cousens, Henshaw, and Ince, like Kalbfleisch, had been under threat of death, and might well have been executed if the war had not been almost over and a new and possibly vengefully victorious power about to emerge in Tokyo. By "arresting" Provoo and Streeter, the others had put themselves in a better light.

This option was not available to Iva Toguri d'Aquino. She could not arrest those more guilty than she, such as Mitsushio, Oki, Yoshii, Reyes, Ince, and Cousens, nor the many nisei who ran other programs, broadcast, or acted as warders to their fellow Americans at Suragadai.

INSTRUCTIONS
TO ALL PERSONS OF

JAPANESE
ANCESTRY
Living in the Following Area:

All of that portion of the County of Alameda, State of California, within the boundary beginning at the point where the southerly limits of the City of Oakland meet San Francisco Bay; thence easterly and following the southerly limits of said city to U. S. Highway No. 50; thence southerly and easterly on said Highway No. 50 to its intersection with California State Highway No. 21; thence southerly on said Highway No. 21 to its intersection, at or near Warm Springs, with California State Highway No. 17; thence southerly on said Highway No. 17 to the Alameda-Santa Clara County line; thence westerly and following said county line to San Francisco Bay; thence northerly, and following the shoreline of San Francisco Bay to the point of beginning.

Pursuant to the provisions of Civilian Exclusion Order No. 34, this Headquarters, dated May 3, 1942, all persons of Japanese ancestry, both alien and non-alien, will be evacuated from the above area by 12 o'clock noon, P. W. T., Saturday, May 9, 1942.

No Japanese person living in the above area will be permitted to change residence after 12 o'clock noon, P. W. T., Sunday, May 3, 1942, without obtaining special permission from the representative of the Commanding General, Northern California Sector, at the Civil Control Station located at:

920 - "C" Street,
Hayward, California.

Such permits will only be granted for the purpose of uniting members of a family, or in cases of grave emergency.

The Civil Control Station is equipped to assist the Japanese population affected by this evacuation in the following ways:

1. Give advice and instructions on the evacuation.
2. Provide services with respect to the management, leasing, sale, storage or other disposition of most kinds of property, such as real estate, business and professional equipment, household goods, boats, automobiles and livestock.
3. Provide temporary residence elsewhere for all Japanese in family groups.
4. Transport persons and a limited amount of clothing and equipment to their new residence.

The Following Instructions Must Be Observed:

1. A responsible member of each family, preferably the head of the family, or the person in whose name most of the property is held, and each individual living alone, will report to the Civil Control Station to receive further instructions. This must be done between 8:00 A. M. and 5:00 P. M. on Monday, May 4, 1942, or between 8:00 A. M. and 5:00 P. M. on Tuesday, May 5, 1942.

2. Evacuees must carry with them on departure for the Assembly Center, the following property:
   (a) Bedding and linens (no mattress) for each member of the family;
   (b) Toilet articles for each member of the family;
   (c) Extra clothing for each member of the family;
   (d) Sufficient knives, forks, spoons, plates, bowls and cups for each member of the family;
   (e) Essential personal effects for each member of the family.

All items carried will be securely packaged, tied and plainly marked with the name of the owner and numbered in accordance with instructions obtained at the Civil Control Station. The size and number of packages is limited to that which can be carried by the individual or family group.

3. No pets of any kind will be permitted.
4. No personal items and no household goods will be shipped to the Assembly Center.
5. The United States Government through its agencies will provide for the storage, at the sole risk of the owner, of the more substantial household items, such as iceboxes, washing machines, pianos and other heavy furniture. Cooking utensils and other small items will be accepted for storage if crated, packed and plainly marked with the name and address of the owner. Only one name and address will be used by a given family.
6. Each family, and individual living alone, will be furnished transportation to the Assembly Center or will be authorized to travel by private automobile in a supervised group. All instructions pertaining to the movement will be obtained at the Civil Control Station.

Go to the Civil Control Station between the hours of 8:00 A. M. and 5:00 P. M., Monday, May 4, 1942, or between the hours of 8:00 A. M. and 5:00 P. M., Tuesday, May 5, 1942, to receive further instructions.

J. L. DeWITT
Lieutenant General, U. S. Army
Commanding

Major Charles Cousens, the Australian broadcaster and POW who wrote scripts for Iva Toguri at Radio Tokyo. He assured her, "All you've got to do is look upon yourself as a soldier under my orders. Do exactly what you're told. . . . You'll do nothing against your own people. I will guarantee that personally, because it's my script." *The Australian Broadcasting Corporation*

Iva Toguri is interviewed by American journalists in Yokohama shortly before being placed under detention in American-occupied Japan. *The Associated Press/Wide World Photos*

Iva Toguri poses outside the Sugamo Prison gates with military prison authorities the evening she was released because of a lack of evidence. The government released her after dark in order to discourage reporters, but they came to take photographs anyway. She holds flowers given to her by her husband, Felippe d'Aquino. *The Associated Press/Wide World Photos*

The Associated Press sent out this photo with the caption, "Mrs. Philip D'Aquino (above), known to American troops in the Pacific during World War II as 'Tokyo Rose,' may be re-arrested. . . . Here she relaxes in her home in Tokyo after her release from Sugamo Prison for lack of sufficient evidence to support charges for which she was being held." *The Associated Press/Wide World Photos*

Toguri is escorted by two burly MP's on her way back to the United States via an Army transport ship, where she would stand trial for treason. *The Associated Press/Wide World Photos*

Toguri leaves the Federal Building in San Francisco with a U.S. Marshal after her arraignment, which took place shortly after her return to the United States. *The Associated Press/Wide World Photos*

Closeups of Toguri as she made an appearance in the Federal Building in San Francisco a few days before her trial began. *The Associated Press/Wide World Photos*

Toguri is escorted by a U.S. Deputy Marshall down a corridor in the Federal Building prior to the opening of her trial. *The Associated Press/Wide World Photos*

The defense for Iva Toguri confers immediately after the guilty verdict is announced. She was convicted of one of eight counts of treason, that of making a broadcast concerning the loss of American ships. Her attorneys are, from left to right, George Olehausen, Wayne Collins, and Theodore Tamba. *The Associated Press/Wide World Photos*

A weary Toguri leaves the Federal Court after her conviction, escorted by a U.S. Deputy Marshal. *The Associated Press/Wide World Photos*

Iva Toguri talks with attorney Wayne Collins after being sentenced to ten years in Federal prison and a $10,000 fine. *The Associated Press/Wide World Photos*

A recent photograph of Frederick G. Tillman, the FBI official who assisted in the prosecution of Iva Toguri as "Tokyo Rose."

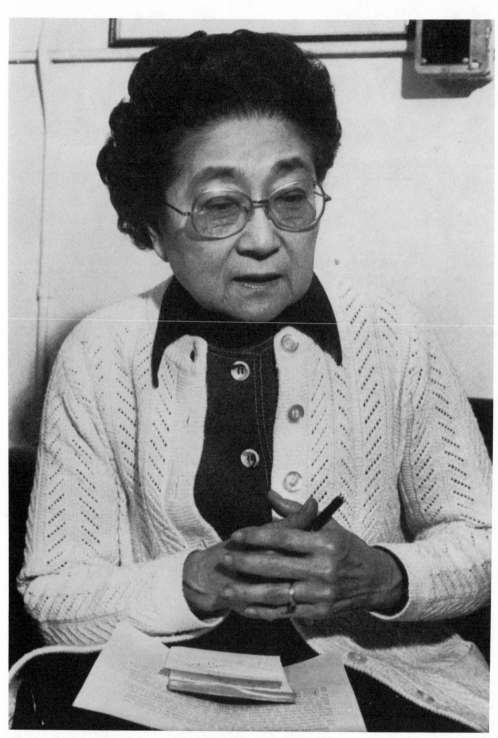

Iva Ikuko Toguri d'Aquino: a recent photograph.

11.

The Audience: Boneheads and Soreheads

THERE IS A FAIRLY CLEAR distinction between murder and man-slaughter, or between rape and seduction, but even in such areas borderline cases crop up. In self-defense, for instance, is killing justified if injury to the assailant would have been sufficient? We know that a drunk driver who kills a child is not a murderer, however angry he makes us feel, and that a girl who gives up her virginity to a man who falsely promises marriage has not been raped; but treason, like self-defense, is more ethereal. Where does the inappropriate end, and iniquity begin? Like pornography, it is in the eye and the troubled mind of the beholder. Was Botticelli's *Birth of Venus* considered porno-graphic in its day, or simply great erotic art? In the American Revolution, the definition of a traitor was the same as the definition of a loyalist.

When Charles Lindbergh urged Americans that Russian communism, not German fascism, was the enemy in the 1940s, the fact that most people today would think him naïve and mistaken does not mean that he was insincere nor, in intention, unpatriotic. Germany had not declared war on the United States; for that matter, it had never declared war on Britain and France.

177

Japan was a horse of a different color. It had attacked the U.S. territory of Hawaii. Would "Lindy" have been a traitor if he had urged Washington to cede the Hawaiian islands to Tokyo and not continue a war to "shore up the British empire?" He could have argued that Hawaii was, then, to America, merely what Algeria was to France—a colony with some limited legislative representation in the motherland, not a part of the motherland as such. Setting aside the protection given to him by his fame, would such pleading have led to his arrest? What if he had gone to Tokyo on an unauthorized mission of peace? There was, after all, no means of resisting Japanese aggression without also fighting Germany, since Tokyo and Berlin were allies. What if he had gone on Tokyo radio and called on Roosevelt to pull out of the war?

Who was and wasn't guilty of treason at NHK? Under what is known, in the United States, as the Uniform Code of Military Justice, Cousens, Ince and Reyes had clearly broken the oath under which they served, in Australia and America. Because they were officers, their guilt was more serious than if they had been enlisted men; because, moreover, they set an example to enlisted men—fellow prisoners—who similarly broke the laws, and because they suborned a nisei civilian, Iva Toguri, their malefaction was further enhanced. Yet, given the circumstances, there are clear and humane attenuating reasons why all three men were exonerated. It had been enough for them to show that they were debilitated and coerced by threats, that they did their best to make their programs ineffective, that broadcasting was not the same as spying or killing.

So much for the prisoners of war. What of the nisei? Among the more culpable was George Mitsushio, who remained an American for sixteen months after Pearl Harbor, while serving Japanese propaganda, and who probably remained one thereafter by not renouncing his U.S. citizenship when he became a subject of Japan. Oki became Japanese in

1940, but it would appear that he never renounced his American nationality either.

A good case could be made that Charles Yoshii, the commentator, if he still had dual citizenship, was America's equivalent of the Englishman at Berlin radio who became known as "Lord Haw-Haw" and whom the British hanged. However, there was no public campaign in America about people like Mitsushio or Oki or Yoshii, because congressmen and columnists and the rest of the public who had stayed behind—and who were now fighting the concluded war vicariously—had never heard of them. They had heard of a GI legend about a girl's voice or voices, about all those killer disc jockeys. . . .

So what of Tokyo Rose? The investigation did accept that there was no such person, that it was a soldier's term for any woman broadcasting in English from Tokyo, or perhaps Manila, or Singapore, or Bandung, or Rangoon, or Wake, or. . . . Just as, for Union soldiers, all Confederate troops were "Johnny Reb"; just as U.S. Marines in Lebanon in 1982 called all Israeli soldiers "Shlomo," and just as all Germans, military or civilian, in both world wars, were "Jerry" to the British, so no one would ever be able to produce Tokyo Rose in court; she was as nonexistent as Johnny Reb, Shlomo, and Jerry.

Logically, since the investigation persisted in saying that it was after "Tokyo Rose," not just Iva Toguri, the Department of Justice, had it wished, could have given the exercise more credibility than it did. In the event, under the guidelines, the FBI did not set out to find if one or more Americans or dual citizens had treasonably devised propaganda broadcasts for the Japanese; it set out to see if it were possible to make a case against one single disc jockey, and one alone.

The announcers who were simply Japanese subjects, like Ken Ishii, were clearly not guilty of anything. The nisei in Tokyo and the Filipina disc jockeys in Manila—still colonial American citizens—might be. If such an investigation had been conducted in a climate amenable to justice, it would have gone looking for commentators and announcers who clearly identified with the enemy and who suffered no coercion from the Japanese. The broadcasts which riled many Americans, mostly congressmen and columnists but even including soldiers who had heard the shows, or said they had heard them, were those announcing bombing attacks on American units or promising a hot reception for a U.S. landing party somewhere. Were such broadcasts ever made? Why would the Japanese give away their element of surprise?

Iva Toguri, today a reluctant expert on Japanese wartime broadcasts in English, doubts if such broadcasts took place at all, despite the fact that a few of those who claim to have heard them were persons of credibility. If they *were* made, she says, it was probably by local commanders on remote islands.

"I seriously doubt if they were made from Japan," she has told the writer. "Why would the Japanese give warnings of attacks? And even if the Japanese air force in the field knew of planned American landings on islands, why would they divulge the extent of their knowledge to their enemies?

"All this comes from the GIs. Their imagination was working overtime. [If such broadcasts were made] why are there no recordings?"

It is significant that the FBIS records, notably those at Portland, Oregon, and a private collection put together at Silver Spring, Maryland, from many sources, contain no broadcasts of this incriminating type. If it is theorized that such broadcasts were made from remote islands, there would presumably be no recordings; but where would Japanese commanders on small islands find female announcers, especially bilingual ones?

What of the other types of broadcast criticized in the legend? Would a broadcast, for instance, be equally demoralizing if it simply asked if listeners weren't worried about their wives remaining faithful—if announcers asked if GIs weren't concerned about the competition from "the 4Fs" earning good money in war factories "while you're out there with the mosquitos?" Reyes made such a broadcast, under orders, and it seems accepted that some female announcers, including one famous one in Manila, used the same line.

Assuming that a skewed decision was taken to put these female announcers in the same boat with "war criminals"—that is, with those who committed vicious brutalities and then lost the war—a serious investigation would have tried to find which announcers made such remarks on the air, which of these owed allegiance to the United States, and how much coercion was involved by the Japanese male military establishment.

What actually took place was quite different. Because she had told two correspondents, for a promised $2,000, that she was "Tokyo Rose," Iva Toguri, the truly "one and original" Orphan Ann, was the only name mentioned for investigation. Had Orphan Ann made pro-Japanese political commentaries or spread demoralizing information about troop movements, impending air attacks, and the like? To discover this, FBI investigators did not confine themselves to Pacific veterans who had heard Orphan Ann, but issued an appeal to all those who had heard "Tokyo Rose"—that is, any female voice on any Japanese-controlled radio. This was all the more contradictory because, since Iva Toguri was the *only* female broadcaster on Tokyo radio to have an identity—"Ann," or "Orphan Ann," or "Orphan Annie"—it could be argued that she was the only one who could never have been the anonymous "Tokyo Rose."

Almost inevitably, the result of the appeal was, for the most part, as farcical as it must have been intensely tedious for the G-men involved. The only interest in the huge pile of interviews with Pacific veterans who had listened to Japanese radio would be for a sociologist studying how a myth begins. Out there in the Pacific, the twenty-seven Tokyo Roses had become a single Ondine, an individual siren luring men onto the rocks. Says the University of Iowa's John Leggett: "In the loneliness of steamy quonset huts and lurching forecastles from the Aleutians to New Guinea, American servicemen were building the fantasy of 'Tokyo Rose.' Hers was so pervasive a myth that for most Americans she was as famous as Emperor Hirohito."

Why not? Did the legend of the mermaid not endure for centuries?

Not surprisingly, those involved with the prosecution, including the attorney who had started all the fuss to begin with, soon urged against going forward with the charges. But of that, later.

Starting in early 1948, Hoover's hardened special agents, justly famous for their long campaign against the vicious leaders of organized crime, began to fan out across the country on a somewhat less challenging assignment—questioning *anyone* who claimed to have heard a female voice on a Japanese radio program in the Pacific. Yet in the appeal to them to come forward, and in the subsequent questioning, agents repeatedly used the mythical term "Tokyo Rose."

The most interesting witnesses were those who remembered broadcasts involving "military predictions." In the following brief selection, many men are referred to as "Blank," because their names are blacked out in the FBI files—probably because, at some time in the now distant past, their request for anonymity was still valid.

One such testimony reads: "Blank, a former Army Air Force lieutenant, and Blank, 883 Bomb [*sic*] squadron, on Saipan from November 11, 1944 to June 5, 1945, advised that Tokyo Rose in broadcasts referred to predicted impending Japanese aerial attacks on Saipan and referred to the B-29 project of the 73 Bomb Wing on Saipan."

There had been, the lieutenant said, a "specific threat of

gas attack which had a definite psychological effect on the personnel." These broadcasts also gave the names of missing aircrew, he said, telling which were dead and which were prisoners. This was obviously news which the airmen on Saipan were glad to have, but the same broadcaster allegedly called her listeners "dogs" and "beasts" for having destroyed churches and an orphanage, according to both of the Blanks.

Another Blank listened to the "broadcasts of Tokyo practically every day, November 22, 1944 through January 1, 1945." Since Iva Toguri was absent from NHK for all or most of that time, this could not have been her, nor was it likely that it was "Zero Hour" at all, since military "predictions" are involved.

"At first our small group of listeners regarded this . . . program as humor," Blank said. But precise Japanese "strafing" of targets was to prove consistent with the predictions, he added. The threat of a gas attack—which, fortunately, did not transpire—had had a "definite psychological effect on the personnel." The fact that this Blank used exactly the same wording as the lieutenant just mentioned suggests that the periphrasis is based more on the FBI agent's question than on the answers, which may well have been "Yes" or "Uh-huh."

Talking of one female broadcaster of military predictions, a different version described her as having "above the tone of an alto" and said that "when she seemed to generate enough anger her voice took on the sound of guttural effects [sic]."

A New Yorker said his unit was convinced that Tokyo Rose was Amelia Earhart, the aviatrix who, it is believed, crashed on Mili atoll during an attempted global flight and who subsequently died in Japanese captivity. He quoted "Earhart" as telling a Seabee group in "October or December [sic] of 1944" that "we are not forgetting that radio tower being built on Leyte. You can expect a visit on Christmas Eve!" The tower, he claimed, was leveled by a Japanese raid on that date. If this story

is authentic, it would reinforce the theory that local commanders ordered such broadcasts.

A former seaman second class with a naval construction
batallion on Ulalope island heard a "broadcast by Tokyo Rose"
in November 1943. She would give the real names of some
sailors' wives and claim that their neighbors had seen them
"dating" other men. Captured letters? This seaman said that
when his group had landed on Manus island in the Admiralties
on March 1, 1944, he remembered a woman broadcaster saying
"Hello there, you boys on Manus island. We know you're there.
. . . You'll be bumped off [the island] next Tuesday." There
was, he conceded, no such Japanese attack.

How serious were such recollections? This man remembered that his Rose had a "cosmopolitan accent similar to what
is heard in Pennsylvania [sic]." It was a "not unpleasing voice,
with no Jap mannerisms."

Often, in the periphrasis, the investigation deceptively
identified Iva Toguri, the "subject," with one or other Tokyo
Rose who was clearly not she. For instance, a former lieutenant
colonel is said to have "remembered listening to subject" frequently on Saipan, where several of the officers had heard her
mention them by name. She had correctly said that one colonel
had arrived late because of "problems with his B-29," and she
had accurately predicted a Japanese bombing of the island. He
remembered her voice as "sexy, sultry," and "somewhat effective," with the "faint trace of an accent." He did not say what
accent, and added: "However, I am not sure that I would
recognize her voice today." Her broadcasts had been regarded
as a joke and "did not have any effect on the men's morale."
Like the others, he was obviously not referring to "Subject"
(Iva Toguri) but to "his" Tokyo Rose.

Special Agent John E. Kelly of the New Haven, Connecticut, office interviewed another Blank, in Connecticut, who
remembered a broadcast of January 2, 1944, which he had heard

in Schofield Barracks in Hawaii. He identified the program as "Zero Hour," but this was presumably in response to a question using that title because January 2 was a Sunday, when there was no "Zero Hour" broadcast. His broadcaster, who he thought actually identified herself as Tokyo Rose, had told him where his unit was headed and had announced that California had been bombed. If this was the "Zero Hour" frequency— NHK—it could conceivably have been Ruth Hayakawa, whose classical-music disc-jockeying replaced "Zero Hour" on the Sabbath; but it could just as easily have been someone else.

Only one of the literally hundreds of GIs interviewed believed that the voice he had heard which "gave the Americans forty-eight hours to get off the island [Saipan] or they would blow up the whole place with bombs" was of someone who called herself "Annie." Since the whole report is periphrasis, it is not clear who brought the name into the conversation—the FBI agent or the veteran. The iconoclast was former Lieutenant Jules Sutter, who told Special Agent Guy Hottel in Washington, D.C., that the broadcast had been made between September 4 and September 6, 1944.

Many GIs were sure, despite all the monitoring by the FBIS and the Office of Strategic Services, and despite other government testimony that there was no broadcaster of that name, that they had heard a "girl" (or two girls, or ten) who actually *called herself* Tokyo Rose. Often, testimony on this point was contradictory. For instance; one veteran said: "At no time was there a formal presentation of a person as Tokyo Rose"; but later, in response to further prodding, he volunteered that "if my memory serves me correct [*sic*], she would end her broadcasts by saying 'This is Tokyo Rose and goodnight and try to sleep if you can.' "

A New York State witness recalled a "high, well-modulated voice." She had called herself both "Rose" and "Tokyo

Rose," and she had announced the bombing of San Francisco, Los Angeles, Seattle, and Reno. Someone who had been at Port Moresby, New Guinea, recalled a broadcast which took place two hours later than "Zero Hour" and which ended with "This is your girlfriend Tokyo Rose signing off from a studio in Tokyo."

Actually, very few believed that Tokyo Rose was a true *nom de théâtre,* although some thought there was only one female broadcaster on the Japanese stations, which were often all thought of as a single transmitter—Tokyo. The vast majority testified that they found the broadcasts more entertaining than depressing—which was precisely why they listened in.

A Colonel Blank is quoted as saying that he made an inspection from October 1944 to April 1945 of "all the bases in New Guinea" to hear "beefs" from the troops. "His duty was to check morale," says the FBI periphrasis. "However, he never came across any adverse effect on the morale of the troops as a result of a Tokyo Rose broadcast."

A former member of the 503rd Parachute Infantry Regiment remembers hearing a "Tokyo Rose" broadcast for three or four weeks in December 1943. She played Glenn Miller and reminded listeners of people back in California who were drinking cold beer in the nightclubs and hearing Miller in person.

This could well be Iva. But, after five years, the paratrooper appears to have got his memories mixed, because he says:

> She would also make nasty cracks and derogatory remarks about different outfits of the American forces, and she reported all [our] setbacks and retreats. She also attempted to lower morale further by telling the numbers and identities of ships sunk and planes shot down. She predicted bombing attacks by Jap [*sic*] planes and shellings by Jap ships. On New Year's Eve

in 1943 she told of a fleet of Japanese ships who [*sic*] would shell the island of Mindoro the following day, New Year's Day. The ships did shell the island the following day.

She was a young woman around twenty years of age who did not sound like an American. She talked with a British accent.

An air force captain with a bomber group said he heard "Tokyo Rose" from September 1944 until "October, 1945 [*sic*]" while on Saipan. Her broadcast was considered a "farce," he said, adding: "We listened to the program merely as a source of amusement." He too recalled an October 1944 warning to evacuate Saipan because it came after the first or second Doolittle raids on Tokyo.

"In his opinion," says the periphrasis, "her broadcasts had no serious effects on the morale of the personnel stationed at Saipan."

The unnamed captain said he did not believe that he "would be able to identify the voice of Tokyo Rose and is not positive that it was the same voice at all times." The periphrasis continues: "He states the personnel on Saipan referred to any female voice coming from Radio Tokyo as that of Tokyo Rose. . . . Tokyo Rose used almost perfect English and enunciated very clearly in what he described as a rather high-pitched voice."

Although the "farce" sounds like Cousens' burlesque intention, this was clearly not the husky contralto of Iva Toguri asking her "onable boneheads" the question: "You are liking, please?"

Another air force captain who had been communications officer with a bomber wing on Saipan from November 1944 until September 1945 [*sic*] said he had heard "Tokyo Rose" often there. She had had a "soft, pleasant voice, not too foreign-sounding." Prompted, he says he "faintly recalls" the names Orphan Ann or Orphan Annie, and he says his "Rose" never made military predictions or named units or individual officers. However, he "also does not recall Tokyo Rose trying to make Americans think of home, their wives or their girl friends."

Taken prisoner late in 1944, he had once been in the NHK studios and he recognized a photo of Iva Toguri as being that of someone he had seen there but whose voice he had not heard. He made no connection between what he heard on Saipan and what he saw in Tokyo.

A seaman who had served on the destroyer *Lansdowne* from August 1942 to March 1943—well before Iva began broadcasting—said he thought he could "positively identify the voice of Iva d'Aquino as the American who broadcast as Tokyo Rose." Confusingly, he said that on the *Lansdowne* he had heard "several women broadcast under the name of Tokyo Rose," but one with a "West Coast" accent "stood out." She was the main broadcaster, but others substituted for her from time to time. "On those occasions, members of the ship's crew would remark that the real Tokyo Rose was off duty," he said.

Another paratrooper, this time with the 505th Regiment, said there had been an "original Tokyo Rose" who had started broadcasting "before 1943." Later, there had been many more voices, but he thought he could identify "the original," whom he had begun listening to "in about January, 1942." There would be music, then an announcer would introduce "Rose," he said. "She would play records and ask if their wives were being faithful . . . when everybody [back home] is making lots of money in war work. 'What do you expect? She's only human?' " he quotes her as saying. His Rose had made mileage out of the coalminers' strike, and the FBI periphrasis quotes the soldier as saying: "She used vile and abusive language when accusing us of hypocracy [*sic*—FBI spelling]."

The tedious task of interviewing every veteran with a

Tokyo Rose memory continued for over a year. Responding to a remark by the author about the evidentiary weakness of the earwitnesses used, Special Agent Fred Tillman says today: "You should have heard those we rejected!"

One of these might well be the navy veteran in California who said that all the female voices on "Zero Hour" were of the same woman, and that none of them used the name Orphan Annie. But perhaps the most typical, after all, was the Saipan veteran in Boise whose testimony is paraphrased as follows: "He knows of no evidence that subject had hindered the United States or aided the enemy in the prosecution of the war."

For the FBI and the potential prosecution, the most useful listeners were those who could remember the sobriquets Ann, Orphan Ann, and Orphan Annie. For the FBI, they were disappointingly few.

In New York, a former enlisted army man whose unit had served with an air force bomber squadron on Saipan said he believed the woman nicknamed "Tokyo Rose" by his buddies was always the same person. This soldier had been one of the first to arrive in Tokyo, where he had met the Eurasian "Bucky" Harris and had asked him if he knew where he could meet Tokyo Rose. Harris, he said, had claimed to know her well and to have worked with her on programs; but he had not fulfilled his promise to locate her, perhaps because he had gone on to become a public relations assistant with the U.S. First Cavalry Division. The army witness had finally tracked down his Rose through none other than Harry Brundidge, who, he claimed, had introduced him to Iva Toguri. However, the periphrasis adds: "He cannot presently state if voice on radio was identical with voice of girl he met through Brundidge in Tokyo. He does not believe the broadcasts adversely affected morale of U.S. troops."

An army sergeant photographer attached to the Eleventh

Airborne Division on Saipan had had only slightly better luck with the resourceful Harris. The Anglo-Japanese again offered to "produce Tokyo Rose so that Blank and others could take pictures," says the FBI report. Harris had taken them on a tour of the NHK studios, showed them "Tokyo Rose's chair," and again claimed to have worked with her on programs. But this Blank had also finally met "Tokyo Rose" only through Brundidge. He and another photographer, a lieutenant, took two shots of Toguri. There was "little conversation." He was unable to say if Toguri's voice resembled that of any Tokyo Rose he had heard in the Pacific. The sergeant and the lieutenant are presumably the photographers who did the freelance work for Brundidge and Lee. One wonders if they were ever paid.

An unnamed reserve colonel from the army contacted the FBI's New York office and recalled broadcasts in which a woman broadcaster had "dwelt on the hardships endured by the boys in New Guinea while the boys at home were having it soft." He could "not recall any specific words of a treasonable nature" in her broadcasts, however. The "majority of the boys laughed at the thought of the program's trying to affect them. As a general rule, he did not think the broadcasts of the subject affected the morale of the men," the report says.

It goes on: "Blank recalled that the men in the Pacific referred to the subject as Tokyo Rose but he could not recall the names Ann or Orphan Ann." He identified her voice as that of a "rich contralto." She had "never expressed a wish that the United States should lose the war or that Japan should win."

Another Pacific veteran, also a colonel, is quoted as saying: "I presumed the voice to be of a single nature [sic], same person broadcasting, and I also wondered many times who this person could be. . . . I was of the belief that it was awfully difficult for her to be severe in her wording and broadcasting. I definitely remember that the crowd would kid that she seemed more upset herself than we were."

A reference to this colonel in the periphrasis says, "Blank

stated hers was the best program in the Pacific until the armed forces radio began broadcasting."

The Japanese felt that "Zero Hour," thanks to Cousens' expertise, was their best program, and the description of the broadcaster could be that of Iva Toguri. But could any listener hear a disc jockey refer to herself night after night as "Orphan Ann" or "Annie" and not remember?

A veritable chorus line of Tokyo Roses was now apparent. Every GI had his favorite—or his favorite enemy. Some of the Roses, according to the legend, had announced forthcoming Japanese raids, and had thereby identified themselves with the Japanese troops. Some of these raids had taken place, either in reality or in the traumatic dreams of the veterans five years later. Some of the women were just, like Iva, disc jockeys in the night, who became affectionately or semiaffectionately known as "Tokyo Rose," in the way all German girls at the time were "Lilli Marlene." Behind all these Roses were men, most of them Japanese but some of them captives like Iva—but prisoners in a different and more formal sense—who wrote their scripts. The prisoners had technically committed treason, especially if they were officers. Some had returned home to hard questioning, followed by understanding, and promotion. Some, like Henshaw, had simply gone from ensign to lieutenant commander without a murmur. Why was Iva lynched?

Probably the key feature in selecting her as the witch of the Pacific war was her decision to keep some of her scripts, with the intention of showing them to radio stations in California when she returned home in search of a job. Innocuous as these scripts are, they are virtually the only "Ann"—therefore, unquestionably, Iva Toguri—scripts that were available at the time to make a prosecution conceivable. She was, in effect, the only woman who acknowledged having done any particular broadcast—because the other announcers had not been asked.

Like the Unknown Soldier in Arlington, the Unknown Fighter under the Arc de Triomphe, and the Unknown Warrior in Westminster Abbey, she was chosen to personify the Unknown Female Disc Jockey on Japanese radio stations in the Pacific in World War II, and to be buried (alive) accordingly.

Her scripts were not incriminating, as far as the wording went, but they were definitely scripts which Cousens had written and which she had agreed to broadcast over enemy radio. They were at least something, in a file which so far contained virtually nothing else of value. Cousens had been exonerated and had returned to radio fame. Ince had been exonerated and promoted. Reyes was on a scholarship to Vanderbilt University. The witch doctor hadn't called for a male sacrifice; he'd called for a witch. Even so, why did the investigation push on, given the unsuitable innocence of the scripts?

The answer appears to be: because the woman had foolishly signed a document, along with a whole series of photographs, as "Tokyo Rose"! She had put her signature to the claim that she was indeed the person who had never existed. It was as though she had guaranteed in writing that she was a mermaid after mermaids had been declared to be vermin. A whole bevy of dubious forces wanted a lynching of "Tokyo Rose", and she had already said with a giggle: "That's I." Ruth Hayakawa, who courageously refused to testify against her, and Miyeko Oki, who accepted to do so although she, like Ruth, was probably a better candidate for the role, never signed anything so silly. People like menacing Special Agent Fred Tillman had said to little women like Miyeko: "Listen, girl!"—and they had listened, and obeyed.

12.

Voices in the Night

ASKING AN AMERICAN soldier to distinguish between one Japanese woman's voice and another, especially one heard on radio and with the usual accompaniment of shortwave static, is like asking most of us to distinguish between the call of a lesser spotted wood tit and that of a crested robin. Although there was already ample evidence of the nature of Iva Toguri's scripts—whether written by Cousens or, later, by herself, with perhaps some unwelcome input from the Japanese army—the fact remained that if any credence was to be attached to the now four- and five-year-old memories of the Pacific vets, some would have to be made to prove that they could distinguish between Iva's voice and all others. In 1948, voice tests were introduced into the investigation, and the G-men were ordered to become turntable spinners themselves.

One man who did not have to listen was former Lieutenant Richard L. Henschel, one of the army photographers who had been at the Bund Hotel for her September 1945 press conference. Henschel, interviewed by the FBI at his office—Disc-of-the-Month, Inc., in the Wall Street area of Manhattan—said he was in charge of an army photographic unit and had taken one of his men, Kingsley R. Fall, with him to shoot pictures when he went to the Bund.

The former officer said he had first heard someone he

thought of as "Tokyo Rose" in July 1944, on New Britain. He was referring to several different programs, however, "anywhere from seven P.M. until midnight." The Tokyo Rose he remembered was a news announcer, so there was little likelihood that he had confused Iva's voice with those of others. In any event, the FBI periphrasis says: "Regarding the possibility of identifying the voice of the subject, Henschel said he was not positive that it was always the same girl broadcasting as Tokyo Rose, and that due to static, atmospherical disturbances, lapses of memory on his part and the length of time between broadcasts, he did not believe he could make a positive identification of the subject."

A former customer of the Wilmington Avenue Market in Watts did recognize Toguri on the air because of his prior knowledge, and without listening to recordings. The unnamed witness, who had been involved a decade before in the original sale of the grocery to Jun Toguri, told Special Agent Michael J. Cassidy of the San Francisco office that it was probably because of the altitude of his mountain home that he had been able to pick up Tokyo in California. Although he insists that Iva was always introduced as "Tokyo Rose," the rest of his testimony seems valid.

He said he had at once recognized the voice as being that of "Toguri's daughter Iva," on the first of "six or seven occasions" when he had heard her, and had called in his wife to listen.

The periphrasis continues:

Blank and his wife repeated previous statements to the effect that they had never heard Toguri make any statement they would consider as disloyal, neither did they hear her say anything during her broadcasts which they would consider as propaganda or which would affect the morale of our armed forces. They said it was their opinion that Toguri would not have performed the broadcasts for the Japanese unless she was forced to do so.

Perhaps because some FBI interrogators were more demanding, other responses were less clear-cut, and assistant attorney general T. Vincent Quinn's entirely responsible idea of making veterans listen to three test recordings created, in the end, only more confusion.

Most former Pacific fans of Japanese radio heard the same three recordings. The first was of someone other than Iva Toguri. The second was a recording of one of Iva's broadcasts, probably taken originally from the OSS files but used in a Hollywood film. The third was the recording of Iva made after the war, at army direction, on the same day as Provoo recorded and Streeter refused to do so; it involved one of her old scripts, but she sounds less chirpy than she actually was when on the air. All the scripts are innocuous.

Whereas former Lieutenant Jules Sutter, cited previously, and a radio operator called Sam Cavnar—both men being radio specialists—correctly recognized numbers two and three as Iva, an Okinawa veteran said number three was "Orphan Ann," but not numbers two and one. A veteran of Saipan and Tinian said number two was "Ann," but that neither number one nor number three had ever been heard on "Zero Hour" at all, while another Okinawa vet said that number two was the voice he had heard earlier in the war predicting troop movements.

Indications such as this—that others might have sounded like Iva, especially to men not skilled in distinguishing one Japanese woman's voice from another—came often. A former seaman who had been on the *Bowditch* when it was lost recognized numbers two and three as "Orphan Ann" but gave a different hour for her broadcast and a different title for the program. Did he confuse two women or, more likely, simply make a lucky guess?

Says the report: "He says this confusion is attributable to two reasons. The first is that all the men referred to all the women who broadcast from Radio Tokyo as Tokyo Rose [whereas he thinks] there were different women on different programs. [The second is that] the program on which Orphan Ann [appeared] was not limited entirely to musical recordings and chit chat, [but] that there were other people on the program who talked in English and often gave news announcements." Two more navy men, one unnamed and the other called Marshall Hoot, said they had never heard numbers two and three before, but they thought number one was "Tokyo Rose."

A tank man said his unit used to pipe "Tokyo Rose" (all such broadcasts) into the movie theater tent and into the rediffusion boxes in individual tents, to entertain the men. He had never heard anything propagandistic, he said. None of the recordings sounded like the girl he remembered, although number three was a bit like her, he said. Master Sergeant Charles Hall listened to number one and to the two recordings of Iva's scratchy voice and pronounced that none of them were the Rose he had heard. His Rose had a "soft, rich, deep voice." Later, reinterviewed at Spokane air base, he plumped for number two after all.

Another survivor of the sunken *Bowditch* said his Rose called herself by that name and had never called herself Orphan Ann. She had talked of herself as "your jive queen," and it was she who had started the chitchat about two-timing spouses and sweethearts back home. But he recognized his Rose as number two!

Similarly confusing was former artillery Corporal Blank of California, who told Special Agents Thomas P. Dowd and Michael J. Cassidy that he had listened to "Zero Hour" on Guadalcanal, in Bougainville, and in the Sterling Islands. Yet his broadcaster called herself "Tokyo Rose" and read the diaries of captured or dead American and Australian soldiers. She would say the Americans were fighting a losing battle against superior Japanese soldiers. Like Iva, however, she referred to her listeners as the orphans of the Pacific. So, which recording was the right voice? All three, he said.

There were many cases of vets remembering a "Zero Hour" and a "Tokyo Rose," but not an "Orphan Ann." Often recording number two was recognized as the voice of a "Rose" who made "military prediction" talks, or as *not* being someone who had used the various "Ann" pseudonyms.

In one case, two marines who had served together took the test: one of the grunts recognized number two as being the voice of Tokyo Rose, whereas the other recognized none of the voices. Of five former signal corpsmen from Saipan, only one could remember an "Orphan Ann," and none could recognize any of the voices. Yet all claimed to have listened to "Zero Hour."

Of four others interviewed separately, again only one remembered the "Ann" names, and he correctly identified numbers two and three as being the real "Ann." Elsewhere, some vets recognized number two, but not number three, or vice versa. Only one *Bowditch* survivor identified numbers two and three as being "his" Tokyo Rose.

An airman identified number two as the voice he had heard when tuning in to Tokyo in his plane in 1942 and early 1943, before Iva joined the program. He said this early broadcaster presented song titles "suggestively." What is curious is that he remembered a record which Iva actually played on "Zero Hour"—Bonnie Baker singing "My Resistance Is Low"—and he remarked: "The broadcast had all the earmarks of an excellent producer and technical staff in back of it, and compared favorably with some of the broadcasts produced in the United States."

But his "Rose," whom he had first listened to six years before, talked about Americans "taking heavy losses in New

Guinea" and "being [let down] by the British and the Australians"—hardly likely to come from a Cousens script. There were also the famous military predictions based on "what appeared to be some advance intelligence."

A Saipan vet interviewed in New York state said there had been several Tokyo Roses, and added frankly that reception on Saipan had been "too poor for any honest person to try to recognize the voices he had heard." Another New Yorker, a paratroop veteran from New Guinea, picked out number 2—Iva—right away as his "Rose," then said, the periphrasis adds, that "he had heard subject *singing* American songs on the radio on a number of occasions."

Normando Reyes, reinterviewed by Agent Hopton in Memphis on August 30, 1948, was played some different recordings and was of course able to recognize all the voices involved—Iva Toguri, Miyeko Furuya, June Suyama, the male announcer Sali Nakamura, and a Mr. Hori, whose given name he could not recall.

The Toguris' old neighbor, Gilbert Vasquez (also sometimes written as Vazquez) Velasquez, when reinterviewed by Chester Horton in Detroit, was less successful, illustrating how unreliable the tests were. He correctly identified number three as Iva Toguri, whom he had heard broadcast as Orphan Ann, but he said number two—one of the very broadcasts of Iva's which he had heard during the war—was of another Tokyo Rose, not her.

The recording used as number two was chosen for the test because it was the only totally clear one of Iva in existence; it had been enhanced by Hollywood techniques and had been taken from the soundtrack of the MGM film *High Barbaree*. It had apparently been recorded directly by an official service (probably the OSS) on August 14, 1944. This is how it went:

Ann: Hello, you fighting orphans of the Pacific. How's tricks? This is the after-the-weekend-Annie back on the air, strictly on the Zero Hour. Reception okay? Well, it had better be, because this is an all-request night and I've got a pretty nice program for my favorite little family—the wandering boneheads of the Pacific islands. The first request is made by none other than the boss. And guess what? He wants Bonnie Baker. Hehhhhhhh! "My Resistance Is Low." My, what taste you have, sir, she said.

MUSIC: BONNIE BAKER—MY RESISTANCE IS LOW

Ann: This is Monday. Washday for some, rifle cleaning for some, and for the others, just another day for play. Let's all get together and forget those wash-day blues. Here's Kay Kaiser, Sonny Mason and all the Playmates, so come join the parade, you boneheads.

MUSIC: SINGING PLAYMATES

Ann: Well, here's a telegram signed just N. S. S., and he wants the song for his favorite sweetheart, R. L. Hmmmmm! Well, here's Bonnie Baker with the usual in the background and the song "Hush, The Baby's Asleep." Quiet now, honey boy.

MUSIC: BONNIE BAKER—HUSH, THE BABY'S ASLEEP

Although POW messages are always thought to have been genuine, the "requests" from the Pacific were, of course, not— although doubtless there would have been many, if there had been some way of writing to Tokyo. It's to be noted here that one request comes from "the boss"—presumably Mitsushio rather than Tsuneishi.

We may note, despite Cousens' retirement from the program, that a Cousens anglicism survives at the end of the first Toguri cut: "My, what taste you have, sir, she said." Americans prefer "as they say" and the French prefer the more logical "as one says"; but the British use the third person feminine singular imperfect without the conjunction—"she said."

We may also note, near the start of the excerpt, the grammatically correct "it had better be," another heritage of Cousens' influence. Americans usually drop the auxiliary verb and say "it better be," as in "you better believe" instead of "you'd better believe." Since the American style is inaccurate, it would not be translatable—notably into Japanese.

Another example of the innocuous broadcasts that cost the little disc jockey so much—and the taxpayers the equivalent of about $7 million today—is the following script, obtained by army filmmaker Robert Cowan in 1945, and signed by Iva. It is dated May 3 (presumably 1944) and begins with a Cousens-style "wipe" from the listeners' memory of the news just read:

> *Ann:* Thank you thank you thank you thank you thank you. Greetings everybody! This is Ann of Radio Tokyo, the little orphan girl, presenting our special program for listeners in Australia and that large but not over-intelligent family, the Orphans of the South Pacific. Good evening, boys! Tonight we have a star performer to open the program, George Scott-Wood with his piano-accordeon. And here he is playing "Speak to Me of Love." Subtle, huh? Orphan to Orphan, over!
>
> MUSIC: SPEAK TO ME OF LOVE   VJA 5010-A
>
> *Ann:* Okay, we're off! Now, here's some music that's easy on the ear. Bajes Bela and orchestra in a Franz Lehar fantasia. Relax, little boneheads, and please to listening!
>
> MUSIC: FRANZ LEHAR FANTASIA, PARTS I & II   P. 15227 A & B
>
> *Ann:* You are liking, please? Well, keep listening because in a few moments you'll be hearing your News from the American Home Front. But first we'll

hear from George Scott-Wood and his accordeon. A
lousy little tune, "In a Gypsy Tea Room," but nicely
played.

MUSIC: IN A GYPSY TEA ROOM   VJA 5010 B

Ann: And now here's your news announcer to
read you the news from the American Home Front.
Come on in!

KEN READS AHF NEWS

Ann: Thank you thank you thank you thank you
thank you. This is Radio Tokyo talking, and your *dear*
little enemy Ann, presenting our regular programme
for Australia and the South Pacific, and it's about time
we heard from that Orphan Choir. Everybody ready
to sing? Okay, let's go. "Love's Old Sweet Song."
Sound effects from this end by Mark Weber and his
Orchestra.

MUSIC: LOVE'S OLD SWEET SONG—VVA 10072 A-B

Ann: Good! That choir's improving. Now let's
settle down quietly to some music in waltz time.
Here's the London Palladium Orchestra playing Victor
Herbert's "Kiss Me Again." Pure propaganda, that is!

MUSIC: KISS ME AGAIN   VJA 531-B

Ann: One more waltz, and then I turn you over
for the next two items in your program—News Highlights, and the Zero Hour with its music made-in-the-
USA. In the meantime, here's Schubert's "Serenade,"
in waltz time. Please to listening, and raising onable
voice in harmony, boneheads!

MUSIC: SERENADE   VVA 10112-B

Despite the departure of Cousens, Iva is still using his Standard
English spelling of "programme." Mostly, she is following his
practice of choosing British music not likely to enthuse the
GIs—accordion solos, the London Palladium Orchestra,

"Love's Old Sweet Song"—while Schubert and Lehar are not exactly soldier fare, in any army. But would the Japanese know? Cousens, however, would probably have ruled that the phrase "lousy little tune" was going too far in self-mockery.

III

A Judicial Lynch Party

13.

Coming Home

DESPITE MEMORANDA WHICH recommended against bringing charges—by special assistant attorney general Thomas de Wolfe and John Hogan, the two federal attorneys handling the case—Justice decided on August 16, 1948, to give way to the emotion-charged congressional and press campaign. Attorney General Clark ordered Iva Toguri's arrest in Tokyo, then still under U.S. occupation.

On August 26, troopers from the Counter Intelligence Corps came to the modest rented room in the Ikejiri suburb where Iva and Felippe lived and took her off to Sugamo once more; there, lights were left on in the cell, night and day, in case she might decide to emulate the prime minister, Hideji Tojo, and attempt suicide. For Iva, the stations of the cross had begun.

A person arrested abroad is tried in the first United States jurisdiction in which he or she arrives. Many ships coming from Tokyo stop at Honolulu, where the government feared that a largely Asian-American jury would be favorable to the tormented little nisei typist. All aircraft crossing the ocean had to refuel in Hawaii or in Alaska, which was an especially inconvenient venue for the prosecutors—indeed, for everyone. So air travel was initially out of consideration. But in Los Angeles, her hometown, it was feared, jurors might also be understanding of the accused's wartime dilemmas, despite the City Council's vote against her. Clark therefore made preparations for a trial on the East Coast, which would mean air travel after all. Landing her on the East Coast before the West was a complicated but far from impossible task, and elaborate plans were laid to transport her through Canada or Mexico. Finally, Clark decided on San Francisco, the American city then most associated with anti-oriental and especially anti-Japanese prejudice. So Iva remained in the brightly lit, six-foot-wide cell at Sugamo until a ship was available that was sailing straight to the Golden Gate. This was to be the U.S. Army transport *General Hodges*.

A United Press dispatch that appeared in papers on August 17 quoted Iva as saying she was anxious to be tried and to get it over with, because "this indefinite waiting is worse than physical torture." She believed that, once back in her own country, she would get justice. She would probably have been heartened to know that the decision to arrest her had not been taken because of any new evidence which had not been available when she had been released in 1946. Her belated, foolish autograph on Brundidge's hyped version of the Imperial Hotel interview had been added to the docket, and Brundidge had bombastically called it a "confession"; but it did not in fact contain anything that was not known when the Attorney General had thrown out the case two years before; it was certainly not an admission of guilt.

A woman army captain, Katherine Stull, and two burly male military policemen brought her from Sugamo to the troopship at Yokohama; Stull was to sail with her as escort. There was a last petty act of mental torture on her final day in Japan: Felippe was not warned of her departure, and she was not allowed to call him. He learned that his wife had been shipped out of the country from the newspapers.

The *General Hodges,* filled with returning soldiers, stopped at Naha, the capital of the Ryukyus, to pick up more time-expired troops, and at a port in South Korea, to take on yet another, smaller contingent of GIs awaiting demobilization. Outside of her sordid cabin-cell, the air on board the ship was festive.

At San Francisco, a huge, cheering crowd was waiting dockside on September 25 to welcome the returning servicemen. Before they could go ashore, however, a solitary figure was led down a gangplank in shame, her head lowered. Iva's thin features were puckered into a mask of pain. For the first time since the whole nightmare had begun two years before, she was finding it hard to fight back tears. It was the disgrace that was proving too much; she knew that her father must be watching, somewhere down there in the mass of faces.

On board, Captain Stull had handed her charge over to two big FBI special agents, each of whom weighed more than twice their tiny victim. These were Frederick G. Tillman and Robert C. Kopriva. They had come aboard as soon as the ship tied up. Tillman and Special Agent John (Joe) Eldon Dunn were to be in charge of the case, which would take a year more to prepare.

She had had dysentery on the journey, and was so thin, she told Duus years later, that she had had to put a safety pin in her skirt to prevent its falling down. When a woman employee of the FBI took it away, as another precaution against suicide, Iva refused to go ashore if her skirt would not stay in place while her arms were held. *The San Francisco Chronicle* reported that she was carried from the ship by two marines, but the press photo clearly shows her walking down the gangway, with the beefy and menacing figures of Tillman and Kopriva behind her. A marvelously bureaucratic compromise had been achieved: since she could hardly run far, or fast, with her hands holding up her skirt, her arms were not pinioned. Her bobby pins were confiscated, and the usually neat figure was embarrassed to feel her hair blowing in the wind as she went down to the crowded quayside.

She was taken into custody once more, this time at Fort Mason. The same day, U.S. Commissioner Francis S. J. Fox arraigned her for treason in his bureau in the Post Office building. He remanded her to the U.S. marshal and set October 7 for a hearing. Although she had no passport and was clearly no danger to anyone, she was refused bail. Finally, in the bleak office, with Fox and the others watching, she was briefly reunited with her father and one of her sisters, June.

"Girl, I'm proud of you!" said Jun Toguri. He had feared that she would give up her U.S. citizenship and become Japanese or Portuguese to put an end to the persecution.

She gave a little, grateful smile. "I'm tired, Daddy," she answered.

The FBI file records that "at the request of Messrs. Thomas de Wolfe and John Hogan, Departmental attorneys handling instant case in San Francisco, subject was interviewed at the San Francisco office [of the FBI] on the afternoon of September 25, 1948, by Special Agent Frederick G. Tillman and the writer [Dunn]. Subject at that time declined on advice of counsel to make any statement."

At last, after three years, she had a lawyer. And he had succeeded in making her close what Tillman had not unfairly called her "big mouth."

Jun Toguri had had difficulty finding an attorney willing to risk opprobrium by taking on a defendant as unpopular as his daughter. The man who had finally agreed to do it, for court and legal costs and no fee, was Wayne Collins, a slim, gray-haired liberal of forty-nine who had first made his name, in 1942, defending Fred Korematsu, a nisei who had refused to be interned. Collins took the Korematsu case all the way to the Supreme Court, and lost. After the war, however, he successfully represented about five thousand Japanese-Americans who had been intimidated into renouncing their U.S. citizenship during the hysteria that followed Pearl Harbor. They were allowed to recover it. He had taken many other Japanese-American cases, refusing to be cowed by the temper of know-nothingism, whether in government, the press, or the public.

Collins was also a forceful critic of the Japanese American Citizens League, the sycophantic nisei organization which Collins acronymically called the Jackals because of their willingness to eat crumbs from Uncle Sam's table. Duus calls him "stubborn, self-righteous and sharp-tongued." He needed to be all those things the first day he met his client in the county jail.

While they were talking, a prison matron came in and told Iva to change out of her prison uniform because a deputy marshal was taking her back to the marshal's office. She said Collins would have to leave. Collins, who knew that the marshal's office was closed, as it was a Saturday afternoon, protested that she could not be removed from the jail except by court order, a copy of which would always be sent to a defendant's counsel. The matron said she was following orders.

Collins called the marshal's office. No reply. He called the district attorney's office. That was empty, too. Clearly, something dishonestly counterjudicial was afoot. When the deputy marshal arrived, Collins went out to the car with his client and found Special Agent J. Eldon Dunn inside. She was obviously going to be interrogated, so the skinny jurist forced himself into the car with her, bumping Dunn to the center of the seat. The driver then went, not to the marshal's office but to the local FBI bureau, where an unnamed agent admitted that Iva had been hoaxed into coming in for interrogation.

Collins insisted that Agent Dunn had breached the Fourth, Fifth, and Sixth amendments to the Constitution and had violated legal ethics. When Iva was asked to go into the next room and meet there with Dunn and Tillman alone, Collins said for the record that she would go under duress and protest. His sharp voice dropping for a moment, he instructed her on no account to answer any questions without presence of counsel, and not to sign anything.

Sure enough, Tillman wanted her to sign a statement which she had made to him at Sugamo. Why he had not forced a signature out of her at the time, we don't know. Iva said in a little voice that she wouldn't sign. Tillman pressed his point, saying she could read it first and would see that it was only what she had truly said at Sugamo. From the next room, Collins, marching up and down, was shouting: "Don't answer any questions, Mrs. d'Aquino. Don't sign anything! Don't answer questions. Don't sign anything!" Tillman and Dunn exchanged glances and shrugged. This was the unsuccessful "interview" referred to in the FBI file. Iva returned to the county jail with Collins, who continued their earlier conversation to enable him to start preparing the case. She had finally won a round.

Collins persuaded two other liberal lawyers, Theodore Tamba and George Olshausen, to join with him, also without fee, although the case looked like being long and arduous. He ensured that she got proper medical treatment for her stomach disorders. Duus records that her father called at the jailhouse daily with gifts of food. But in many ways the American prison was to prove much worse than Sugamo: American prisoners can be barbarically noisy, and it was difficult for the little nisei to sleep.

The Japanese witnesses who were to testify for the government, and against her, had already arrived by air. They were interrogated and put before a grand jury. What they told the FBI as they were coached for the grand jury experience will be related in the next chapter. The grand jury was told that the evidence on which the CIC and the FBI had decided in favor of her release in Japan had been destroyed. There was no mention of the FBIS transcripts, and only six recordings of Iva were played. By October 8, the grand jury was ready to find a bill of particulars against her.

There were eight counts. In each count, she was accused of acting "with treasonable intent, for the purpose of, and with the intent in her to adhere and give aid and comfort to, the Imperial Japanese Government." Intent is key, because the Constitution says that "Treason against the United States shall consist only in levying war against them, or in adhering to their enemies, giving them aid and comfort."

All the counts were blissfully trivial, and Iva read them with relief. Because treason is such a "special" crime (it is the only one defined in the Constitution), it can be proven only by "overt acts," and there must, as noted earlier, be two witnesses to each act.

The eight counts were as follows:

Overt Act One: That on a day between March 1, 1944, and May 1, 1944, the exact date being to the Grand Jurors unknown, said Defendant, at Tokyo, Japan, in the offices of the broadcasting Corporation of Japan, did discuss with another person the proposed participation of said Defendant in a radio broadcasting program.

Overt Act Two: That [within the same time frame and in the same place] said Defendant . . . did discuss with employees of said Corporation the nature and quality of a specific proposed radio broadcast.

Overt Act Three: That [within the same time frame and in the same place] said Defendant . . . did speak into a microphone [to introduce] a program dealing with a motion picture involving war.

Overt Act Four: That on a date between August 1, 1944, and December 1, 1944, the exact date being to

211

the Grand Jurors unknown, said Defendant, at Tokyo, Japan, did speak into a microphone in a studio of the broadcasting Corporation of Japan referring to enemies of Japan.

Overt Act Five: That on a day during October, 1944, the exact date being to the Grand Jurors unknown, said Defendant, at Tokyo, Japan, did prepare a script for subsequent radio broadcast concerning the loss of ships.

Overt Act Six: That [on the same date and in the same place] said Defendant did speak into a microphone concerning the loss of ships.

Overt Act Seven: That on or about May 23, 1945, the exact date being to the Grand Jurors unknown, said Defendant, at Tokyo, Japan, did prepare a radio script for radio broadcast.

Overt Act Eight: That on a day between May 1, 1945, and July 31, 1945, the exact date being to the Grand Jurors unknown, said Defendant, at Tokyo, Japan, did speak into a microphone in a studio of the broadcasting Corporation of Japan, and did then and there engage in an entertainment dialogue with an employee of the broadcasting Corporation of Japan for radio broadcast purposes.

It was an astonishing bill of particulars, by any standards, especially compared with those of similar cases against Axis Sally, Lord Haw-Haw, and other "radio traitors." *The San Francisco Chronicle* summed it up for readers by saying that it merely meant that Iva had worked for NHK during the war. It is still not clear how some of the counts represent treason at all, unless all the Bunka prisoners should have been indicted for refusing to be beheaded. Most of the counts would hardly seem to justify the more than one year Iva had already spent incarcerated in Japan, and the additional year she was about to spend in prison in San Francisco, waiting for the FBI and the prosecutors to put together a fragile case with rusty pins and bailing wire.

The only halfway serious count was number four—assuming that it meant that Iva had presented the enemies of Japan as being her enemies too, and had not just used the term, without treasonous intent, as a joke. Rather less serious was count five, in which she is said to have written a script "concerning the loss of ships." Count six—reading that script—would seem to mean anything only if she had written it (the previous count).

Special assistant attorney general Tom de Wolfe, put onto this Alice-in-Wonderland case because of the public furor attached to it, said wearily in a memo to Ray Whearty at Justice: "I understood my instructions in the Toguri case." Only two of the twenty-three jurors had voted against indictment, he said, but it had been "necessary for me to practically make [sic] a Fourth of July speech in order to obtain [it]."

Reporting to assistant attorney general Alexander Campbell, he had said: "I told the Grand Talesmen that the case as to Colonel [sic] Ince, Mrs. d'Aquino's superior on Radio Tokyo, would be presented to a Federal Grand Jury here in the immediate future." De Wolfe said that if he had not made this promise (which was to turn out to be mendacious), "I believe that the grand jury would have returned a no true bill against Mrs. d'Aquino."

De Wolfe, who had made his name as a war crimes prosecutor in the Internal Security Division of Justice, and who had got life sentences for Douglas Chandler and Robert Best, two Americans who had broadcast for the Nazis, had earlier pleaded to be allowed to withdraw the case against Iva Toguri. On May 25, 1948, he had told Campbell: "There is no evidence upon which a reasonable mind might fairly conclude guilt beyond a reasonable doubt, and consequently a motion for . . . acquittal . . . would probably be granted."

On October 11, when Iva finally appeared in court for the

first time, she was again refused bail, on the bizarre ground that treason was a "capital" (i.e., death penalty) offense. By then, the witnesses from Japan, including several U.S. citizens who had broadcast in English on NHK, had been given a brief tour of the United States and sent home, with a two-day stop-off in Honolulu, where everyone wanted to see Pearl Harbor—still a magnet for Japanese tourists, today. They would come back the next year for yet another paid vacation—the trial itself.

Only twelve Americans were indicted for treason after World War II. None was executed—a punishment exclusively reserved for one case of desertion from the field of battle: pathetic little Private Eddie Slovik, one of many less than warriorlike soldiers who panicked under fire, but the only unfortunate chosen by General Dwight Eisenhower as a scapegoat to intimidate others.

Seven of those indicted for treason were "radio traitors"—the previously mentioned Best and Chandler, who got life terms; Martin Monti, who was sentenced to twenty-five years; Herbert John Burgman, who received six to twenty years; Mildred Gillars, who got ten to thirty years; John David Provoo, acquitted on appeal; and Iva Toguri. The first five were all Nazis. Gillars, converted to nazism by the love of her life, Max-Otto Koischewitz (Germany's equivalent of Colonel Tsuneishi), received her sentence for the only count on which she was convicted: she had narrated a highly realistic account of D Day, before it happened, complete with the groans and screams of dying and drowning GIs.

Iva Toguri faced no such heavy charges, and no one alleged that she was anti-American or pro-Axis, only that she had been persuaded to broadcast for the enemy. The grand jury, as de Wolfe had recounted, had agreed to indict her on some possibly disloyal misdemeanors only because de Wolfe had falsely promised that the government would indict Ince.

The trial of Gillars, known as Axis Sally (she had used the name Sally on the air), was to precede Iva's by only a few weeks. So was that of Tomoya Kawakita, the tubby nisei who, stranded in Japan in 1941 at the age of twenty, had become a brutal prison-camp guard. Although he had taken Japanese nationality, he had returned to California without difficulty after the war, but had been recognized by a former prisoner, in 1947, while shopping in a Los Angeles department store.

"That's Meatball!" the enraged former POW shouted, holding on to the struggling fat man until police came. "Meatball" Kawakita finally got eight years for brutalizing American prisoners.

Gillars had been allowed to bring five defense witnesses from Germany at U.S. government expense. Although Germany was a foreign country, it was still under Allied occupation, which made American subpoenas possible. Japan was also under U.S. occupation, but when Collins asked for forty-three witnesses from there, including General MacArthur and his G-2, General Willoughby, the court refused to allow any of them to be subpoenaed.

Judge Michael Roche, who in 1943 had denied habeas corpus to Mitsuye Endo, an American woman who had held that her detention on the basis of her ethnic descent was unlawful, now denied Toguri's right to compel witnesses under the Sixth Amendment. One defense attorney, Ted Tamba, was given funds to pay for a trip to Japan to take depositions, but not to pay for an interpreter. Tetsujiro Nakamura, a nisei who had been one of the five thousand to whom Collins had helped restore American citizenship, offered to go with Tamba for no fee, but at Jun Toguri's expense, to translate. But Nakamura had never been to Japan before and his Japanese was not fluent. The two soon found that, by now, nobody was anxious to testify for Iva—that is, to testify against the United States Government.

Fortunately, Tamotsu Murayama, the friendliest of the Japanese officers at Suragadai, who had become what Duus calls "an informal liaison between prime minister Kiyuro Shidehara and General MacArthur" after the war, offered to help. He was now the star reporter on *The Japan Times,* Tokyo's main English-language daily. He could see how invidious was the notion of picking out Iva, the solitary American patriot at NHK, as the sole scapegoat for NHK English broadcasts, and he used his muscle as a member of the new Japanese elite to persuade thirty-one Japanese to make depositions which Tamba could use. Depositions are not as useful as a good witness in the box, especially in a jury trial, but they were something. The defense used nineteen of them.

Justice had sent Tillman, in Tokyo, a list of the forty-three people whom Collins wanted, and what evidence they were expected to generate. Tillman or CIC agents, or both, had called on most of them, and cajoled many of them into making statements which could be used to contradict whatever Collins or Tamba might get from them later. It was the old story of "When you fight the government, the government won't fight fair."

Tillman went everywhere accompanied by armed MPs— all about twice lifesize by Japanese standards. By the time Tamba got to Tokyo with his Americanized Japanese interpreter, they found that most of the people on Iva's list had been successfully intimidated. Some were working for the Occupation authorities and did not want to prejudice their jobs. The fact that Tamba was accompanied everywhere by the Justice Department's Noel Storey, who had the right to cross-examine all the deponents, also didn't help.

Tamba was to write later, in 1954, in support of the unsuccessful pardon petition to President Eisenhower, Eddie Slovik's nemesis, that the people they questioned "appeared to Mr. Storey and to me to be genuinely frightened of our troops in Occupied Japan. A number of them had been led to believe that if they testified against Mrs. d'Aquino, our government might react favorably to requests on their part to return to the United States as American citizens, without being charged and put on trial for their own admitted treasonable utterances and conduct."

MacArthur, ever political, ordered his staff to be uncooperative. He had Iva's Yokohama and Sugamo statements classified Top Secret, so that the defense could not even read them. When the defense team protested, the court ruled that martial law prevailed in MacArthur's Japan and the court had no power to oppose the generalissimo. The same documents had, however, been given to Tillman.

Tamba's work went slowly. He had to prolong his stay in Japan. The trial, set for May 16, was postponed *sine die*.

Collins had not been informed that Charles Cousens wanted to come from Australia to testify that Iva had broadcast only because he had persuaded her to, that she was totally pro-American, and that she had never acted treasonably. Cousens, the English gentleman, had thought that telling the U.S. Embassy in Canberra would be enough—but it had been enough only to warn Justice. Cousens made his offer in November 1948, but Collins did not learn of it until May 1949. Another Australian from Suragadai, Kenneth Parkyns, also offered to come. Jun Toguri borrowed the money to pay their fares and expenses.

Cousens had spent five days defending himself before a magisterial inquiry in Sydney, after an investigation that had lasted two months, so he knew to some extent what Iva was going through, although Australia had never ridden roughshod over his rights in the way that the United States was doing over Iva's. The case against Major Cousens had been dropped partly because he had been able to prove that biased commentary attributed to him was actually a broadcast by Ken Ishii, and because he had taken on Iva, whom he had chosen because she was a "completely loyal American citizen."

The charges against Cousens, however, had not been officially withdrawn until November 1946, and some of the stigmata of the accusations had remained; it required an act of loyalty by such a public figure to stir up criticism again by defending Iva.

Collins and Tamba went to the airport to meet Cousens and Parkyns and to make sure Fred Tillman did not get to them first. When the Australians did not emerge from Immigration and Customs, Collins barged in and found that Tillman and Dunn were in one of the customs rooms, trying to ask the visitors questions. He roared at them and drove them out.

The case was becoming more and more like a Hollywood movie about a corrupt prosecution than about "disc jockey treason." One can only imagine the reactions of Cousens and Parkyns. Both men probably already had a jaundiced view of the justice system in the United States, a country where judges and prosecutors were often elected like other politicians. Yet surely, they must have thought, the notion of the FBI sequestering defense witnesses must be beyond the pale. Cousens was to say later, for the Australian press, that he had had to contain his temper because he feared seeing Tillman and Dunn going one inethical step further and putting him and Parkyns back on the plane. Jun Toguri had borrowed heavily to bring them to San Francisco, and Cousens had to be there in court to save his "soldier." Cousens was to tell the Australian press that he had played for time and had been very relieved to see the skinny, balding figure of the defense attorney crashing improbably through the door.

Duus records that when Iva met her father in 1948, after seven years' absence, she had controlled her emotions, but that when she saw Cousens for the first time since 1945—a brief glimpse on what was to be his last day at the studios—she had broken down and wept. Her mentor figure, whose intellectual and moral bearing so surpassed those of anyone else she had known in Japan, Allied or Japanese, had come to the rescue of his young protégée. Apart from Cousens and Parkyns, the only other defense witness brought from abroad was Felippe, who had to pay his own fare. (In fact, it was his father-in-law who had once again borrowed money to help.)

Twenty-seven years later, in 1976, Felippe d'Aquino recalled his only visit to America for Ronald Yates of *The Chicago Tribune:*

"I arrived in Seattle aboard a ship and immediately I was taken into custody by the FBI and the immigration authorities. When I told them I had come to testify at my wife's trial in San Francisco, they said I wouldn't be allowed to, unless I signed a paper saying I would never return to the United States."

Yates said that "d'Aquino was kept in jail under suspicion of being an illegal immigrant and harassed for two days until he signed that dubious paper."

American jails are frightening to Americans. They are devastating to foreigners, especially those from smaller races. Felippe signed, thus virtually ensuring permanent separation from his wife. For Yates, d'Aquino also recalled the twenty-six-year-old he had met and courted—"typically American, happygolucky, not Japanese at all." The war years had taken their toll and increased her homesickness, he said, but they had looked forward to a life together in America; that life, however, was to be limited to seeing her in court each day for several weeks.

As the trial neared, the government luxuriated in once more bringing nineteen witnesses from Japan at American taxpayers' expense. Seven were nisei who had taken Japanese citizenship and who had been warned that, if they did not cooperate, the best they could hope for was never to be allowed to return home to California; the worst would be to find themselves in Iva's situation, charged with treason. The other twelve were Japanese, not all of whom had been grand jury witnesses; they were predominantly lured by the promise of a free American vacation.

Some nisei, despite the threats, had refused to be disloyal to their former colleague. Prominent among these was Ruth Hayakawa, the sultry beauty who had read whatever she was ordered to read and who, at least among those who broadcast from the Tokyo studios, most nearly corresponds to the image of the legendary "Tokyo Rose" siren. Mitsushio and Oki, however, lacked Hayakawa's courage and had even helped Tillman to persuade others to come and load the case against their former subordinate. The foreign witnesses were paid $10 a day for expenses and fees. By living with relatives, many managed to save most of that and could take advantage of a phenomenally artificial exchange rate which made the salary of a young Japanese executive, then, the equivalent of about $7 a month. Some witnesses, Oki among them, saved $150 or $200, went home, and started businesses. Others bought American goods and sold them on the Tokyo black market. Fifty dollars' worth of saccharin, for instance, being minimal in volume, could be hidden in one's pockets. In Japan, where sugar was scarce, it could be sold on the black market for enough yen to buy a small apartment. Only the brave and the honest refused to join Tillman's army. The war was over; Japan had surrendered; the Californian nisei in Tokyo had mostly gone over on their backs and pawed the air.

14.

Drilling the Witnesses

BECAUSE THE PROSECUTION had virtually no case at the time of Iva Toguri d'Aquino's arrest, and since Tom de Wolfe had coaxed a true bill out of the grand jury only with great difficulty, the task of preparing witnesses for the trial had begun even before the *General Hodges* had docked with the puny, sickly prisoner. After her arrival, the pace quickened.

Tillman and Dunn went through several key interviews on September 24, 1948, using Louis M. Howe as their interpreter. The first was Yukio Ikeda, who had been in charge of personnel records at NHK. He confirmed that Iva had been a *rinji shoku-taku*, or temporary employee. He said he did not think there was any record to show that she had been employed at the written behest of the Japanese army; any such request would have been verbal, he thought. Her regular salary had originally been ¥80 a month, plus allowances of ¥20 and ¥10; this had been increased to ¥140 plus an allowance of ¥40 on August 31, 1944. Ikeda said he had never met Miss Toguri, who was carried on the payroll until the foreign broadcasting section was abolished on September 26, 1945.

Having thus earned his passage money and expenses, Ikeda bowed and departed. The seat was taken by a very different figure, Shigetsugu Tsuneishi, the trim, wiry career colonel, still in his thirties and now turned island teahouse owner.

Tsuneishi recounted his service in Manchukuo (the name given to Manchuria during the Japanese occupation), where he had earned sufficient distinction to be sent to the military academy for two years in 1938. During the nearly four years of war with the United States, he had held his "propaganda" post, as he called it, with the rank of major. Shortly before the surrender, he had been posted to his home province of Shikoku with the recently acquired rank of lieutenant colonel.

He defined his task as being the army member of the committee for overseas broadcasting of propaganda, the other representatives being from the navy, the Foreign Office, the Great East Asia Ministry, the Ministry of Communications, and the Cabinet Information Bureau.

"It was realized [in 1942] that Tokyo radio's handling of propaganda was unsuccessful and not achieving its purpose," Tsuneishi barked candidly. The answer, "Zero Hour," was started sometime in the spring of 1943, he added, after generals in the occupied territories were instructed to select "prisoners of war with ability that could be used on such programs." This had brought in Ince, Reyes, and the especially valuable Cousens.

The account he gave in San Francisco of his first dramatic interview with Cousens was predictably bland.

"I believe that Cousens immediately expressed great dislike at having to do any such things [as coaching a propaganda program]," he said. Cousens had finally acquiesced and had been given accommodation at the Dai-ichi Hotel, without a guard. In all, he calculated, Cousens had worked at NHK for a total of thirty-eight months. Tsuneishi remembered approving the title "Zero Hour," but once again could not recall who suggested it. Because of his almost nonexistent English, he said he was unable to make a good judgment of the program's quality and relied on the advice of others; but he had sometimes complained that there was too much music and "not enough propaganda," and this, he claimed, had been corrected.

In the FBI periphrasis, he had first "met" Iva at an office lunch party in 1944 and had decided she must be the person whom the American press was calling Tokyo Rose. He had been introduced to her and to many of her colleagues by George Nakamoto (Mitsushio). The only other guests he remembered were Kenkiichi Oki and June Suyama. He said he had "encouraged" all his radio staff but had not personally complimented Iva Toguri or engaged in any conversation with her. He had warned them all that Japan was "being defeated" and had said that it was their role to "discourage the enemy and thereby assist us." There had been another such luncheon about six months later; this, he claimed, was the only other time that he had seen Toguri-*san*.

Asked the purpose of "Zero Hour," he said it was to make American frontline troops, especially those in the islands, "homesick" and to "discourage them from carrying on the war." Broadly speaking, he said, the politics of programming was discussed only with the male staff, because "as you are well aware, females in Japan are not taken into confidences nor are persons of that category told what the purpose of things are for."

One of Tillman's cleverer questions was to ask if her pay raise had been the result of her becoming famous as Tokyo Rose. Said Tsuneishi: "I did hear subsequently that she got some reward for having attracted the recognition of an American magazine." Although he did not say he ever gave her a "Tokyo Rose" bonus, this answer at least confirms his own belief that Iva was the source of the early "Rose" stories in the American press. This belief was to exercise some weight in the thinking of the trial jury.

Tsuneishi confirmed that from time to time the army

would "require that certain broadcasts be made," notably inserts into programs. He said he knew that Miss Toguri was a nisei Californian, but he again claimed that he had not known until after the war that she had retained her American nationality.

No date appears in the files for the interview with Mitsushio, but since it begins at the bottom of the page on which Tsuneishi's ends, and concludes immediately before Oki's, which is dated September 24, it seems to have followed Tsuneishi's and to have taken place on the same day. Today, both Mitsushio and Tillman say they cannot remember, and Oki died before the author could ask him.

Mitsushio said he had been born in San Francisco in 1905, the son of Sanzo Mitsushio and Shizuko Tanabe, and had been given the name Hideo. George was his schoolboy name. His father had died of an illness while on a visit to Japan in 1911. His mother had remarried Kanehiro Nakamoto, an issei, who had adopted George and his brother Iwao. Mitsushio said he had first visited Japan in 1926.

Because his mother had no brothers, he had also taken the name Tanabe, thus becoming the putative adopted son of his maternal grandparents—in effect, his mother's brother—and their heir. He had acquired dual U.S.-Japanese nationality, and as a putative family heir he could escape conscription into the Japanese army, he explained.

He had revisited Japan from October 1938 to March 1939, working as a "copy reader" for the Domei news agency in Tokyo and in occupied Shanghai. Back in California, he had worked for the Japanese-language newspaper *Rafu Shimpo* and had become a correspondent for NHK. On January 3, he had set sail for Yokohama again, to join the English-language staff of Tokyo radio. Shortly before, he had given up his Japanese citizenship, as an added insurance against being drafted while in Japan.

The periphrasis reads: "On April 2, 1943, he was restored on the family record as an independent family. He stated this [Japanese renaturalization] step was taken on the assumption his United States citizenship [had been] automatically revoked by the Nationality Act of 1941."

His first U.S. passport, issued in 1926, described him as Hideo Tanabe. The passport issued for his second trip to Japan, in 1938, described him as George Hideo Nakamoto. This document had expired in 1942, the FBI report notes. He had registered with the Japanese police as an American until April 1943. In 1944, he had officially dropped the name Nakamoto and reassumed that of Mitsushio.

From June 1942 until October or November 1944, he had been "in charge of the commentaries and features of the English section [division?] of Tokyo radio, of which the Zero Hour was a part." "Zero Hour," he confirmed, had started in March 1943, "at the time of the Guadalcanal operation." It had become part of the Front Line Section of the English division, when this section had been created in August 1944, to broadcast to American troops in the islands; he had been appointed its chief, with Kenkiichi Oki as production supervisor.

What was different about "Zero Hour," he said, was that the foreigners—the prisoners and Iva Toguri—were allowed to prepare their own scripts. He confirmed again that the "major purpose of the program was to induce a spirit of homesickness, discontent and nostalgia in the American troops stationed in the South Pacific islands, in order to discourage them from fighting against the Japanese troops." Mitsushio said he was held responsible for the content of the programs by his immediate superior, Shinojo Sawada.

Tillman then took Mitsushio slowly and methodically through repetitive explanations that sought to show that the stocky San Franciscan had explained the program's purpose to his staff in English, and that Iva had understood it and been cooperative. Mitsushio also recalled the March 1944 lunch with Tsuneishi, except that he first described it as a dinner (which, in March, would mean after dark) then refers to it only later as a lunch. It had been held at the To-kyo Mai-kan restaurant, he said. Tsuneishi had explained to his guests that American forces had landed on several formerly Japanese-occupied islands and that his broadcasters were a psychological weapon against a now stronger enemy. Tsuneishi had been in uniform at the time and had of course spoken in Japanese, so that Iva would have understood his words only partially. Tillman, however, has Mitsushio saying she understood all of the major's remarks. Today, Mitsushio agrees that that was not true, and that Iva's Japanese at the time was "incoherent."

An explanation of two of the counts in the indictment then follows, with Mitsushio recalling that "sometime between the dates of March 1, 1944, and December 1, 1944," the "Zero Hour" staff was invited by the Japanese Army General Staff to attend a showing of *Gone With the Wind* and that he decided to do a program based on the film. Later, Kenkiichi Oki distributed scripts to the staff for such a show.

The periphrasis of this part of Mitsushio's interrogation contains the odd plural in the phrase "the exact date of which *they* do not recall" (emphasis added), which, as the reader will see later, has a special significance. Iva, Mitsushio remembered, had criticized Oki's send-up of the Margaret Mitchell novel-film as being "corny" and had said Cousens' Orphan Annie creation was better; but she had been ordered to play a role in the Oki script that evening, and had done so. The show emphasized the "discouraging phases of warfare."

Two more counts in the indictment are explained in what follows. According to Tillman's periphrasis, "Mitsushio stated that he further recalled that shortly after the battle of the Leyte

Gulf, the Imperial General Headquarters of the Japanese armed forces [had] handed him an official announcement . . . which . . . reflected (*sic*) that a great number of American ships had been sunk."

Here, the word *him* is made to occupy the space of four typewritten letters, suggesting once again that the word *them* had been typed in first, that Mitsushio and Oki were interviewed together, and that Oki had only later pretended to have given a separate testimony.

The periphrasis of Mitsushio's interview goes on:

> He stated he received this announcement about five o'clock in the evening and that it was timed just right for them to use in their "Zero Hour" broadcast, and that they were the first to use the news of the Leyte Gulf battle in their broadcast program.
>
> Mitsushio stated that on the same day, after six o'clock in the evening and before seven o'clock in the evening, he saw Toguri at the microphone in the broadcasting studio and that she in substance made this remark, the exact words of which he does not recall. . . . "Now, you fellows have lost all your ships. You really are orphans of the Pacific, and how do you think that you will ever get home?"

Mitsushio said these words, or something like them, had been inserted into Iva's script that evening at the insistence of the Imperial General Headquarters.

Recently, the author asked Ken Ishii if it were feasible that the imperial staff had insisted on announcing a pretended major victory in Orphan Ann's platter chatter.

"Mitsushio was lying," Ishii said. "What he was recalling was part of a news broadcast, not Iva's patter. If headquarters had wanted a victory announced, Iva would have been their last choice as announcer."

In any event, there is no trace of such a script in the files. More significantly, neither the FBIS nor the OSS heard it, either in the "Zero Hour" news or as an introduction to Iva's music. None of the "soreheads" among her listening audience recalled such a broadcast—which would surely have been good for a laugh at the time, since the battle of Leyte Gulf was the most important American naval victory of the Pacific war. And to make a charge of this "overt act" stick, there had to be a second witness. As readers will see later, the prosecution produced a clone.

Mitsushio, under further questioning, then recalled that "sometime between the dates of August 1, 1944 and December 1, 1944," he remembered that Iva had "stood" before the microphone and, describing herself as "your favorite enemy, Orphan Annie," had announced the song "Goodbye Now." He remembered that it was the fall of the year, because it was after the program had been made longer but before Miyeko Furuya left NHK to marry Oki.

Then comes what later transpires to be a very important remark: "George Mitsushio recalls that Kenkiichi Oki, Production Supervisor, Front Line Section, Broadcasting Corporation of Japan, was present at the time all of the above incidents occurred."

It defies belief that Mitsushio would have repeated Oki's job title, even down to spelling out NHK word for word, but his insistence that Oki was present at the dinner-lunch, at the *Gone With the Wind* screening and subsequent discussion, and at the "sunken ships" broadcast was to decide the result of the trial and finally ruin Iva Toguri's life. Oki was to become the crucial "second witness" by what seems to have been a dubious trick.

Next Mitsushio recalled a visit by Kenneth Ishii to the studio, on his first furlough from the army, and puts the date at "about May 23, 1945." He and Ishii both saw Iva preparing a script for that night's broadcast. Coincidentally, Oki also was "present at the time the above incident occurred."

Oki's interrogation, which follows, is also dated September 24. He described how he had sailed for Japan in March 1939, aboard the Nihon Yusem Kaicha vessel *Kamakura Maru*. He had stayed at his grandparents' home in the fashionable Shiba ward and had spent a year learning Japanese and touring the country. He had done some freelance sports reporting for *The Nippon Times* and later, with the help of Mitsushio, whom he had known in California, he had gone to work at NHK. He had started work as a production supervisor at ¥100 a month, and had eventually occupied that post on "Zero Hour."

At the request of his father, Kenjio Oki, who had died in Tokyo in 1943, Oki had taken Japanese nationality in 1940, he told Tillman. (In 1986, he said he was a dual citizen from then, meaning that his father had registered him in Japan at that time.) Oki said he had registered as a Japanese resident at the Shiba police station and had been entered on the family registry in their home prefecture, Hiroshima. From the FBI periphrasis, it appears that Tillman never asked him the crucial and embarrassing question as to whether he had renounced his American nationality at the U.S. consulate general in 1940, and Oki did not mention this; so we may reasonably conclude that he was a dual citizen throughout the war. If "Zero Hour" was treason, Oki was as guilty as Mitsushio—and perhaps more so than their more intimidated fellow Americans, Iva Toguri and Captain Ince, who were not dual citizens.

Then, beginning from the sixth paragraph of Tillman's periphrasis of Oki's interrogation, a strange thing happens. His entire interview becomes word for word (except for the change of names) the same as everything in the periphrasis of Mitsushio, from the third paragraph of the seventh page of that interrogation onward. This astonishing pretense—it can hardly be anything else—goes on for about two thousand words. (See appendix 1.)

In Mitsushio, the long passage begins: "Mitsushio recalls that at the time the Front Line Section was organized, they called together a meeting of the Front Line Section for a conference concerning the radio broadcasts. He recalls that Toguri was among those present."

With "Mitsushio" replaced by "Oki," the passage begins in exactly the same way in the Oki periphrasis, including the awkward repetition of "Front Line Section."

In Mitsushio, the next paragraph begins: "Mitsushio recalls that one Norman Reyes. . . ." In Oki: "Oki recalls that one Norman Reyes. . . ." All the wording thereafter remains identical.

Where it says, in Mitsushio, that "Mitsushio recalls that he gave these instructions in the English language . . ." so in Oki it says that "Oki recalls that Mitsushio gave these instructions in the English language. . . ." Where it says, in the Mitsushio periphrasis, that "Mitsushio recalls that Toguri assented specifically as to her understanding of the instructions . . ." so, in Oki, it says that "Oki recalls that Toguri assented specifically as to her understanding of the instructions. . . ."

Each of the two men remembers the first staff party under Tsuneishi as a "dinner" which later becomes a "lunch." Each remembers only five of the guests—the same five, in the same order.

And so it goes on, word for word, with only those word changes that are necessary to make it look as though Oki actually said exactly what Mitsushio had allegedly said earlier. In the key "Leyte Gulf" sequence, Mitsushio said that headquarters had handed him an official announcement. Curiously, presumably because of a slip by Tillman, the Oki periphrasis does not say "handed Mitsushio" but remains "handed him" (that is, Oki) as though both men shared the same hand. This clearly indicates that it is Mitsushio's testimony, signed by Oki. Oki's recollection of what Iva said on the air is word for word the version that came out of Mitsushio's memory, even though both men are recorded as stating that they cannot recall the words exactly. Oki similarly remembers the "Goodbye Now" recording, and similarly dates it to just before he and Miyeko Furuya were married. (Just before his death, Oki still claimed that Miyeko had already left the station by that time, although, as noted earlier, NHK records show she remained there almost until the end of the war.)

The whole cloned two-thousand-word passage, which ends, in Mitsushio, with him recalling that Ishii and Oki were present at "the above incident," ends, in Oki, with the latter recalling that Mitsushio and Ishii were there.

Earlier, on September 22, either Tillman or Dunn, or both, had interviewed a Japanese travel agency employee named Hiromu Yagi, who recalled being given a wartime tour of NHK by a friend and being shown someone he could recognize from photos as being Iva Toguri; she was doing a broadcast. His friend had told him that she was "Tokyo Rose." He did not hear all of her broadcast, but she had "stated in effect that the soldiers' wives in the United States were going out with war workers."

The periphrasis ends: "After vacillating considerably, Yagi advised that the friend mentioned was Toshi Kodaira, an employee of the Associated Press in Tokyo, Japan." There is no Kodaira testimony in the FBI files. The embarrassing reason for this becomes apparent later, when Kodaira's testimony to the grand jury was read at the trial.

Kenneth Ishii was interviewed on September 27. He said he had been born in Tokyo in 1924, and he is quoted as saying his mother had been born in London. Today, he notes that his parents met when both were students in Leeds, in northern England, and says this was his mother's birthplace.

In 1943, he recounted proudly, he had been one of more than a hundred applicants for a single post as an English announcer at NHK, and he had been ordered to start work in October. He notes today that he was trying to avoid the draft, which eventually caught up with him in December 1944. On "Zero Hour," he had read war news and "American Home Front News," which would follow Iva Toguri's sequence, he told Tillman. His salary had been ¥150 a month. After being conscripted, he had been trained, then seconded to a regiment designed for the defense of the Japanese home islands.

Ishii's interview is brief—just over one typescript page. His main reason for being flown to the United States comes toward the end, when he recalls the incident of Iva preparing a script "around May 23, 1945," when he was visiting the studios on leave. He thus furnishes a third testimony to one of the counts. He predictably recalls that Mitsushio and Oki were there as well. Although the count seems innocuous enough, the trial jury was not to believe Ishii's testimony.

Ken Ishii's sister Mary said she had been born in England. Although her brother says today that he was never a dual citizen, Mary testified that she was still both British and Japanese. She had got the job as announcer after her brother had introduced her to Mitsushio, before leaving the station. Until then, like Iva, she had been an NHK typist. She recalled a program in which Mitsushio and Iva had exchanged joking remarks, and which she said Oki could confirm. This was not, however, one of the counts proposed to the grand jury, presumably because the jurors would have asked why Mitsushio was not being similarly charged.

Another apparently unused witness was a nisei and dual citizen, Emi Matsuda, a Japanese Foreign Office employee, who said she had seen someone referred to as "Toguri-*san*" broadcasting from a booth at NHK.

Had de Wolfe, Hogan, Tillman, and Dunn known it then, the government, although hopelessly unprepared for a treason trial after three years of on-and-off investigations, was as prepared as it would be a year later. But it now began interviewing and reinterviewing American witnesses, giving more "voice tests" to veterans who had heard "Tokyo Rose," and checking yet again on the citizenship of the woman who had been born in Los Angeles.

The prosecution turned back first to the POW witnesses. With Cousens absent in Australia and clearly hostile to the persecution of the typist who had read his scripts, Tillman concentrated his attention once more on Reyes and Ince, who had both been bound by American law during the conflict and were therefore vulnerable.

Reyes was reinterviewed on October 1, 4, and 5, 1948, and once more retraced his short life history. On February 13, 1942, he said, his employers, the Far Eastern Broadcasting Company, had sent him to Bataan to try to procure a transmitter crystal from the Signal Corps of the U.S. Army. He had been unsuccessful there but had resourcefully pushed on to Corregidor, where he had been blocked by the Japanese advance from returning to the capital. On March 1 he had joined the Filipino army as a private, was soon promoted corporal, then sergeant. On April 9, after barely a month in uniform, he was commissioned a third lieutenant. By then, the Filipino army had been absorbed into the U.S. Armed Forces for the Far East, USAFFE. Reyes became an announcer on America's "Voice of Freedom" radio, but a month later, on May 7, the American and Filipino forces surrendered.

He again related his journey in captivity to Japan with Ince, and the beginning of their collaboration with Major Cousens.

Under the Geneva Convention, the Japanese paid him ¥70 a month, plus board and lodging. The three men had shared a room at the Dai-ichi before being given separate rooms at a better hotel, the Sanno. When Reyes had become a friendly alien and qualified for a higher salary, he had lost his free accommodation and had moved in for a few weeks with a missionary group consisting of Genevieve "Ma" Topping, Ruth Ward, and Henry Grizzard, later moving back to the Sanno at his own expense, paying ¥150 a month. After four months, he had taken a room in the house of a Japanese widow, until he had finally moved in with his nisei bride, Katherine, at her mother's house in Meguro; this house had burned down in an American raid in May 1945, and they had several different addresses in the following weeks. When he returned to Manila in October, he and his wife had parted.

Initially, Cousens, Ince, and Reyes were not allowed on the streets of Tokyo without an interpreter—which they needed for shopping, anyway—but eventually, Reyes claimed, this restriction was relaxed. Reyes said his early work at NHK had been mostly editing and correcting pronunciation. When "Zero Hour" started as a fifteen-minute program in March 1943, he was the first and only announcer. Nineteen at the time, Reyes had thought "Zero Hour" meant "the hour of doom," but Mitsushio had explained that the program was intended to create homesickness—feeling like zero. When the program was expanded to include a five-minute round-up of American news from Domei, Ince became the announcer for that. By this time, he recalled, Cousens was reading POW messages to families and "commentaries" on a different program.

Questioned about the recruitment of Iva into the show, Reyes now changed his testimony radically because, as he was to explain in court, he had been threatened with a treason trial of his own if he did not "play ball." The FBI periphrasis now has Reyes saying that, in her questions to him, Iva had "implied that she wanted to do her work well and that she was pro-Japanese in attitude, so much [so] that Reyes was afraid to talk a great deal to her." In this coerced testimony, strikingly different from all the others he had given over the previous three years, Reyes also said that he did not know at the time that she was American, although this must have been obvious from her accent and her fractured Japanese, apart from everything else. But Reyes agreed that Iva had not been involved in the destruction of the NHK English-language scripts at the end of the war; that had been done by Kenkiichi Oki, Hasashi Moriyama, Seizō Hyuga, and himself, Reyes said.

At the second reinterview, on the fourth, Dunn and Tillman found the intimidated Reyes even more cooperative. He could now recall Major Tsuneishi telling the entire staff about an American magazine article on "Tokyo Rose" which described the Orphan Annie broadcast. Tsuneishi, he said, had singled out Iva for compliments at the To-kyo Kai-kan ("Mai-kan" elsewhere in the FBI file) staff party. Reyes also claimed that Iva had mentioned her spoof U.S. Navy citation in one of her broadcasts, implying that she accepted that she was the "Tokyo Rose" mentioned in that citation. (There is no record of such a broadcast.)

Reyes now began to move further away from the accounts he gave in Manila and Nashville. He is quoted as saying: "I recall a conversation very shortly after [Tsuneishi addressed the staff] in which she stated to me in substance that she was afraid of what might happen to her because she was broadcasting Japanese propaganda to American front-line troops. My answer to her was noncommittal. I did not trust her, having gained the impression that she was pro-Japanese."

Reyes again contradicted his earlier testimony by saying that he had been under no threat or coercion to work at NHK and knew of no duress exerted on Iva. As a Filipino citizen in 1948, after his country had become independent of the United

States, Reyes should have known that it would have been difficult to pursue him in the U.S. courts, even though he had been a colonial national when the ordeal in Tokyo began. His U.S. student visa, however, along with his right to continue living with his mother and siblings in Nashville, was something which the FBI could always spitefully endanger if he did not cooperate.

Reyes now also reversed his testimony on Cousens, saying: "During the time I was associated with him, I became convinced that he believed that the political problems of Asia and the Pacific islands could only be solved through the domination of this territory by a strong power, namely a benevolent Japan." He said he thought Cousens had consented to work at NHK in order to convert "Zero Hour" listeners to this view! More and more, the terrified Reyes seems to resemble Peter Lorre in his pre-execution scene in *Casablanca*.

Only Ince, who had a Filipina wife, comes off relatively well in Reyes' new metamorphosis. Ince, he said, had not objected to working at NHK but had protested at some of the commentaries. Ince also, however, had been subject to no coercion, Reyes claimed.

Dunn and Tillman quote Reyes as saying:

> With reference to Ince, I wish to state that never in my presence were any overt or implied threats of torture or death made to him to influence him to continue his broadcasting activities. On the contrary, during the time that we were at Radio Tokyo, the influence was one of inducements of better living quarters and more freedom. I also wish to state that we were treated with courtesy and consideration by the officials of Radio Tokyo.
>
> With respect to Toguri, I believe that she joined Radio Tokyo because she was desirous of increasing

her income and because the idea of being a "radio character" was not repulsive to her.

Her concerns were "inspired by what might happen to her after the war, [not by] what her treatment might be if she had not engaged in such work."

The two FBI men apparently did not press Reyes to incriminate himself, but he did admit that "at the time I became connected with Radio Tokyo, I was nineteen years old and had an obsession for being engaged in radio work."

Reyes had now become so cooperative that he was called in again the following day, the fifth, and asked for details of specific broadcasts by Iva Toguri, with dates. Those he produced can hardly have been what they hoped for. He recalled that on November 11, 1944, the anniversary of the Armistice which ended World War I, she had "said in substance it was time to forget about the war and remember the dead." On the Fourth of July, 1945, which he remembered because it was America's and Iva's birthday, Reyes recalled her telling her listeners to forget the war and try to have a good time. On another occasion, she had made fun of the Japanese army: when they had finally admitted to having lost Saipan, she had allegedly quipped: "Saipan toothpaste—good for bleeding bums. You don't have to rub it in."

This was about the time when she had returned to the station after her long absence. At that time, orders had been received to leave anything remotely propagandistic out of the program. "Zero Hour was to represent the Japanese as losing like good sports," Reyes said.

He claimed that in the summer of 1944, Tsuneishi had ordered Mitsushio to tell Iva to make remarks about the delights of cold beer and even of water that evening. The reason, Tsuneishi said, was that Japanese intelligence had reported a platoon of American soldiers on a small island without drinking water. The anecdote was not used by the prosecution, so may have been untrue.

With the prosecutory investigation still trying to establish a case, Collins appealed for bail for his client, but this was turned down on October 14.

The questioning of Americans switched briefly to Iva's new hometown of Chicago, where Special Agents W. Rulon Paxman and George H. Murphy questioned Shigemi Mazawa, a Seattle-born nisei who had been stranded in Tokyo as a twenty-year-old student by the outbreak of war. It had taken him until May 1947 to be readmitted to the United States. From November 1943 until that date he had been a reporter on *The Nippon Times*. From September 1944 until August 1945, he had also worked at NHK, where he had met Iva. He had sometimes done the monologue in the "Amos an' Andy" takeoff, replacing Mitsushio, he told the FBI.

Mazawa comes across as a very positive witness, and fortunately he had been—along with Cousens and the Danish minister—one of the few to whom she had not been afraid to confide her pro-American views.

Mazawa said: "I have no recollection of any remarks made by her on [those] broadcasts which were of a political nature. . . . I accompanied her from the station to her streetcar on a few occasions. I recall no remarks . . . that . . . referred to the United States or its Allies unfavorably. I do recall remarks she made to the effect that she was sick of the war and homesick for the United States."

The next day, Tillman and Dunn reinterviewed Ince. This was to become a three-day interrogation, the most intensive of them all. In the periphrasis, it is about thirteen thousand words long and would fill nearly thirty pages of a book. About half of it relates to Ince's own experiences at Suragadai and was related in chapter 9. It also incorporates a fresh copy of his 1946 testimony to the CIC quoted in chapter 7.

The interview of the second day, October 19, filled ten closely typed pages and must have gone on for many hours. It is a periphrasis, but in the first person singular. In the preamble, he is made to say, ominously: "I have been advised that I am not required to make a statement and that any statement I may make may be used in a subsequent criminal proceedings [*sic*] against me." He was presumably aware of de Wolfe's promise to the grand jury to charge him with treason. Now, suddenly, he began to distance himself from Iva.

When she had joined "Zero Hour," he now said, he had objected because she appeared to be Japanese and might not be sympathetic to their aims, as well as because of her lack of experience and her unsuitable voice, which he calls "harsh and strident." What he most feared was that the "introduction of an outsider" would hinder their "control" of the program. Ince explained how he had initially distrusted Cousens because he did not know him, and recounted how, slowly, the three men—he, Cousens, and Reyes—had combined to render the "Zero Hour" show innocuous.

"Reyes and myself . . . finally decided that Cousens was trustworthy and loyal [and] was actually taking measures to modify Japanese propaganda given to him for broadcast purposes. . . . We [all] agreed that the Japanese were not nearly as clever as we had always been led to believe and could be fooled."

Ince said that, initially, both he and Cousens would select the records for Iva's sequence from the NHK library, which had been augmented by discs from Manila radio after the Japanese capture of the Philippines. Cousens would write Iva's script in longhand. Ince would type it and make carbon copies. The two copies retained at NHK were for Iva and for either Ince or Reyes on the turntable.

Under Cousens' constant coaching, Ince said, Iva had

learned technique and become more confident at the microphone, so Cousens "began writing the introductions in a
lighter, more personal vein." This was all the more true after
the "Orphan Ann" pseudonym was coined, and Cousens invented such phrases as "forgotten men," "boneheads," and
"little orphans of the Pacific" to describe the listeners. Cousens
also invented for Iva a boyfriend, called Abe, a Japanese family
name, to whom she would refer from time to time in her script.

Ince confirmed that he spun the turntables for "Zero
Hour" all the time he was with the program, sitting a few feet
from Iva during her sequence, and doing news broadcasts both
before and after it. Ince identified a number of scripts from the
period of February to May 1944, recognizing phrases used by
Cousens and reused by Iva after Cousens fell ill. He specifically
recalled typing ten of the March scripts, and two each from
February and April.

One script bore a mention of "Stephen Foster's Melodies"
in Ince's own handwriting. Others bore such typical Cousens-
isms as "Sergeant, where the hell's that orphan choir?" or
"This is your little playmate, Orphan Annie," jokes about
"ABC" (the Australian Broadcasting Corporation), and Pacific
puns like "not bad atoll, atoll."

Ince went through Iva's personal collection of fourteen
scripts. There was the classic patter of Cousens' style, the
appeals to the "celebrated featherless songster, the singing
bonehead," the Japanisms like "please to listening!" and the
remarks about "wicked propaganda" such as "Right now, I'm
lulling their senses before I creep up and annihilate them with
my nail file!"

Ince said he could identify the scripts by their "unusual
phraseology" and by the fact that he either typed them or
watched them being broadcast, or both. He talked about
Toguri's desire to return home to America, and said:

"I believe that her sympathies leaned more toward America

than Japan for the following reasons: she consistently referred to the Japanese as 'Japs,' and brought us as frequently as she could reports of intercepted American news which gave the true picture of the war in the Pacific." Once, she had arrived with the news that American troops had captured an island before the Japanese had even admitted, in their own bulletins, that there had been a U.S. landing there. Iva, who had received the news at the Danish legation, had said of the Japanese General Staff: "Who do these people think they're kidding?"

But Ince put less emphasis than he had at the previous session on her American loyalty, clearly not wanting to be seen as wholeheartedly defending someone who might be convicted. From Ince's testimony that day, it would appear that Iva was coached only by Cousens, not by the others, about efforts to sabotage the program by the way the scripts were written. Ince, who had a hatred of the Japanese, now insisted that he had never been able to bring himself to trust her completely. This is a totally new development in his testimony. He now said that most of the *doubles entendres* in phrasing were in the commentaries, rather than in Iva's disc jockey scripts, since it was believed that few would be listening to Iva's patter for information. This makes sense. He agreed that he and Iva Toguri had shared their concerns about what reactions might be when they returned home, after the war, from broadcasting for "the Japs." He had, however, never confided in her in the way that Cousens had done, he now insisted.

More testimonies were being collected around the country: from a former vice consul in Tokyo; from Major James T. Reitz of the CIC who was by then in Oberammergau; from one of his former CIC subordinates, now in Charlotte, North Carolina; from a former GI in Buffalo, New York, who had a one-yen note autographed "Iva Toguri, Tokyo Rose"; and a longer statement from James Keeney, who had helped Dale Kramer with the *Yank* interview. Keeney, now working in Philadelphia, said he had been convinced that her NHK work was innocuous.

In Denver, Elizabeth Mitsuru Hashii remembered Iva from UCLA and from seeing her working in her father's grocery in Watts.

"I helped Iva get her sewing done before she went to Japan," where she had gone mainly to "please her father," Betty Hashii said.

On April 5, 1949, Special Agent Thomas McShane of New York interviewed the writer Robert Ruark about an article he had written in the Washington *Daily News* two months before, recalling "Tokyo Rose" broadcasts he had heard at sea in the Pacific and on Guam. But Ruark, questioned at his New York home, was unable to remember details and it is not clear from the periphrasis which "Rose" he heard.

Most of the other minor interviews were of similar former listeners to Japanese radio programs, and involved testing them on the three recordings mentioned earlier—one of another woman, one of a real Iva program, and one of Iva reenacting a broadcast later at army request.

A former radio engineer in Honolulu, now in Butte, Montana, recalled that "Tokyo Rose" had begun broadcasting *before* the war. "She used excellent English and had a smooth, cultured voice," he said, identifying the number one recording as being his "Rose." He also remembered "another female voice (which) announced herself as Annie, sounded like a teenager and was irritating to listen to." He correctly identified numbers two and three as being that voice, and said "Annie" was not political like the real "Rose."

A former marine sergeant in Oklahoma City also said that the "real" hostile Tokyo Rose had been broadcasting at least as early as 1942. An El Paso veteran recognized numbers two and three, and said "Orphan Annie's" broadcasts were nonpolitical. So did a former marine in Riverside, California.

Special Agent Gary Sawtelle in Los Angeles reinterviewed Jules Sutter, Gilbert Vasquez Velasquez, Sam Cavnar, Charles Hall, and Marshall Hout (sometimes described as Hoot). Sutter once more distinguished between the "Rose" who had threatened to blow up Saipan island, and who played no music, and the very different program of music by "Orphan Annie." But Sutter seems actually to have confused Iva's show with another program which came on much earlier in the day.

Even Gilbert Vasquez Velasquez, her former neighbor, who had already slipped up earlier, seemed to have more than one program confused. Hall still had no recollection of "Zero Hour" or "Ann." Cavnar thought "Ann's" voice resembled that of Sonja Henie, the Scandinavian skater who had become a film star.

Hout, who had earlier said he remembered hearing the voice in recording number one, which was not Iva, now revealed that he had been the chief boatswain's mate on a high-speed rescue launch, from where he had heard "Zero Hour" and a woman broadcaster who called herself Orphan Ann or Annie. However, he said that he remembered Annie saying: "Congratulations, Commander Perry, on the safe landing of your squadron on Albamama; but you'll be sorry." The little island had been bombed three nights later. Bizarrely, this confused bos'n was one of the few serviceman witnesses called at the trial; even more bizarrely, his testimony was said by reporters at the time to have turned the jury against Iva. A Hollywood screenwriter, Red Sherdeman, had similarly confused memories, but he was not called as a trial witness.

A former classmate from UCLA who had been on field trips with Iva, Dr. Clair Steggall, said she had told him she hoped to study medicine in Japan.

"She said that because of her race and the fact that she was a woman she would probably have difficulty gaining admittance to a medical school in this country," he had told the FBI. He, like many of the veterans interviewed, had never heard an "Orphan Annie" broadcast. A former sergeant remembered "Annie" announcing Doolittle's first raid on Tokyo in 1942— two years before the first raid took place. One of the survivors of the *Lansdowne* identified recording number one as Annie, but not numbers two and three. This was the same mistake that Hout had made. A brigadier general and an AP correspondent had difficulty recognizing any of the recordings; the journalist said he thought that, not only were there many announcers called "Tokyo Rose" by the Americans, but also many announcers who had called themselves Orphan Annie.

Sergeant John David Provoo, the accused traitor, then under psychiatric care at Walter Reed Hospital in Washington, said again that he had seen Iva Toguri at the studio and learned her name. Only after the war did he learn that some people thought that she was a legendary figure known as Tokyo Rose.

They had been in different wings of the prison at Sugamo, he said, and had spoken only briefly—once when both had gone to a dentist, and on the occasion when they had both made test broadcasts for the army. She had never done him any favors while he was a prisoner, Provoo said. This was presumably because he was considered a turncoat by his comrades. He also said that "I never heard her make any statement which I would consider treasonable."

On January 3, 1949, Judge Michael J. Roche refused the defendant's new request for bail and set a trial date for May 16. The delay was mostly because the FBI was still collecting reports from former listeners to Japanese radio, and still questioning her nationality.

The Toguris' family doctor, Donald Raffington, told agents he had known the family since the 1930s. He had treated Iva's mother for a stroke in 1937 and he had given Iva smallpox, diphtheria, and typhoid immunizations in April 1941, prior to her journey to Tokyo. In October of that year, he had received an eight-page letter from her, describing conditions in Japan and—in connection with her passport application—asking for an affidavit saying he had been present at her birth. He had still been in medical school at the time, and the birth had been handled by a midwife, so he had been unable to fulfill her request.

Also put into the file was Iva and Felippe's residence registration in the Setagaya ward office of Tokyo on July 16, 1947. She had registered as an American and he as a Portuguese. Amusingly, she had given her birth date as 1918, making herself two years younger and only three years older than her spouse.

Charles Dubois, the chargé d'affaires of the Swiss Embassy in Tokyo, sent in her letter of April 21, 1947, in which she had asked for proof of her request to be evacuated during the war, which he appended. The Portuguese chargé d'affaires in Tokyo, Alberto Nogueira, confirmed that, so far as Lisbon was concerned, she was a dual American and Portuguese citizen.

There were other consular and State Department records, a copy of an imperial order for aliens to register—which she received shortly after Japan and the United States found themselves at war—and her *taiho-kyokasho,* or alien residence permit.

There were her passport applications, a certificate of her attendance at Japanese language school, documents proving her employment at the Danish legation, Domei, and NHK, her wedding certificate, her request to reenter the United States, correspondence between Iva and the U.S. consulate general in Yokohama, along with various documents proving that she was not Japanese.

The correspondence with Vice Consul Harry Pfeiffer, Jr., is lengthy and detailed but adds nothing to what we already know. She had stressed to him her obstinate refusal to give up her U.S. citizenship during the war, her health and survival problems, and the fact that she had "never at any time read news and commentaries over the air," adding that "this has been confirmed by the CIC and the FBI." She spoke of her close links with the POWs and almost apologizes for mentioning the help she gave them with food, tobacco, and medicine, and by supplying them with news of Allied victories.

She adds in one of her letters to Pfeiffer:

> What good these things did for the POWs I learned from the CIC after they had been furnished such facts by the same POWs who were kind enough to give the CIC this information before I myself even mentioned all the details of my activities outside of Radio Tokyo.
>
> The Prisoners of War as well as myself were, putting it plainly, forced to survive this war and this fact was expressed freely among us, who gained each other's confidence. . . .
>
> Had it been my intention to commit so-called treason against the United States, I certainly would have followed the normal procedure [and] applied for and received Japanese citizenship papers.

She related the disabilities under which she had lived because she had remained American.

Shigemi Mazawa, her NHK colleague, was reinterviewed and emphasized that Iva had "tried to make the best of it because of the unfortunate circumstances." A former army colonel said: "I never came across evidence of ill effects on the morale of the troops as a result of 'Orphan Annie's' broadcasts." Lieutenant Henschel, the photographer, again stressed the innocence of her programs. Former Ensign Henshaw, also reinterviewed, reminded the FBI that everyone at Bunka worked under threat of severe punishment or death, implying that this applied to the American civilians outside as well; he said once more that he had never met Toguri or heard "Zero Hour" and knew about it only from Ince and Cousens.

There seems a flash of irritation in his final comment: "I am in no position to state the purposes of Zero Hour, by whom it was designed or conducted, and in whose cause it was carried on." He was, he said, unwilling to testify for either the defense or the prosecution.

Clearly, Tillman was trying to "stiffen" the prosecution but was getting only occasional positive reaction. His main success: he had apparently neutered Reyes.

A New York newspaperman said his "Rose" had been broadcasting in January 1943, so could not be Iva. Kramer, of *Yank,* questioned again, said that it was "practically impossible to identify a recorded voice unless you have had a great deal of experience listening to this voice." He described the reluctance of NHK staff, when he had called there in August 1945, to identify anyone as a possible "Tokyo Rose;" but someone at the station had finally introduced him to Felippe, and Kramer had persuaded Iva to disregard her contract with Lee and Brundidge.

Kramer said she had told him that the first time she had heard the name Tokyo Rose had been when a copy of *Time* magazine had reached NHK; it referred to broadcasts starting in 1942. The Japanese press, which had seen the magazine, had taken pictures of all the female English-language announcers at NHK.

The investigation pushed on into May as prosecutors tried to strengthen a weak but already very expensive case. The trial was postponed again. Former marine Corporal Albert Powhatan Rickert, now a lieutenant, was questioned once more and confessed to having played the role of General Wainwright, leading a surrender party in the Philippines, in a Japanese propaganda movie, after he and the other POW "actors" had tried to refuse the task. What relevance this unrelated testimony had comes at the end: "I did not see any woman . . . connected with this film in any way whatsoever."

All of the main defense witnesses, and some of the minor ones, were visited again, and attempts made to turn them around. One of these was May (or Mae) Hagedorn, the radio ham who had first entered "Tokyo Rose" in her log in mid-1943. A young man who had been like an adopted son to her and to her husband, she said, had been reported missing in the Pacific that year, and she had listened in vain to Japanese programs for news of his capture, passing on the lists of prisoners she heard about to their families. Mrs. Hagedorn testified that the "Orphan Ann" broadcasts had been innocuous and nonpolitical.

Another ham, Ira Hayden of San Diego, also knew a "Rose" who sponsored POW messages. An FBIS monitor said firmly that Tokyo Rose was not on the "Zero Hour" program. More witnesses were now able to remember Tokyo Roses who gave battle information; after all, these, if they in fact existed, were the Tokyo Roses who had stimulated the witch hunt in the first place.

Katherine Morōka Reyes was discovered in Chicago, where she was working for the Veterans Administration. She had been in Japan from 1936, when she was thirteen years old, she said. She was a defense witness whom Collins had asked not to make a statement to anyone, and as a clerk in the NHK business office who rarely used a mike, she did not seem to be vulnerable to harassment; but she did respond to some questions.

"Miss Toguri introduced musical recordings," she is quoted as saying. "These were principally of popular music. . . . Her introductions were not of a propaganda nature. . . . I have no recollection of her broadcasting news [or] information concerning alleged conditions in the United States or other material which might tend to demoralize the U.S. troops."

Mrs. Reyes said she knew from conversations with her husband that Iva did not prepare her own scripts. She remembered Cousens coaching her.

Not everyone was negative, however, from Tillman's point of view. Master Sergeant Hall was reinterviewed, and he suddenly remembered broadcasts about troop movements in December 1943 and February 1944 (but, curiously, not in January), and he thought that the "Rose" in question referred to her listeners as "boneheads"—Cousens' and, therefore, Iva's word. This, of course, was what Tillman's vacuum-cleaner approach was all about: a half dozen like this, out of the cast of countless thousands who had served in the Pacific, and perhaps the lady could be snared.

The most recalcitrant American POW at Suragadai had been Edwin Kalbfleisch, and he was now reinterviewed twice more. Although neither Mazawa nor the intensely political Streeter (whom Tillman refers to today as a "typical barrack-room lawyer") had been helpful to the FBI, they too were subjected to more questioning.

Kalbfleisch, interviewed in St. Louis, Missouri, where he was now a captain and an army information officer, said he had never met Iva Toguri or spoken to her. She was not the woman once pointed out to him at NHK doing broadcasts to American troops, he confirmed. He produced his earlier statement for the army which, like Ince's, was meant to demonstrate that everything done by Americans at NHK was under duress, and at a time when the prisoners had been very weak from undernourishment. Like Iva, he had had beri-beri.

When the prisoners had complained about the poor food, Lieutenant Hamamoto had lined them up and raged at them. "Among other things," Kalbfleisch recalled, "he told us that we were only alive through the magnanimity of the Japanese army; that we really should all have been killed when we surrendered. . . . He then lined up [separately] those of us who had complained and . . . gave every man a substantial blow on the jaw. . . . I reeled under the blow. The last man in the line was almost knocked down. After finishing this, he told us that if he ever heard that one of us [had] complained about anything at all he would immediately . . . behead the person."

When Kalbfleisch had later refused to read a script about India, "Buddy" Uno had told him: "You read it or you'll go the way of George Williams." Kalbfleisch had changed the script as he read it, and Uno in retaliation had deprived him of food for a day.

Kalbfleisch again discussed the report which he had made for Major Tsuneishi, and which had enraged the Japanese. He recalled Hishikari, at the camp meeting afterward, saying that everybody had cooperated "with one exception! Number 2804, step forward!"

Kalbfleisch then recounted the dramatic episode that followed: "I was left alone in the middle of the room. I was ordered to pack my belongings, and then I was transported to Camp Ōmori to be placed in solitary confinement." He was transferred from there, still in "solitary," to Camp Shinagawa. During the second week in confinement at Shinagawa, he was intensely questioned by an interpreter, who told him: "I have been sent here to gather the necessary data for your court-martial and execution. This information will be forwarded to the court which is to try your case."

He was told that his offense was disobedience to a civilian employee of the army—Kazumaro Uno—and that "disobedience is punishable by death." He said he had been told that the trial was a formality and that he could expect to be put to death "in a few days." He repeated that he had discovered after the end of the war that he had been saved by the intervention of Tamotsu Murayama.

250

Also reinterviewed, Shigemi Mazawa said he had worked at NHK only to avoid the draft, which he felt would jeopardize his American citizenship. It seems, however, that Mazawa too had come under pressure to be more helpful to the prosecution, because he remembered Iva typing her own scripts unaided, and he was "unable to recall [that] Subject ever made any remarks indicating her preference for United States or Allied cause over that of Japan, or that she ever expressed sympathy for or befriended prisoners of war from Bunka Prison Camp." All his previous recollections of conversations on the way to the streetcar had suddenly been "wiped" from his memory.

This sort of statement could of course be trotted out to contradict any evidence to the contrary which he might give for the defense at the trial. When witnesses protest that they have been badgered by the FBI into saying something untrue, juries rarely believe them. Yet Mazawa still said in that final interrogation that he was himself "coerced into working at Radio Tokyo by forces of circumstances [*sic*] beyond my control."

Streeter, interviewed in Idaho Falls by Special Agent Joseph I. Hart of the Butte office, "refused to furnish a signed statement, and manifested considerable reluctance to furnish any details concerning this matter," the report said. Streeter intended to testify for the defense, when he would "again relate all he knows concerning this case," Hart added. Streeter noted that he had already been interrogated by the CIC and four times by the FBI, in Seattle, San Francisco, Phoenix, and Washington.

One gets some taste of the flavor of Streeter's admonitions to Hart from the latter's next paragraph:

"He further stated that, in his opinion, he has been libeled and slandered so many times by Army officials [*sic*] and the Department of Justice [that] he does not feel disposed at this time to extend the least cooperation to the Government in this or other matters."

Nevertheless, Hart had coaxed Streeter into retelling the story of his capture on Wake and transfer to Tokyo. He said he had first read about "Tokyo Rose" in *Stars and Stripes* sometime around September 1, 1945, when he was arrested and taken to Yokohama prison. There, three days later, he was visited by General Eichelberger, who asked him if he knew Iva Toguri. He quoted the general as saying: "She done us a hell of a lot of good when we needed it."

As a prisoner of war, Streeter said, he had been forced to make broadcasts, which had enabled him to meet Miss Toguri before encountering her again in Yokohama and Sugamo prisons.

Hart, in his periphrasis, goes on:

> It was further pointed out by Streeter that he had never heard Iva Toguri make any broadcasts which were in any way detrimental to the United States or the Allied cause. On the contrary, he stated that in personal conversations he had heard her make remarks severely criticizing the Japanese. He advised that Toguri's life was in constant jeopardy and that her broadcasts were made under duress. . . .
>
> Streeter advised that the Government should not have indicted Subject in this case, but . . . Captain Wallace E. Ince [instead]. . . . Streeter concluded by stating that this cause of action against Subject is a gross miscarriage of justice and that he is willing to testify in her behalf. He advised that he prefers not to be interviewed any further in this matter.

Although Streeter's own ambiguous position, caused by his anti-Roosevelt attitude and his willingness to broadcast it from Tokyo, made him a witness of dubious value to Iva, he did in fact testify at the trial—where he called for Tsuneishi's arrest as a war criminal.

For three days, June 15, 16, and 17, Kalbfleisch was called in to the St. Louis office of the FBI once more and questioned by Special Agent John S. Bush. The trial had now been put off until July 5. However, Kalbfleisch, who had been the bravest of the Americans at Suragadai—after Williams' supposed execution had terrified the others—was getting almost as irritable as Streeter. Part of his new statement reads: "I have no knowledge whatsoever of the identity or identities of any announcer or announcers on the Zero Hour, or of any other programs which were broadcast in the English language." In something of a contradiction, he recalled that he had taken part in "Hinomaru Hour" himself.

"I am aware that Charles Cousens, formerly Major, Australian Army, and Major Ted Ince, U.S. Army, were connected with other programs which were broadcast in English," he said. "However, I do not know the nature of these broadcasts, the titles of the particular programs, nor any circumstances regarding their presentation."

Kalbfleisch, who claimed that he had not expressed willingness to appear for the defense, said he had written and read scripts and taken part in plays under repeated threats of punishment, adding: "It was my constant endeavor to write these scripts in such a manner that information for use to our government might be incorporated."

In a second interrogation, Kalbfleisch described the Bataan death march; on the third day, he made a summary of the contents of the report to Tsuneishi which had landed him on "death row" for several weeks.

On June 21, an obviously intimidated young woman called Yoneko Matsunaga Kanzaki was interviewed in New York. She

253

had been one of the nisei announcers at NHK and had already been called for the defense; Collins had told her that she did not have to talk to the FBI.

Mrs. Kanzaki, long before her marriage, had met Iva through Chieko Ito at the Waseda Institute and had followed her to NHK; but the frightened girl now had no recollection of what Iva, Miyeko Furuya, and Mary Ishii—her friends—had done there; she said, however, that when a Japanese newspaper had referred to the "Rose of Tokyo," she had immediately identified Iva as being "Rose." She had been subpoenaed by both sides but said that she did not want to testify at all. Only twenty when the war ended, the then Yoneko Matsunaga had been still at finishing school during her few months of work at NHK, where her task was to introduce the commentator, Charles Yoshii. She had been forced to take a job by the authorities, she said, and had consequently packed food supplies for the Japanese army and painted torpedos for the navy. At NHK, she had only seen Iva "socially" about three times, but "I never heard her say anything against the United States," she concluded.

At the end of June, the last five witnesses were all former officers of the FBIS, interviewed in San Francisco, Reseda, and Portland, Oregon. All either gave Iva a clean bill of health, politically, or could not recognize her voice. This should have been significant to the investigators: the FBIS had a full collection of all "Zero Hour" broadcasts, and enough of them were sufficiently audible to know who, if anyone, had committed treason on the show.

There was a final reinterview with Rickert, who said the only women in Japan whom he could remember were "Ma" Topping, who had played "Mother Christmas" at the camp, and the mama-san—the wife of the prison caretaker who "gave us castor oil and medical assistance from her own meager supplies."

The Government was now ready to go to trial—or as ready as it would ever be.

15.

The Trial

THE TRIAL OPENED ON July 5, 1949, the day after Iva's thirty-third birthday. It was a reminder of how many years had been brutally removed from the young Californian's life by her parents' request that she visit Aunt Shizu in Tokyo.

The judicial proceedings won banner headlines from the start. The government attorneys had said the trial might last as long as two months. In the event, it stretched to nearly three. Reporters like figures, so the prosecution had trotted out the sum of half a million dollars as their budget and had noted that it was the most expensive federal trial in American history. In the end, the cost was to run to over $700,000, or about $7 million at 1989 values, far more than was spent on the trial of Bruno Hauptmann for the kidnapping of the Lindbergh baby, an even more horrendous miscarriage of justice. Only in the United States, perhaps, could so much wealth be wasted to satisfy someone like Walter Winchell, who had spent the war in Lindy's and Romanoff's, to convict a part-time disc jockey for reading patter written by Allied prisoners of war under threat of death.

Justice is for the rich, says a French proverb, and the profligacy of the prosecution underscored the burdensome poverty of the defense—although none of the papers and wire services mentioned that. Iva's three lawyers, Wayne Collins,

Theodore Tamba, and George Olshausen, were all working for nothing. All the expenses—court costs, deposition costs, sending Tamba and Nakamura to Tokyo, and bringing Cousens and Parkyns from Australia—were carried by Iva's father, who had to borrow money against his struggling shop.

Ten reporters covered the entire trial: five were from local papers, three from agencies, and two from local Japanese-language journals. All had noted the flimsiness of the grand jury indictment, and all predicted acquittal or the sort of modest sentence that the two years spent in durance vile, in Japan and California, would easily cover.

On the bench was Judge Michael Roche, himself a nisei of sorts—the American-born son of poor Irish immigrants. Roche was to display little patience with a defendant who seemed to him exotic, or with witnesses who explained that wartime Tokyo was a different and more frightening place, especially for Americans, than wartime San Francisco.

Had Roche but known it, however, the prosecution team of Frank J. Hennessey and Tom de Wolfe had made an appraisal of the case similar to that of the press. Hennessey had recommended in a memorandum to Attorney General Tom Clark that charges be dropped. In effect, he had agreed with the earlier memoranda by de Wolfe, who had advised against Mrs. d'Aquino's arrest before she left Japan. But Clark was afraid to back down, because of the razzmatazz in the papers and on Capitol Hill.

The result was a boilerplate bureaucratic decision: the prosecution would go ahead, and Hennessey would pass the buck to de Wolfe to lead the team in trying this apparently hopeless affair. De Wolfe appears to have understood that he would have to use courtroom theatrics and to try to bully witnesses to overcome the burden of a feeble case. The other prosecution lawyers were John Hogan and James Knapp. The FBI witness team was led by John Eldon (Joe) Dunn.

The public, like the GIs in post–victory Tokyo, was surprised at how poorly the defendant matched the image of the siren which the sobriquet "Tokyo Rose" suggested. She sat, effaced, in an old plaid two-piece suit which she had bought before the war, which she ironed each night in her cell and had cleaned at weekends. It had been her "Sunday best" when she had sailed for Yokohama eight years before.

On the trial's opening day, the newspapers described Iva Ikuko Toguri d'Aquino's features as sharp, drawn, or "unattractive." She and her family, seated nearby—her father; sister June; June's husband, Hiroshi Hori; Hiroshi's brother, and, eventually, Iva's own husband—kept a composed expression, conscious of the stares which are so common in the West but which are seen as the mark of primitive behavior among the Japanese.

There were few other Japanese-Americans in the audience; for her fellow nisei, Iva Toguri was an embarrassment, helping to revive the extreme racial prejudices against the community in California. The Japanese American Citizens League had refused to help raise funds for the defense, and Collins, once again punning on their acronym, had dismissed the group as "jackals."

The inadvisability of juries in emotional cases is self-evident, and need not be labored here, but the prosecution, with its weak case, naturally wanted one. The medieval institution of the jury system, introduced to ensure that accused persons should be tried by their peers and not by the peerage, had become obsolete with the creation of a world of jurists five or six centuries ago in the West, and juries have now been abolished in most countries; but American and some other cultures have clung to them because of their democratic symbolism and because they have become the last best hope of guilty defendants pleading innocence and for prosecutors and plaintiffs with frivolous cases. Surprisingly, jury selection took only two hours.

All the jurors chosen were white. The prosecution dismissed six blacks and two Chinese-Americans. Collins dismissed anyone who had lost a relative in the Pacific war, and questioned others about their attitude to Japanese-Americans, interracial marriage, and Walter Winchell. Both sides agreed on six men and six women. De Wolfe, a graduate of the University of Virginia, kept white witnesses in one room, Asian witnesses in another, and he rarely gave Asian witnesses courtesy titles.

Press coverage was considerable, aided by the fact that the Alger Hiss trial was still going on when the Toguri proceedings began. It was the treason season. The public seats were packed; when viewers went to lunch, others grabbed their places and waited patiently for the proceedings to start again.

De Wolfe outlined the government's case to the jury. He would, he said, show that Iva Toguri had betrayed the United States with malicious intent, and had urged American troops to lay down their arms, after she had voluntarily stayed in Japan after the outbreak of the Pacific war and voluntarily made radio broadcasts.

In his May 25, 1948, memo that sought to head off her arrest, de Wolfe had written: "The government's case must fall as a matter of law, because the testimony . . . will disclose that Subject did not adhere to the enemy or possess the requisite disloyal state of mind. There is no proof available that when Subject committed said acts she intended to betray the United States by means of said acts." That this was what de Wolfe, as a lawyer, truly believed explains how hard he realized it would be to carry out Tom Clark's orders and make a prosecution stick.

The only point on which de Wolfe was still sure was that the defendant was an American, born in the United States, and who had voted in 1940. Collins was to make a bid at having her declared Portuguese, to try to stop the proceedings right away; but de Wolfe was able to argue that she had never renounced her nationality—quite the contrary—and that she had not even been Portuguese by marriage for most of the time that she had worked at NHK.

Perhaps the hardest thing to understand is why there was so much effort to prove something that was not only unprovable but irrelevant—that Iva Toguri d'Aquino was "Tokyo Rose"—when the real issue was one that could legitimately be considered, namely whether Mrs. d'Aquino had committed treason. The FBI had concentrated on the "Tokyo Rose" issue, and now de Wolfe was stuck with it. Proving intentional treason was not enough, under these self-imposed guidelines; de Wolfe virtually had to prove that she was the legend.

Inevitably, therefore, de Wolfe's case began on a somewhat frivolous note. As his first witness, he called Corporal Richard J. Eisenhart, a stony-faced MP who had been a Yokohama prison guard, to testify that at his request in 1945 she had signed his one-yen note as "Iva Toguri—Tokyo Rose." Iva was later to testify that Eisenhart had come with two other guards, all wearing guns, and asked for the autograph, that she had refused it, and that Eisenhart had then said: "Well, you'll change your mind in two or three days." The guards had then left the lights on in her cell, night and day, for six days. She had signed.

De Wolfe also offered as exhibits the scripts she had similarly autographed for the armed forces film crews, at the time that she thought that they looked upon her as the "GI sweetheart."

A more inspiring witness came next. Colonel Tsuneishi stalked superbly to the witness stand, his eyes apparently almost closed, and came trimly to attention to take the Shinto oath. It was Friday, July 8. The preliminary alarums and excursions of the attorneys were over, and the trial was getting down to business. The day before, the incorrigible Streeter had gone to the press, insisting that Tsuneishi be arrested as a brutal war criminal. Streeter had said he could personally claim to have been beaten by the colonel; but it seems likely that Tsuneishi had been promised immunity if he came to the United States to help the prosecution.

Tsuneishi said "Zero Hour" was "psychological warfare." Besides Tokyo, he listed from memory other Japanese stations which employed English-speaking women broadcasters: Arai, Bandung, Bangkok, Hsinkiang, Manila, Nanking, Rangoon, Saigon, Seoul, Shanghai, Singapore, Soerabaja, and Taipei.

Under Collins' cross-examination, he admitted that

> at that time Japan was suffering rapid defeat and it was satisfactory to me to produce any program appealing to American soldiers. . . . I calculated that we would wait until Japanese troops went over to the offensive, and then the propaganda would be greatly increased. . . . It was unfortunate, but the opportunity did not present itself to do the real, true propaganda program that I wanted.

Tsuneishi also admitted that there were thirteen other female announcers in his English-language program at Tokyo radio, not counting the score or more at other Japanese stations in the Pacific. Since the prosecution said it was prosecuting "Tokyo Rose," and Tsuneishi said he had personally grown fourteen of the species in his NHK garden, this was clearly another point for the defense.

Streeter had wanted to help Iva; but by getting *The San Francisco Chronicle* to call for Tsuneishi's arrest on war crimes, he had done her a disservice, because the colonel, now made nervous, proved cautious and elusive when questioned about the brutalities at Suragadai. He denied having ever threatened Cousens or any of the other prisoners. He made Bunka sound like a holiday camp, implying that those who went there were happy to collaborate. The trucks which took the POWs to

NHK daily became, in his testimony, "Packard sedans." He had never allowed any guards to beat prisoners, he said. Such action would be against his "personality," he added stiffly. He also noted, no doubt truly, that he did not know everything that went on in the camp.

Tsuneishi had been grilled by Australian interrogators as to how much pressure he had put on Cousens. To protect his superiors, Generals Seizō Arisue and Yatsugi Nagai, who were candidates for war crimes trials, he had denied his public statement at NHK that he would behead Cousens if he did not cooperate, despite the large number of nisei witnesses, and similar broad hints at Suragadai; in so doing, he was also protecting himself.

David Seizō Hyuga, a government witness, had told the defense attorneys that he was prepared to testify that Tsuneishi had told him to tell Iva that if she backed out of "Zero Hour" the army would conscript her. During the trial, after Mitsushio and Oki had testified, he approached the defense and asked them to put certain questions to him that would enable him to show that the two NHK officials had lied. But the prosecution, which had seen Hyuga talking to the defense, never called him, and when Collins tried to call him as a defense witness he discovered that the government had hastily sent Hyuga home.

Conscripting Iva would have been illegal, of course, since she was American, and it might well have been a Tsuneishi bluff—but, as Ince had put it, in the circumstances of the time "no one was going to say no to a mad Jap." The Japanese had conscripted Korean girls into a concubine corps for the soldiery, and there was virtually nothing that they might not have done to this traitorous (that is, American) Japanese, Iva Toguri, if the generals had wanted to.

One senses, even today, when he is in his dotage, a certain honorability in Tsuneishi, a man of codes and discipline. When asked at the trial whether he had passed such a threatening message to Iva through Hyuga, Tsuneishi appears to have been reluctant to say no, which would presumably have been an outright lie; but he was also reluctant to say yes, which would have been a breach of his deal with the prosecution—a deal which protected his superiors, two generals, as well as himself. So, he took refuge in a truism: "This is a matter which happened a considerable time ago, and I don't recall all the details." Because all questions and answers went through an interpreter—and not a simultaneous one—it was to the beleaguered colonel's advantage to drag out his responses and thereby force another question, until the judge grew impatient and asked Collins to bring his cross-examination to an end.

Calling Clark Lee for the prosecution was clearly a risk. He was not as flaky as Brundidge appears to have been, but the role of both journalists had clearly been less than ethical. De Wolfe, in his memo advising against prosecution, had said: "The so-called confession . . . given by Subject to newspapermen Lee and Brundidge was given only after those gentlemen offered Subject $2,000 for exclusive rights to Subject's story."

A researcher notes at once the mocking use of the word *gentlemen* and the preference for the less prestigious word *newspapermen* over *correspondents*. De Wolfe concluded: "The methods by which these newspapermen obtained the so-called . . . 'confession' from Subject appear at least questionable and of doubtful propriety."

De Wolfe now led Lee through this document, which he had held at arm's length a year before. At one point, he made Lee address the sixth count in the indictment, and the stocky reporter replied: "She said that in the fall of '44, at the time that Japan claimed that they had sunk a number of American ships off Formosa, a major came to her from Imperial Headquarters and bluntly suggested that she broadcast as follows: 'Orphans of the Pacific, you really are orphans now. How are you going

to get home now that all your ships are sunk?' " This was the
apparent reference to Tsuneishi which had impressed the grand
jury, although there is no reason to disbelieve Tsuneishi when
he says that he never spoke directly to junior subordinates,
especially women.

Masaya Duus, in her own research of how the prosecution
was put together, observed that the notes taken by Lee at the
Imperial Hotel, which she obtained, said something far less:

> Sometimes fighting news, admit defeat in typical Ger-
> man fashion, well planned defeat [presumably Lee
> meant to write "well planned retreat"] like seritorious
> [sic] advance to the rear, exaggerate your lossed [sic],
> minimize ours. Formosa claimed sunk American fleet.
> They sent major from GHQ who wanted to play up
> great victory wiping our [sic] u.s. fleet. i get inside
> news and we add up ships claimed sunk and they
> wouldn't add. would be suicide say truth. after this
> time last year we just mouth piece of GHQ. they'd
> bluntly suggest "you fellows all without ships. what
> are you going to do about getting home?" "Orphans
> of the pacific. you really are orphans."

Cassette recorders were not in use at the time. Lee, who knew
no shorthand, was using a typewriter, which is slower than
writing. Lee's typos are understandable and, one would have
thought, correctable. But without shorthand or a recording
device, it is virtually impossible to conduct a serious interview
for more than a few minutes, unless one continually asks the
interviewee to slow down or repeat, which soon destroys spon-
taneity. What is principally obvious to any ethical journalist is
that she clearly never told Lee and Brundidge that she had said
the last two sentences herself. In what she was telling the Hearst
reporters, she was making fun of the staff officers when they

had tried to disguise defeats as tactical withdrawals, as she had done when she had remarked to Ted Ince: "Who do these people think they're kidding?" The journalistic defects here compete with the flawed attitude of the judiciary: the notion of using such garbled notes to present a case is a mockery of justice. If an irresponsible prosecutor wanted to use such raw jottings, to interpret them at will, what should a responsible reporter do? Destroy them and say truthfully that they no longer existed? One has to remember that these typed notes appeared in the prosecution file more to try to salvage Brundidge's reputation than for anything else. Iva recalls today that the major's suggestion to refer to the sinking of U.S. ships had been made to Oki, who had passed it on.

"I don't know if it was ever said at all [on the air]," she told the writer. "I never said it on my program. It might have been said on another program, or over the weekend and at the same time as my weekday program. I don't know."

Under cross-examination, Lee told Collins that he had been informed by intelligence sources that "Tokyo Rose" was Canadian, perhaps meaning June Suyama, and that he had first heard of "Rose" in 1942. Roche ruled that this was inadmissible hearsay evidence.

Suddenly, there was a moment of drama.

Collins said: "Now, Mr. Lee, isn't it a fact that you and Mr. Brundidge requested me to go to the St. Francis Hotel on October 25, 1948, because you wished to ascertain from me at that time whether or not I knew that Harry Brundidge had gone to Japan in 1948 and while in Japan [had] advised Yagi to come before the grand jury and testify falsely in this case?"

De Wolfe shouted: "You know that's nonsense!"

"We'll demonstrate it in this court!"

"No, you won't!" de Wolfe responded.

"I will."

"You're talking through your hat!" de Wolfe exclaimed.

Judge Roche sustained de Wolfe's objection and directed the jury to ignore the question; but another of the grave defects of juries is that they're human, and they rarely ignore any-thing—which in this case was to Iva Toguri's advantage, since it helped to establish the unreliability of both Lee and Brun-didge.

Outside the court, Brundidge was asked by reporters if he had tried to suborn Hiromu Yagi, the Tokyo travel agent, and he denied it; but de Wolfe changed his mind about calling Brundidge as a witness; it is unlikely, however, that the jury saw the importance of that change of plan.

Deprived of Brundidge, it would not be until July 27 that Collins would get the opportunity to produce this evidence again. With Tillman of the FBI on the stand, he asked if the G-man had not told Collins' fellow counsel Ted Tamba that Yagi had confessed that he had been bribed to lie to the grand jury.

De Wolfe objected. Collins said the court should know if there had been an obstruction of justice. Roche agreed, and all eyes turned to the burly Tillman.

"Yes," he said.

There was a ripple through the audience. Roche, however, then prevented Collins from developing the point further.

What had happened was this: in April 1948, Brundidge had called on Hiromu Yagi, who in turn had called on Toshikatsu Kodaira of the Associated Press bureau and asked him if he wanted a free trip to the United States. The next day, Yagi had taken Kodaira to the Dai-ichi, where Brundidge was staying. Brundidge had offered them whisky and asked them both to testify that they had jointly witnessed Iva making certain broad-casts. They would be the two witnesses needed to certain "overt acts." Kodaira had asked to think about it, and accepted Brun-didge's offer of a bottle of whisky, but he came back the next day and turned down the request. Brundidge gave him a three-piece suit from his wardrobe and asked him to consider again.

Kodaira had his wife cut the suit to fit him, but still refused, and sent Brundidge a hanging scroll in return. On the way home from the third visit, according to Duus, the two Japanese stopped at a coffee shop and Kodaira berated Yagi for trying to get him to commit perjury. Yagi, apparently shamed, said he wouldn't go to San Francisco, either; then as narrated in chapter 14, he had changed his mind and had told the grand jury how a "friend" had got him into NHK one day, during the war, and how he had seen Iva telling listeners that their wives back home were going out with war workers. Why Brundidge hadn't invented some more spectacular lie about Iva's broadcasts isn't clear.

In September 1948, after the grand jury hearing, Tillman had asked Yagi who his friend was. Yagi had said—as he'd told the grand jurors—that he had promised to keep his friend's name secret, but finally he revealed that it was Kodaira. Attorney Hogan had asked the CIC to persuade Kodaira to come to the grand jury hearing, but Kodaira had then told the CIC the whole story—that Yagi had perjured himself at the grand jury hearing and had tried to get Kodaira to commit perjury also.

Yagi had finally broken down and confessed to the FBI that he had lied, and that he had done it at the instigation of Harry Brundidge. He had then sworn out a statement to that effect. Questioned by assistant attorney general Alexander Campbell, Brundidge denied everything.

Campbell had sent Tillman back to Tokyo on December 28, 1948, and Tillman had reported that both Yagi and Kodaira had agreed that Brundidge had tried to bribe them to lie. Tillman, when questioned by Tamba at the time, had conceded that this was the case. Why de Wolfe ever considered calling Brundidge, after that, is not clear; indicting him would have made more sense, and given an aura of probity to the investigation of Iva Toguri. But in a memo, Campbell told Attorney General Tom Clark that arresting Brundidge for "subornation of perjury" would "completely destroy any chance of a conviction in her [Iva Toguri's] case." Campbell also thought that no Californian court would convict a white man on the testimony of two Japanese.

Collins, however, was unable to get much out of Kodaira's responses at the grand jury, because Judge Roche was constantly to sustain de Wolfe's objections: of Kodaira's 131 replies, 103 were to be stricken.

The Kodaira caper inevitably raises the first doubts about the two key witnesses in the trial, Mitsushio and Oki; but, as they admitted in 1976, and again to this writer ten years later, they had been threatened with treason trials if they did not cooperate and if they did not confirm each other's rehearsed testimony. Not surprisingly, both repeated everything which Mitsushio had said to the FBI, and to which Oki had signed his name also.

But Mitsushio's memory had been bad, and having Oki copy it did not make the perjured testimony any truer. Reyes was to testify that the meeting of the Front Line Section had taken place at the end of 1944, not in March—when the Front Line Section had not yet been formed. Mitsushio and Oki had had Cousens leaving "Zero Hour" in "December 1943," a month after Iva joined, whereas everyone else, including Cousens, remembered that his departure had not taken place until June 1944.

The terrible twins recalled the famous screening of *Gone With the Wind* as having taken place between March and June 1944, when Shinichi Oshidari had written a script which Iva had reportedly called "corny." But Oshidari, Reyes recalled, had not joined "Zero Hour" until later; he recalled the *Gone With the Wind* episode as having taken place around the time of his marriage—November 1944. Henshaw was to agree that there was no movie projection room in existence until September 17, 1944—it was in his diary. Reyes said that the Atlanta "hospital scene" from the film, which Mitsushio and Oki so clearly remembered, had in fact been unusable, because of a scratchy soundtrack, and both he and Iva testified that she and the others had never used the Oshidari script at all.

The press, reporting all this, concluded that it would be virtually impossible for the jury to find the defendant guilty of any of the first three "overt acts."

In lockstep, Mitsushio and Oki testified to Overt Act Four, the most serious of the counts, in which she is said to have referred to the United States as the "enemy." They set the night of this broadcast as December 1, 1944, saying it was the same night as Miyeko Furuya's farewell party. It will be recalled, however, that the NHK records show that Miss Furuya did not leave for another five months, staying on long enough to become another candidate for "Tokyo Rose." Curiously, Iva, scripted by Cousens, had in fact laughingly called her fans "enemies" about a year before, but the government never used this to produce another spurious count.

Mitsushio and Oki once more confirmed that Iva had written a script about ship sinkings and had broadcast it—that is, Overt Act Five, (the second most serious count) and Six. Iva would testify that she had overheard Oki telling Reyes about a naval battle and suggesting incorporating this into one of the "Zero Hour" scripts. Reyes said he remembered something about a naval battle, but it had not been put into Iva's script, which he had written himself, because it was not disc jockey material. She herself was sure that she had never read it. Reyes appears to have taken responsibility, in his court testimony, for Iva's script that night, and for any dubious content which it might have had, to make amends for his false testimony against her in San Francisco, before the trial.

Iva today recalls that she had used an old Cousens script that night, adding: "Very little was written outside of my rewriting old Cousens scripts. . . . Reyes was a very confused young man."

Iva had told Brundidge and Lee about how Imperial General Headquarters had wanted radio news of a naval battle to be bowdlerized, and Reyes, from his testimony, also seems to have remembered something along these lines; there was no evidence, except the suspiciously cloned statements of Mitsushio and Oki, that it had been in her script and that she had read it. The jury's crucial verdict was to depend entirely on how much credence it attached to these two men's testimony; the jury, of course, did not know that Oki had simply countersigned Mitsushio's responses, pretending to have said them himself, to satisfy the FBI. Oki, who turned out to be the most important witness of all, had told Tamba, however, in a deposition given to the defense, that the news of ship sinkings had been made in a news broadcast, not by Iva and not on "Zero Hour" at all.

The vague and flimsy Overt Act Seven was testified to by Oki and Ishii, while Act Eight was confirmed by Mitsushio and Oki, although the patter referred to in the court was never played to the jury.

The key prosecution duet, Oki and Mitsushio, did not impress the reporters, who inevitably reflected that they were American-born traitors who had served Japan. But no one could say in print that this had made them vulnerable to pressure by the prosecution, since this would be contempt of court, implying that the government was open to suspicion.

Collins could not be sure to what degree Reyes' testimony would throw out that of Mitsushio and Oki, but he could see that he should concentrate on the most serious counts, four and five, and on six, which was an echo of five. Both men had not only remembered the same things, in the same words, but they had remembered astonishing detail—especially considering that

271

they had the dates wrong! Iva today recalls Collins saying to Oki in court: "Are you a man or a parrot?"

Collins questioned them both about what else they could remember that had stamped one day so indelibly in their memory. The slower, fatter Mitsushio was harder to hook, but the slim and shifty-eyed Oki had clearly dismayed the jury; Collins, when he cast out his line, decided to play him the most. What had he had for breakfast that day? The question was too American, inapposite. Oki said probably rice, since that was all there usually was. He couldn't remember what he had had for dinner, what clothes he had worn, what records were played, what the other news items were, or what the weather had been. Soon, beads of perspiration broke out on Oki's brow and Collins drew the jury's attention to them by saying: "I'm sure it wasn't as hot that December as it is here now, eh?"

Finally, Collins offered, tartly: "So, your recollection of what transpired that day is reduced to the fact that you had rice for breakfast and that you read this one release from the Dai Hon Yei?"

"That is correct," said Oki.

With Mitsushio, Collins emphasized even more that the witness was a traitor. Referring to him by the name under which he had grown up in California, he said: "Mr. Nakamoto, would you please recite that pledge you made in grammar school?"

De Wolfe justifiably objected that this was irrelevant, but Roche overruled him, saying that it addressed the question of justice.

Flushing, Mitsushio began: "I pledge allegiance to the flag . . ." When he reached "one nation indivisible" he suddenly stopped, and Judge Roche completed the pledge: "with liberty and justice for all." It was one of Collins' rare uses of cheap theatrics.

Mitsushio agreed that, since he had arrived in San Francisco, he had met de Wolfe, the other prosecutors, and Fred
Tillman almost every day. In the *Chronicle,* Stanton Delaplane
wrote: "On the face of his letter-perfect, unchanging word
structure, it was a damaging admission."

Ishii, the young playboy, testified against his old friend Iva
on count seven, but the jury was not to believe him. The other
government witnesses were mostly even less effective, according to the press reports. One admitted that his English was so
poor that he could not understand what Iva said on her broadcasts anyway. As mentioned earlier, a witness waiting to be
called, David Seizō Hyuga, had told Collins and Tamba during
a recess that he could prove that Mitsushio and Oki had
committed perjury, and had been sent home by the government
for talking to the defense. The prosecution's nervousness, however inethical its outward manifestations, was understandable,
because Mitsushio and Oki had been their only witnesses of
value.

The defense did not know that the FBIS in Hawaii and in
Portland, Oregon, had recorded all "Zero Hour" broadcasts. A
great number of the recordings were poor, but if Iva Toguri had
made any broadcasts about troop movements or unfaithful
wives, or implying her support for Japan, as so many other
English-speaking Japanese female voices of the Pacific night
were said to have done, there would have been enough left to
pin such charges down. Instead, the only recordings played by
the prosecution to the trial were those that corresponded to six
of the innocuous, bantering, friendly scripts which she had let
Felippe hand over. Curiously, even those bits of her scripts
which might have been called demoralizing, such as "Wouldn't
you like a cold beer?" were not included. The selection was
even more innocuous than that. In retrospect, it seems regrettable that Collins did not have the clairvoyance to subpoena the

273

head of the FBIS and ask if there were any recordings of "Zero Hour."

Ostensibly, the GI witnesses did mostly more harm to the prosecution than good. Marshall Hout was maudlin about the sufferings of the soldiers and sailors in the islands. The press, however, reported that he got a good response from the jury for reading an irrelevant letter which he had sent to his wife from the Pacific theater, and which had made no mention of radio broadcasts. Questioned on these, Hout remembered "Zero Hour" as being broadcast between 6:00 and 7:00 P.M. in the Gilbert Islands, whereas that was the hour of transmission in Tokyo, three time zones away. Tillman or Dunn or de Wolfe had injected the wrong facts into his "memory." None of the words attributed by GI witnesses to Iva were on the tapes played, and even some prosecution witnesses denied ever having heard her say them.

From Monday, August 8, until Friday, August 12, the defendant was sick with a recurrence of dysentery. When she returned, Hennessey and de Wolfe concluded their case, and half a million words of testimony were soon to be on their way to the National Archives. Now, the defense would add its own portion, and the jury would have to decide whether Iva had in fact committed some offense.

Tamba outlined Iva's case: that she had broadcast under duress and with no treasonous intent. Then he called his first witness, who stood in marked contrast to the prosecution's prison screw who had left the lights on in a cell for six days in order to get an autograph.

Charles Hughes Cousens strode, tall and erect, to the witness stand. Masaya Duus quotes Katherine Pinkham, who covered the trial for the AP, as calling him "articulate and assured," in enormous contrast to the perspiring Mitsushio and the flushed Oki. But as memories of Singapore and Suragadai came back, he was also deeply moving.

Collins led him through testimony to show how much terror they had all lived under. His voice broke for a moment as he recounted seeing a Singaporean Chinese "coolie" beaten to death on the quayside by two Japanese guards for taking some food, and an Australian soldier thrashed into unconsciousness for taking onions. When Cousens—like Tsuneishi, every inch an officer, but more in a mold that Westerners could understand—began to tremble at the memory of the battered Aussie, Iva, for the first time at the trial, began to sob. All of the memories of the stress under which they had both lived in wartime Tokyo were coming back.

De Wolfe tried to do a "wipe" of Cousens' testimony by ceaseless objections, but Roche reluctantly agreed that his recollections went to the question of duress. Collins now phrased the questions differently, to associate them with the defendant, and Cousens said:

"We told her men were being starved, beaten and tortured, that the Japanese had discarded every semblance of civilized behavior, if you can apply that word to war, sir—that you did what you were told to do or you died."

He confirmed that he had told her that she was a "soldier" under his command, and that he intended to stay on the program until Japan was defeated—that she could rely on him. He had written her scripts, and when she had objected to him, when he was in hospital, that Reyes was not as capable as Cousens of keeping the scripts silly and frivolous, and did not have enough rank to resist Mitsushio, he had advised her to keep recycling his old ones. He explained how he had coached her to make words mean something different, according to the way in which they were spoken, and how to do a "wipe."

James Knapp, who cross-examined Cousens, was sarcastic with the long-suffering veteran and, to demonstrate that life as a POW was not all that bad, he produced Cousens' first restaurant bill from the Dai-ichi; but this showed that he had thin soup, curried rice with no meat, fish, or vegetables, and coffee. Spectators tittered.

Although Cousens impressed the reporters, and probably the jurors, much more than had the prosecution witnesses who had preceded him, no case usually hangs on one witness alone, however good, because jurors are not jurists, and there are twelve of them. The major's most signal service to his old "soldier" in trouble had been to assume his former Suragadai command again and to browbeat Ince and Reyes for their disloyalty in being so mealymouthed before the grand jury. He persuaded them to be defense witnesses, not prosecution witnesses, as the government had hoped they would be.

Both were clearly scared. The army had accepted Ince's arguments of attenuating circumstances and was protecting him against de Wolfe's shallow promise to the grand jury that he would be tried for treason; but he could never be sure if his life and career—he was up for promotion to lieutenant colonel— might not disappear, to satisfy somebody's political ambition. A generation later, the U.S. Navy was to pillory a captain for allowing his boat to be captured by North Korea, despite physical sufferings which surpassed those of Ince.

Reyes had altered his testimony radically in San Francisco, in obvious fear of losing his student visa and being separated from the rest of his family in Nashville, and he had always been the most impressionable of the three, largely because of his age. His brief marriage was in tatters, and Ince's had not survived the long separation. Both men were traumatized, but Cousens got to them anyway.

De Wolfe had noted, in his historic memo to Tom Clark, that both Ince and Reyes were "just as much or more culpable than Subject," and both clearly knew that. But Cousens, his health restored, now edging fifty, and once again the commanding personality—his Sandhurst confidence much different from the style of the two former privates who had become officers only because of war—seems to have convinced both of them to do no further lying to save their skin. Ince, however, did take one wise precaution: he was the only witness to bring a lawyer to court with him.

American officers tend to acquire more medals and other ribbons than almost any others, especially in time of war, and Ince walked into court with a tunic breast as colorful as a male bird in estrus. The jurors appeared to be impressed by that.

Collins led him through testimony similar to that given by Cousens. Ince had had his share of brutalities, which he had recounted to the army earlier. He also told again of how Iva had supplied the prisoners with food, tobacco, medicine, and the cheering truthful news from the Pacific front. He remembered how she had broken the law to enter Suragadai to tell him of the liberation of the Philippines, where his wife and children were.

De Wolfe, slow and drawling and insolently sarcastic in the Southern manner, and possessing no experience of war of his own, insisted that Ince had had an easy time in Suragadai; so when Collins reexamined him, he asked the tough up-from-the-ranks major if he had ever been beaten.

"Yes," said Ince. "By Lieutenant Hamamoto, Imperial Japanese Army."

It was to be the occasion for yet another searing scene. Ince covered his face and began to sob at the recollection, remembering the humiliation and the impotence and the pain, and raging inside. It was several minutes before he could resume testimony, and by then his flat, military tone had gone.

"I beg the court's pardon for breaking down," he said. "It's not so easy to speak so matter-of-factly of death and brutality."

The prosecution was noticing that Ince, being American,

was attracting the jury's sympathy even more than Cousens had done.

"You are not telling us what happened," Knapp said impatiently.

"I am telling what happened," Ince said, angered at the civilian's remark.

"Was your life threatened?" Collins asked gently.

"Yes." There was a pause. Collins waited for him to recount the beating during calisthenics in the wintry yard; and perhaps Collins wondered if the jury, in the comfort of San Francisco years later, would be able to imagine the degradation and quasi-starvation and constant fear of Suragadai, and whether they would consider being knocked to the icy ground with a bamboo stick brutal enough to justify the officer's tears.

Ince began to say: "Lieutenant Hamamoto, Major Tsuneishi, Kazumaro Uno, Hishikari, Ikeda—"

Collins, knowing that a jury trial is as much theater as fact, cut in while the drama was still there.

"No more questions," he said.

It was another of the rare occasions when Collins deliberately used "courtroom psychology."

The prosecution had by now learned that it was counterproductive to cast civilian aspersions on the bemedaled Ince, and had been unable to break through Cousens' steely if polite contempt for those who were persecuting Iva Toguri. They decided to concentrate on Reyes, the American juvenile who had been frightened into "hyping" his pretrial evidence in San Francisco and who had now challenged the FBI by going over to the defense. One would like to think that de Wolfe, Knapp, and Hogan found it a distasteful task—to bully a veteran of Corregidor and prison ships, and of a situation in Tokyo which, though better than that of Ince and Cousens, had been a frightening initiation into life at nineteen, for someone who could not speak a word of Japanese. He told of seeing two of his friends beaten to death at Sant Iago prison in Manila, and of being given the choice of going to Tokyo or losing his head.

Reyes said boldly that he was officially responsible for all of Iva's scripts after Cousens' heart attack, and that it was he who inserted headquarters items into some of them, but that none of these included news propaganda. She had broadcast under duress and had often expressed the wish to leave NHK. He remembered Felippe and Iva coming to dinner with him and Katherine in the Meguro district of Tokyo on December 19, 1944, his wife's birthday. The American air raids were intensifying. He was worried about Katherine and wanted to move away from Tokyo, but he had noted that this would mean giving up the radio work. Iva had said that there was nothing that she would like better, but that "she was afraid for fear of what the army would do to her."

It was de Wolfe, the University of Virginia graduate, who grilled Reyes, the "colored" witness. He called the former officer "Norman" when he wanted to be smooth and "Reyes" when he wanted to sound angry, but never Mr. Reyes. He raised the point that Reyes was the result of "miscegenation" and had himself contracted an interracial marriage with a Japanese.

Reyes' last FBI testimony in San Francisco was of course fuel for the prosecution. Facing threats, he had said that he "did not trust [Iva]," that he had "gained the impression that she was pro-Japanese." To protest that he had been threatened by the FBI would get him nowhere, even if what he said was not simply stricken from the record. Reyes, like Ince and Kalbfleisch, had learned the hard way what every child should be taught at school: do not answer questions from an FBI agent, even a friendly one, without an attorney present.

After the ordeal with the prosecutor was over, Collins was to ask Reyes the obvious question to rescue the young witness from the mess he had created in his last interrogation before the trial. "Did you trust her?"

"I would have trusted her with my life," said Reyes.

But de Wolfe had already skillfully sapped the young man's credibility. Reyes had testified that, like every other prisoner, he had been threatened with death.

De Wolfe had added: "Now, we have this statement—'I wish to state at this time that, during my employment at Radio Tokyo, I was never conscious of threats of death or torture if my radio activities stopped.' Then, that statement was false, wasn't it?"

"Yes, sir."

"How many other lies have you told here, Reyes?"

Collins was to say later that, at that point, he regretted having put Reyes on the stand at all. But in Collins' redirect examination, Reyes said: "The [FBI] agents told me [that] Ince and Collins and the defendant aren't going to worry about you—you are in a highly questionable position."

De Wolfe objected and was overruled; Judge Roche knew that refusing to accept evidence of suborning a witness would make a great case for appeal.

Reyes said that, after agreeing to testify for the defense, one of the agents had told him, on October 2, 1948: "If you want to go over to the other side, all right. I want you to know we [have] got a lot of stuff on you. I'll pass this on to my CIC friends in the Philippines and you won't like it a bit. . . ." Said Reyes: "I was extremely frightened. I could see them building up [overt acts] and I thought that if overt acts were all that was needed for a case of treason, I might be held as guilty as the defendant."

The FBI had made him alter his testimony, word for word, until it fit their format, he said, and the agents had invented dates. He had signed "to get rid of these people. I had had enough of it. I would sign anything to get out from under.

Secondly, I was afraid. I was afraid of these two men [Tillman and Dunn], the atmosphere under which the questioning was conducted and of my own status."

If you read the newspaper reports years later, Reyes seems to have saved both himself and his credibility by saying, in effect: I have taken back the lies you made me sign; now, do your worst. Duus, in her book, admires his belated courage. But how does a jury weigh a witness who changes his mind? If you admit to having lied once, is your repentance believed? Roche was to disqualify *all* of Reyes' testimony, along with the evidence given by Ken Murayama (Myrtle Lipton's script-writer), Suisei Matsui, who did similar work in Java, and even that of Captain Edwin Kalbfleisch, who testified from experience that you could get the death penalty for refusing to cooperate with the Japanese radio propaganda program.

The defense called fewer GI fans than the prosecution had called GI critics, but their memories were of broadcasts "Orphan Ann" had actually made. A Seabee and a marine lieutenant remembered how popular she had been. The Seabee said the radio tent in the Admiralties was filled each day, and that people stood in the rain to hear "your playmate, Ann." A warrant officer in the judge advocate's office in Juneau said that staff officers had been informed that the Orphan Ann broadcasts were good for morale in Alaska.

The prosecution was left with little to do but question the loyalty of such witnesses, an invidious and tasteless tack for civilian lawyers to take, but by then all the defense witnesses had been badgered by the FBI.

The last defense witness was Ruth Yoneko Kanzaki, who had also been the last witness questioned by the FBI, after she had agreed to testify for Iva. Readers will recall that, under FBI pressure, her answers hardly sounded like those of a defense witness. Now, she revealed that, while in finishing school, she had been obliged to be the disc jockey for the "German Hour"

281

at NHK—which was broadcast in English. The scripts had been written by a British traitor, Reginald Hollingsworth, and had been full of propaganda. She feared that she might be, if not the "Tokyo Rose" of legend—since she had broadcast only for the final months of the war—at least a better candidate than Iva Toguri. It was because of that fear, she explained, that she had said earlier what the FBI had wanted her to say.

Because the government had refused to pay for defense witnesses to travel, Jun Toguri had had to borrow to bring Cousens and Parkyns to America and to send Tamba and Nakamura to take depositions in Tokyo. Tamba had decided to use nineteen of these. Ruth Hayakawa, the beautiful announcer who had made "political" broadcasts but who had refused to be intimidated into testifying for the prosecution (thus perhaps showing that their threats to the others were bluff, as Iva believes today), and Lily Ghivenian, who had often typed "Zero Hour" scripts, both said in their depositions to Tamba that there was nothing political or damaging in anything the accused disc jockey had read into the mike.

A more interesting deposition came from Ken Murayama, a nisei who had worked for Domei during the war and who said he had been stationed in occupied Manila. There, he had written scripts for Myrtle Lipton, the Eurasian of legendary beauty who had once been Miss Manila, and whose disc jockey program had been, like Iva's perky one, designed to create homesickness among the GI listeners. Murayama said his scripts for Miss Lipton had inaugurated the style of referring to the possible unfaithfulness of wives and sweethearts back home, a factor which—being unlikely with Japanese wives—appears to have impressed the Japanese general staff by its psy-war quality. Murayama said Miss Lipton had a "low-pitched, husky" voice which corresponded to the voice remembered by many of the

GI fans, in contrast to what Cousens had called Iva's "comic" tones.

Yank reporters had interviewed Myrtle Lipton at the liberation and had been bowled over by her beauty. She had had a secondary school education, then had followed an American soldier to Shanghai, then returned home. She had taken the radio job even later than Iva—June 1944—winning an audition, she thought, more on her appearance than on her voice. Coincidentally, after the Suragadai prisoners had managed to persuade Tsuneishi to transfer the brutal "Buddy" Uno, he had ended up in Manila working with Murayama on Myrtle's show, "Melody Lane." Tamba had of course, taken a deposition from Uno, also.

"I thought her program was wonderful," the old Bunka brute enthused. "It carried a punch. It was sexy. She had everything in it. She had her heart and soul in the program. . . . She painted horrible pictures of jungles, of bombs . . . [contrasted with] the 'good old days' back home." Myrtle Lipton had played slow, belly-to-belly music. However, after the U.S. fleet had won the battle of Leyte Gulf in local waters, Lipton, perhaps weighing the future, had played the Notre Dame fight song on her program, which brought a rebuke all the way from the general staff in Tokyo. Myrtle's lover, the Japanese head of Manila radio, had been sent back to combat duty in Java, and Uno had taken his place, keeping up the pro-Japanese propaganda.

Miss Lipton seems to have been more sophisticated than most of the other English-speaking announcers in Japanese service. When Manila radio was liberated in June 1945, she told *Yank*: "I'm neither pro-Jap nor pro-Yank, I'm pro-Filipino." She conceded that she had worried about the propaganda aspects of the job but had been warned by Uno that she could "lose her head" if she quit the station; she had taken to drink. Uno confirmed to Tamba that she had frequently arrived at the station drunk, but could still do a credible disc jockey show, sometimes extemporizing rather than reading Uno's script. Duus, in her book, calls Myrtle Lipton "the strongest candidate for the title of 'Tokyo Rose' "—even though she had never been in Tokyo.

Later in 1945, the FBI sent Nicholas Alaga, a San Francisco attorney, to Manila with Tillman to investigate Filipino collaborators (the Philippines were still an American colony). Alaga described his only meeting with Myrtle Lipton:

"When I walked into the interrogation room, there was a lovely young woman sitting surrounded by a CIC colonel, a major and a lieutenant. The interrogation seemed to have gotten along pretty well, and everybody seemed to be having a good time. But when I walked in, the fun seemed to quiet down a bit. I felt as though I was intruding on something," Duus quotes Alaga as saying.

The lieutenant was asking the questions. Alaga said she was calm, "beautiful," and "quite aware of that herself." Eventually, Alaga was asked if he had any questions. He asked her about her broadcasts.

"All of a sudden she got tense and looked offended and started to stutter and cry," Alaga remembered in an interview by Duus. One of the CIC officers went for a glass of water. Alaga asked three more questions, and she began to cry again. The colonel said gruffly that she was tired, and "why don't we take this up some other time?" Alaga agreed, and later learned that Miss Lipton's file had been closed, with the mention that "FBI liaison agent Nicholas Alaga agreed further investigation not required."

Alaga told Duus he had complained to FBI Director J. Edgar Hoover, who had not bothered to reply. A rumor soon spread that the gorgeous Myrtle had died, then another that she had simply "died" diplomatically, married an American officer (the colonel? the major? the lieutenant? the colonel, surely) and gone to live in the United States. That certainly saved a lot of money in pursuing another tiny and insignificant case. And, after all, surely all the defense would have needed would have been an all-male jury? The present writer apologizes for having been unable to trace a photo of Myrtle Lipton in her prime.

Collins called Murayama as a witness to show that Myrtle, not Iva, had made the sort of broadcasts described in the government's complaint. Judge Roche disqualified Murayama's testimony.

It was September 7, the forty-sixth day of the trial, and it came as something of an anticlimax when Iva Ikuko Toguri d'Aquino took the stand in her own defense. Racked by dysentery, a skinny, thin-featured young woman with a gritty voice, she had nothing going for her except that de Wolfe had perhaps overplayed his hand. But she was far too American to see it thus.

She told Duus: "I thought about it this way: if I got on the witness stand and told only the truth, then the truth would win, I thought. My family was very worried . . . but I wasn't all that worried. I did not feel the least bit as though I had betrayed America. If I had felt that way . . . I would have run away to Lisbon. I had the chance to do so."

The Portuguese legate in Tokyo, impressed with the muscle which Washington was putting into persecuting her, had offered her a ticket "home" via Macao. She had found the proposal kind but absurd. To begin with, neither she nor Felippe could speak a word of Portuguese.

To say that Roche handled the case with prejudice would be an understatement. He sustained objections to her telling about her experiences with the *kempeitai,* which would have shown duress, or talking of her work with the prisoners to show her attitude, or even referring to her clean bill of health from the CIC.

The press noted that she was "pale" and "haggard" and that her voice did not resemble the one described by the prosecution, as she recounted her childhood, her trip to Japan, and her misfortunes there. At the start, her voice was strong; but by the third day, it began to falter as the long ordeal and the prospect of cross-examination began to get to her.

Collins, frustrated by Roche's animus against the defendant, got around to the question of duress in another way. Led by Collins, Iva was able to tell of how, in the late summer of 1944, Seizō Hyuga had told her that Major Tsuneishi wanted a verbal assurance from her that she would cooperate with the army; otherwise, she would be conscripted. Hyuga had told her that Kenkiichi Oki and Miyeko Furuya had already given such assurances. This was the key evidence of duress, which the prosecution had prevented Hyuga from giving in court by sending him home suddenly, and which Tsuneishi had said he could not remember.

Iva went on: "I told him to tell Major Tsuneishi that he could never get an oral agreement from me. I told him I would quit that day and suffer the consequences." Hyuga had advised her to give the agreement, but she had refused.

"I told him I was only on the Zero Hour for one purpose," she told the court. "I told him I was going to stick by the POWs until the house collapsed." Then she had the same reaction as Cousens and Ince when memories of terror returned; she collapsed into tears. She bit her lip to stop crying and, in a little voice, told how Hyuga had urged her to say something accommodating, but had finally made up something himself, in her place.

She told how she had refused to buy war bonds or contribute to the Japanese Red Cross. When old clothes were called for, she again refused to give but sold some to buy food for the prisoners. She had refused to take part in air drills, using the excuse of her poor knowledge of Japanese.

Collins then read her a number of questions concerning specific broadcasts mentioned by GI witnesses for the prosecution. She denied ever having made any of the broadcasts.

Then there were formal questions about giving "adherence" or "aid" to the enemies of the United States, to which she responded: "Never."

Like Collins' examination, de Wolfe's cross-examination was to last four days. It began with the largely irrelevant question of nationality. De Wolfe then established that the duress under which she worked was emotional and mental and derived from threats, not actual physical punishment. The rest of the first day of cross-examination was devoted by the prosecuting attorney to trying without much success to get Iva to admit that some of Clark Lee's interview notes were accurate.

De Wolfe's racist manner became more insolent and sarcastic on the second day. He began to snap at the defendant, insisting on "yes" and "no" answers. He succeeded in irritating Iva.

In his redirect examination, Collins established that Iva didn't know if she was American, Portuguese, or both, but she said she still wanted to be American.

The case went to the jury on September 19. There had been ninety-five witnesses, including the nineteen defense affidavits from Japan. Someone calculated that there had been nearly one million words of testimony—equivalent to just over twice the length of the Bible.

Hennessey summed up for the government, rejecting the arguments of duress and even denying that the prisoners had tried to sabotage the Japanese programs. He did concede that no actual "Tokyo Rose" existed and that the case depended on whether the treasonal statements alleged had been made by Iva Toguri as "Orphan Annie." This left some confusion as to why so much importance had been attached to Iva's autographs as "Tokyo Rose."

For two days, George Olshausen summed up for the defense, pointing out that, to find Mrs. d'Aquino guilty, the jurors must have no doubt about any of the government's three points: that she was an American, that she had given aid and comfort to the enemy, and that she had intended to betray the United States. He pointed out the contradictions in Mitsushio's testimony, and in Oki's, and said the government had called the confused GI witnesses only because, despite possessing recordings of "Zero Hour," it had no material evidence that she had ever made a treasonous broadcast. This was also the point being hammered by the press—that the prosecution had managed to produce only recordings which proved the defense point that her chitchat as a disc jockey was innocuous.

Olshausen pointed out that Lee's interview notes had not indicated that the broadcast about ship sinkings had ever been made; they merely implied that she or one of her colleagues had been asked to make it. Olshausen concluded, looking at Iva and thus encouraging the jurors to do the same: "This isn't really a treason trial at all. It's a story of intrigue of the kind you see in the movies but hardly ever in real life." Iva, he said, had been the heroine, working behind enemy lines.

"I think she served the United States very well," Olshausen said, "and all she got for her trouble was a year in jail. The least—and the most—we can do at this time is to acquit her."

De Wolfe followed, accusing Iva of being "smart" and "clever." In the sort of emotional and rhetorical style that would turn most Western juries off but which seems to remind Americans of familiar church sermons, he called her a "female Nipponese turncoat and a female Benedict Arnold." He rejected all of the evidence of her work for the POWs.

Judge Roche gave his instructions to the jury on September 26, first addressing the question of citizenship. He noted that dual citizenship was not admissible in the United States. (It is now tolerated, if still illegal, because so many Americans have taken Israeli nationality, but that was not an issue in 1949.) He told the jurors to distinguish between intent and motive. Even if her motive—to help the POWs—had been good, it would not excuse her from having made treasonous broadcasts if she had made them "intentionally." Sympathizing with the enemy was not treason; there had to be "overt acts," and two witnesses to each. However, he said that whether the acts succeeded in helping the enemy was not the issue, only whether they were "treasonable."

In both of these areas, Roche in effect made it easier for the prosecution to secure conviction on *something*. His definition of duress was even more damning to the defense. He said:

> In order to excuse a criminal act on the ground of coercion, compulsion or necessity, one must have acted under apprehension of immediate or impending death or serious and immediate bodily harm. Fear of injury to one's property or of remote bodily harm do [*sic*] not excuse an offense. That one committed a crime merely because he or she is ordered to do so by some superior authority in itself is no defense, for there is nothing in the mere relationship of the parties that justifies or excuses obedience to such commands. . . . It is not sufficient that the defendant thought she might be sent to a concentration or internment camp or that she might be deprived of her food ration card. Neither is it sufficient that such threats were made to other persons and that she knew of such threats, if you find, in fact, such threats were made to her knowledge.

The press related that this instruction to the jury left Iva slumped, unbelieving, in her chair. Roche, she seemed to feel, had saved the case that the prosecution had lost.

The jury retired. In the afternoon, John Mann, the fore-

man, asked for a copy of the judge's instructions and a transcript of the trial. He was given the instructions and told to ask
for transcripts of the testimony of specific witnesses.

Despite the controversial summation, reporters found that
most spectators thought that she would be acquitted—reflecting
more their own beliefs than the contest of legal theory which
the jury faced.

The next day, Mann asked for the testimony of Oki,
Mitsushio, and Clark Lee regarding the "loss of ships" broadcast. Again the jury went on deliberating after dinner. Just after
10:00 P.M., they returned to the courtroom and Mann said they
could not reach a verdict. They were, Mann said, a hung jury.
Roche told them the trial had been long and expensive and
refused to order a mistrial.

"Like all cases, [this one] must be disposed of some time,"
John Leggett recalls him saying. "There appears no reason to
believe that another trial would not be equally long and expensive [or would be] tried better or more exhaustively."

He told them to sleep on it and try again the following
day.

When the jury entered the court on the morrow, they
asked for some depositions, including Ruth Hayakawa's. When
they wished to continue into the evening, Roche wanted to send
them home but agreed to let them continue. He too was clearly
tired. On the fourth evening, just before six o'clock, the jury
asked Roche for a definition of something in his instructions:
"Overt acts of an apparently incriminating nature, when judged
in the light of related events, may turn out to be acts which
were not of aid and comfort to the enemy." What, Mann asked,
did "related events" mean?

Roche's response provided perhaps the clearest indication
of all that the judge—who could obviously see that some jurors
were seeking an attenuating circumstance for Iva—was anxious
that they bring in a conviction. He declined to fill their request,

but urged them, bizarrely, "not to single out any portion of my instructions for special attention." Then he counseled them to go to dinner, and to stop work for the day. The jury, however, insisted on continuing.

Half an hour later, the jury returned. Exhausted and under strain, they had reached a verdict. Meanwhile, the ten reporters had taken a poll among themselves: Frances Ogara, a nisei reporter on the *Examiner,* thought the judge had forced the jury to find the defendant guilty of something; her colleagues all thought the government's case too weak for anything but acquittal. Mann handed a paper to James Welch, the court clerk, who read it and handed it to Judge Roche.

Welch announced: "Guilty."

Spectators were stunned. Reporters—except for Ms. Ogara—were astonished. The Toguri family seemed frozen. Iva looked numb.

After nearly eighty hours, the jury verdict was not quite as outrageous as reporters and the public might have believed from Welch's one-word announcement. She had been found innocent on seven of the eight counts, including the most serious—Overt Act Four—and the next most damning, Act Five. In what was obviously (and was later disclosed as being) a compromise, the jury singled out Overt Act Six—that she had made a broadcast about "the loss of ships" herself but had not been responsible for the script (which Reyes had denied had even been in the "Orphan Annie" material.)

That it was a compromise by a tired jury that had spent twelve weeks away from jobs and family was perhaps clearest in what the finding meant: that the jurors believed that Mitsushio and Oki, under threats or inducements from the FBI, had lied about seven of the eight counts and had told the truth about only one. If there was a rationalization for the jury's belief that Mitsushio and Oki had acted out of character and told the truth on one point, while lying everywhere else, it was perhaps that the jurors actually misread Clark Lee's jumbled Imperial Hotel notes the way he himself had done.

Collins told reporters that it was "guilt without proof." Hennessey announced that Iva would lose her citizenship—apparently unaware that, by writing and signing the United Nations Charter, the United States had agreed not to create stateless citizens.

Mann said the jurors had agreed not to tell the press how they had arrived at their verdict. Informed that the reporters had been nine to one for acquittal, he said: "We were about the same, at the start." Pushed, he said: "If it had been possible, under the judge's instructions, we would have done it [found her innocent]."

Later accounts revealed that, for the first day, the jury had been ten to two, then eleven to one, then ten to two again, for acquittal. Then, the two holdouts began to emphasize the judge's narrow instructions. Even if she was logically innocent, they said, she was legally guilty because of a quirk in the law. By the end of the second day, fatigue began to work for the prosecution, and the jury was split six to six. By the end of the fourth day, Iva had only three defenders left, including Mann. The other nine, anxious to get home, began to berate the three for perhaps supporting a traitor. It was then that Mann asked for a definition of "related events" and was turned down by Roche.

The final compromise, confirmed by Mann much later, was that the three agreed to find her guilty of a relatively minor count, with the nine arguing that, since Iva had spent two years in prison in Japan and California already, the judge would not send her back to jail. Mann said later that, when he heard the sentence, he was unable to sleep for days.

On October 6, Roche gave Iva Toguri ten years and a $10,000 fine.

The unpaid defense team bravely said they would appeal,

still without fee. Local editorials supported them, and at least one editorial lashed out at the judge, risking contempt of court.

Interviewed twenty-seven years later by *The San Francisco Chronicle,* foreman Mann said: "I should have had a little more guts and stuck with my acquittal vote." He said all of the members of the jury were shocked by Roche's savage sentence, and that the "three hold-outs," including himself, "instantly regretted our compromise." The next year, after Mrs. d'Aquino was pardoned by Gerald Ford, Mann told Morley Safer of *60 Minutes* that he had had the conviction on his conscience ever since; he was then seventy-six.

The resourceful Masaya Duus found evidence that Roche had prejudged the case. Katherine Pinkham told her that Roche had revealed as much in loose-tongued moments.

Once, in a theater lobby, the agency reporter said, Roche expressed surprise to Pinkham that his son, a Pacific vet, thought the Tokyo Rose case was a waste of time and money about nothing. On another occasion, in his chambers, Roche had told Pinkham: "You know, I always thought there was something peculiar about the girl's going to Japan when she did. I always thought she might have been up to something."

One can only ask: What? A broadcasting career for a young woman with a hacksaw voice? It should be noted that, professionally, Pinkham had a duty to reveal what she knew, at the time, initially to the Department of Justice and then, if they covered up, in the press. A lot of people, not only Roche, appear to have been guilty of misconduct in this case.

However, the Ninth Circuit Court of Appeals refused to reverse the conviction or even to reduce the sentence. The Supreme Court threw the case out repeatedly. On one occasion, while the court was deliberating, Justice William O. Douglas agreed to a bail of $50,000—a large sum at the time, but one which the JACL could easily have raised if required, since no financial risk was involved. But the money was never raised, and she remained in prison while Collins fought her case.

Collins argued that his client had been denied legal counsel, had been unlawfully detained, and had been denied speedy trial; that there had been destruction of evidence, perjured testimony before a grand jury, denial of defense witnesses, misconduct by the prosecution, and prejudicial instructions by the judge.

Only the "unlawful detention" claim—given the martial law that prevailed in the occupied country—had some weaknesses; but viewed dispassionately, the other complaints seem hard to resist. Nevertheless, the Supreme Court did so, three times in as many years. In contrast, Provoo was released because he had mistakenly been tried in New York instead of Maryland. He had the clear advantage of being white.

On his way home by ship, Iva's husband, Felippe, had been forced at the Honolulu stopover to sign yet a further statement that he would never return to the United States.

The Californian press, for the most part, now rightly said that she had been a victim of the prevailing hysteria, the Tokyo Rose myth, and of the lingering animus toward persons of Japanese descent. But again the press was wrong in its prediction that she would have to serve only about three and a half years, of which she had served two already. In the event, she was to spend six years and two months in the Federal Reformatory for Women at Alderson, West Virginia, for a total of just over eight years' incarceration in all. This is approximately the average that someone sentenced to twenty years for multiple crimes or espionage might serve.

When she was released on January 28, 1956, at six o'clock in the morning, she found the press waiting. So, fortunately, were her father, her brother, Fred, and her sister Inez.

"I have no future," she told a reporter in response to a question. "I am going into darkness." To another, on a more hopeful note, she said: "All I ask is a fifty-fifty chance to get back on my feet."

The door of the car closed and she set off for Chicago, where the *Tribune* headed its story: "Tokyo Rose Quits Jail, Shows No Repentance." In the car, as Jun Toguri drove her home, she opened the papers which she had been handed as she left prison. They were a deportation notice. Ignoring the U.N. Charter, the notice was served under the McCarran-Walter Immigration and Nationality Act of 1952, which was passed after she had been sentenced.

Wayne Collins called this move "cruel and needless." Under the terms of the deportation order, she could not move more than fifty miles from Chicago until it was executed; but she was finally allowed to move to Collins' house in San Francisco and spent most of the next two years with the Collins family. Her future pardon lawyer, Wayne Merritt Collins, was eleven years old when she first met him at the breakfast table.

After two and a half years, the government admitted defeat on July 10, 1958, and withdrew the notice, but for a rather lame reason: there was no country to which to deport her. Still contrary to the U.N. Charter, however, she was declared a stateless person. With no passport, she could not even visit her husband, who had been forced to agree never to return to her in America. Indeed, if she went anywhere, in the improbable event that she could obtain a visa, she could probably not come back. As Catholics, she and Felippe wrestled with their consciences for over two decades longer before getting a divorce. It was a made-in-USA situation designed for Kafka.

The government continued to pursue her for the $10,000 fine—the equivalent, in 1949, of over $100,000 today. Two insurance policies on her life, taken out by her father at the Chicago Japanese Civic Association Credit Union, were seized and cashed in for $4,745. She insisted that her father should not go into debt again to settle the rest, which she resented seeing paid; but when he died in 1972, at the age of ninety, there were directions in his will that the balance be paid from his estate.

Iva Ikuko Toguri had by then overpaid her dues to the United States, but she still remained stateless.

Tamba died of a heart attack the year after her father, 1973. Collins died the same way a year later, on a flight from Hong Kong to San Francisco. A lonely and, she admitted, bitter woman, Aunt Iva (as her sales assistants in the family store now refer to her) seemed further than ever from recovering her citizenship, her attachment to which had brought her only decades of trouble. But now the "jackals" whom Collins had apostrophized were changing their colors. A new generation of Japanese-Americans, encouraged by their arrival on the American scene, notably in politics, felt ashamed of the sycophancy and disloyalty of their elders. Now there were Japanese-Americans in the state assemblies, even in Congress, and some were almost as angry as Iva had been.

16.

The Pardon

SOME BELATED EFFORT to redress the poor showing by Iva Toguri's own generation of Japanese-Americans had emerged in 1957, shortly after her release. A member of the Japanese American Citizens League, William Hosokawa, had suggested in the League newsletter that "Perhaps it is time to acknowledge that she does indeed exist, and [to] say firmly that we are interested in seeing that she gains justice."

However, Mrs. d'Aquino had been sentenced at the inception of the McCarthy era, and, for most Japanese-Americans, it was still too close to memory for comfort. The formidable courage of their forebears in the ancestral land was matched only by the formidable attachment to invisibility which the descendants had learned in America. It was true that some of this was due to the queer ambiguities of American political fads: the first voices raised in support of Iva Toguri had been branded as *supporters of General Tojo* and therefore *communists*. Where does one get one's intellectual footing in the University of Oz? But when Hosokawa spoke, there were already moves afoot in support of Alger Hiss—who was ultimately (much later) restored to the bar.

In 1977, Iva told Elaine Markoutsas of *The Chicago Tribune* that the first sign of public opinion swinging to her side had come after Bill Kurtis, a CBS reporter in Chicago, had done a short documentary on her. Her initial reaction to the pardon movement when it gathered momentum, she told Markoutsas, was that her father would have been proud of her again for not changing her nationality.

But she remained chary of getting directly involved. "I'd go to Mass from Chinatown to Evanston," she told the *Tribune* reporter. "I was afraid to join anything for fear someone might say 'We don't want you to be associated with us.' That [was a] hurt I wanted to avoid."

Apparently asked if she sometimes cried, Iva said: "We Japanese are stoic by nature. Hysteria doesn't accomplish much in the end." She quoted the jailhouse maxim: "I did the time. I didn't let time do me. I did a lot of reading. I still do."

She also said that it was the family business, with its fourteen-hour days, that had prevented her from "going to pot."

At the time, she and Felippe, now a copy editor, had still not divorced, out of deference to their faith; but they had ceased to correspond shortly after she came out of prison and he had found a companion to look after him.

Ted Tamba had first petitioned for executive clemency on June 7, 1954; President Eisenhower did not even reply. Fourteen years passed. On November 4, 1968, Wayne Collins made a similar plea to President Johnson. Nixon beat Humphrey in the election the following day, so neither Johnson nor the Democrats had anything to lose. In his letter to the president, Collins said:

> There was no trick or device to which the government's agents would not or did not resort in seeking an undeserved conviction. . . . They seized two of the Australian witnesses who had notified the Attorney General that Iva was guiltless of any act against the

interests of the United States and that they offered to testify on her behalf. Both were former prisoners of war held . . . in Tokyo. Two FBI agents seized them on their arrival from Australia and secreted them in a locked room at the Pan American Airways Terminal at the San Francisco Airport and subjected them to interrogation and attempted to browbeat them into refusing to testify for the defendant. They held those Australian ex-soldiers incommunicado until counsel for the defendant was informed by a Customs officer that the agents had taken the Australian passengers to that room. Thereupon, counsel for the defendant broke through the locked door, irrupted [*sic*] into the room and brought the *tête-à-tête* to an abrupt climax and halt. . . .

On March 1, 1949, the defendant filed a notice of motion for an order of court of the issuance of subpoenas to be served on 43 witnesses for the defendant in Japan for the taking of their depositions. To obtain such an order on behalf of the impoverished defendant at government expense, the defendant was required by court rule to file an affidavit specifying therein the name and address of such witnesses and a statement of the testimony expected to be elicited from them. Immediately following the service of such a notice and affidavit on counsel for the prosecution, the names and addresses and contents of the affidavit revealing the testimony expected to be elicited from each of the 43 witnesses was [*sic*] teletyped to the Justice Department and relayed to F.B.I. agents in Tokyo. Thereupon, F.B.I. agent Fred Tillman accompanied by one or two M.P.s called upon a majority of the witnesses and coerced them to sign statements containing a multitude of falsities.

Again, there was not even a response from the White House.

In both 1954 and 1968, Iva had questioned whether it was

wise to try at all, because as soon as the petitions were reported in the press she received hate mail and abusive phone calls.

By the mid-seventies, however, most of her old persecutors had gone to their reward. Clark Lee had died in 1953, having told friends that, had he known what would have happened, he would have written his story differently. Brundidge died in 1961. De Wolfe had died two years before. Judge Roche lived on until 1964, and Hennessey and Hogan until 1968. Of the defense team, only Olshausen survived; he was writing a book in Yugoslavia.

The moving force for a pardon was to be Dr. Clifford I. Uveyda, a now retired San Francisco pediatrician who headed the National Committee for Iva Toguri and who later became national president of JACL. In 1973, Uveyda learned that retired Lieutenant Colonel John Hada had just done a master's thesis at the University of San Francisco on the "indictment and trial of Iva Ikuko Toguri d'Aquino." Uveyda invited Hada to speak to the San Francisco Center for Japanese American Studies in September that year. This, however, raised only a minimum of consciousness, and it was not until the March 1975 dinner of the San Francisco JACL chapter that a move to grant a pardon to Iva Toguri became reality. David Ushio, the national executive director of JACL, told Uveyda shamefacedly, in answer to a question, that the League was doing nothing about the case.

Uveyda recounted later: "I said to John 'Let's form a committee to see what we can do. You be the chairman, because you know more about the case than anyone else.' "

The retired colonel said he was a busy man; so Uveyda, who was as busy as Hada, offered to be cochairman, and Hada agreed to help him start something. Although eventually Hada took a job in Tokyo and dropped out of active work, he and Uveyda set the wheels in motion. Iva Toguri was approached.

When the committee which Uveyda formed met her for the first time, its members were astonished that she had not simply "gone under" in the ordeal. Uveyda later quoted her as saying: "I shut everything out. I set up a mental block about everything that [had] happened to me." She said that she was afraid that the campaign for her rehabilitation might backfire, and warned that "I'm responsible for the livelihood of numerous employees and their families." She urged them to adopt a low-profile strategy.

As she later recalled for Linda Witt of *The San Francisco Chronicle*: "Who would believe? There is supposed to be justice in this world, but even when my story is told right, there are still those who think I started the war. You wouldn't believe the caliber of people who attack me. I have had salt poured in my wounds."

She still feared the media. Uveyda understood this; but how do you correct an injustice in America without some of the razzmatazz that brought about the injustice in the first place? America is Ringling Brothers, Barnum and Bailey, not discretion—not Japan. Uveyda and his friends assured Iva that the mood of the country had changed considerably since 1949. Iva admitted that her experiences had to some extent made her paranoid. Since her release, she had received so many hate letters from cranks that she had ceased opening any letters whose origin seemed uncertain—thereby, she had learned later, sometimes burning checks from sympathizers. She authorized the issuance of a booklet.

Iva Toguri: Victim of a Legend, which came out in May 1976, is remarkable for its spare, unemotional style. Uveyda says today that it was refined from a more emotional document put together by a group of authors. Perhaps this is just as well, for it is not only as dispassionate as a judicial summation is supposed to be (but wasn't in Iva's case), but also a pamphlet which covers all the angles thoroughly.

The booklet stressed how ill-prepared the all-American Iva had been for the ordeals that lay ahead when she landed at

Yokohama in 1941. It outlined her ill-fated efforts to get back to America by ship, the battle for survival as an enemy alien in Tokyo, and how she had been virtually forced to leave the Hattoris.

"From that time on, Iva Toguri was on her own," the pamphlet told a carefully selected audience. "Without an income and without a food ration card, she faced the possibility of starvation. She asked Japanese authorities to imprison her with other American nationals, but was refused." With her inadequate Japanese, job hunting had been difficult. On the pittance paid to her by Domei, she had fallen sick from malnutrition and beri-beri. Nursed back to health by Felippe, she had found a second typing job at Tokyo radio, which had led to her association with Cousens, Ince, and Reyes. As the pamphlet put it: "The POWs needed a trustworthy companion because they were covertly burlesquing the Japanese program intent."

For most Americans, it was the first time they were learning something of the true story of Iva Toguri. The pamphlet went on to describe how, in December 1943, she had been forced to leave Domei "because of constant arguments over her pro-American statements," and because Felippe had become involved in a "fistfight defending her position." The pamphlet said of her "Orphan Ann" disc jockey appellation that it was a "bitter-sweet, self-mocking name for the young woman who felt lonely and foresaken, but who had thought she was resisting the enemy while waiting to be rescued from her predicament."

The authors related the events of the American occupation and how Iva's interview with the armed and uniformed Hearst correspondents had led to her arrest. It went on: "During her twelve months imprisonment, she was never informed of the charges against her, was denied legal counsel, was denied speedy trial, and was prohibited from sending or receiving mail. She was held totally incommunicado for over two months

until a Christmas visit from her husband was allowed. Thereafter, the only person permitted to visit was her husband—for
only one twenty-minute session per month."

The pamphlet then dealt with her attempts to return home
after she was cleared of all charges:

> The State Department was caught in a bind; if she was
> permitted to return, there might be a public uproar;
> but there was no legal means to prevent her entry
> because she was a native-born citizen cleared by the
> Army and the FBI. Moreover, the Justice Department
> was in an embarrassing position of having lost or
> destroyed evidence which originally cleared her.
> Hence, the government issued a statement to the press
> that 'Tokyo Rose' had applied to return to the United
> States. The public outcry was immediate and impas-
> sioned.

Newspapers, including *The New York Times,* had appealed for
witnesses able to identify Iva with "Tokyo Rose"; but the
pamphlet conceded that it was presumably on the basis of
having foolishly signed Brundidge's notes that she was rearrested on August 26, 1948.

The pamphlet outlined the countless ways in which her
rights had been once more abused, the litany of defects in her
trial and judgment, the spiteful harassment afterward by the
immigration service, and so on.

The low-key campaign began to draw results, beginning
with an editorial in *The Denver Post.* In early 1975, the pamphlet
was circulated to all publications with a circulation of over two
hundred thousand. A dozen more sympathetic articles and
editorials appeared.

In January 1976, JACL's then 30,000 members offered Mrs.

d'Aquino a "belated apology" for its "helplessness to do anything . . . in hostile, postwar America."

Rex Gunn was to recall that she hesitated even to acknowledge the apology but finally did accept it from Dr. Uveyda in
San Francisco. She was still afraid that news of the apology
would draw hate mail from those she called "the crazies."

"If I were alone, I wouldn't care," she explained to Gunn.
"But what if someone throws a bomb in my shop? I have all
my family and the people who work for me to worry about."

On March 22, 1976, *The Chicago Tribune* published the first
of two articles by its Tokyo correspondent, Ronald Yates,
quoting Mitsushio and Oki as saying the FBI had threatened
them in order to force them to perjure themselves at the trial.
In his stories, Yates did not say which of the two men had made
which statement. But Oki, before his death, identified himself
to this writer as the one who had said: "We had no choice. U.S.
Occupation police came and told me I had no choice but to
testify against Iva, or else. Then, after I was flown to San
Francisco for the trial, along with the other government witnesses, we were told what to say and what not to say two hours
every morning for a month before the trial started."

Oki also identified himself as the man who told Yates: "She
got a raw deal. She was railroaded into jail."

Mitsushio says today that he was the former witness who
told Yates: "We were told that if we didn't cooperate, Uncle
Sam might arrange a trial for us too. All of us could see how
easy it was for a mammoth country like the United States to
crucify a Japanese-American—all we had to do was look at Iva."

Both men said in 1986 that, having fulfilled their Judas
mission in San Francisco, they were told that if they ever
revealed why they had testified in the way they had, they would
not receive visas for the United States.

Mitsushio said it was he who had told the *Tribune* reporter
a decade before: "I've heard Iva is very bitter about our testi-

mony. I understand her bitterness and I think she has a right to feel that way. I just wish I had the opportunity to talk with Iva and tell her why we had to do it."

Ruth Hayakawa, who had refused to testify against Iva but who had been a witness against Provoo, called Mitsushio's and Oki's statements cowardly evasions. By then, Hayakawa, along with Miyeko Furuya Oki and Katherine Morōka Reyes, had all recovered their U.S. nationality.

Yates quoted Teruo Ozasa, who had been "Zero Hour's" sound engineer and had been present for about half of Iva's broadcasts, as saying: "A lot of people who testified against Iva did it to save their own necks. I never heard Iva make any treasonous statement. All she did was play records and make small talk."

Ozasa, who was born in Utah and who testified by affidavit in her defense, told Yates: "She was very popular with American GIs. Just how popular was made evident after a broadcast in which Iva apologized for playing the same records over and over again." Ozasa recounted how a B-29, on Lieutenant General Eichelberger's orders, had dropped records by parachute for her, but how most of them had broken on impact.

He agreed that she enjoyed using the name "Orphan Ann" because it summed up her exile situation in Tokyo. Of the POWs, he said: "Those guys wrote the scripts, they read the censored news and gave the propaganda commentaries, yet they were all exonerated by their respective governments. Only Iva was made a scapegoat."

Yates' series, which had considerable impact, noted that "Other witnesses who testified during the sensational Tokyo Rose trial have told [me] of FBI harassment and threats if they didn't 'do what we were told.' Two of them told of government witnesses being bribed by American officials to give harmful testimony. They asked not to be identified 'for fear of harmful repercussions.' "

Yates went on: " 'Iva never made a treasonable broadcast in her life,' asserted one of her former superiors, whose testimony nevertheless helped nail down the prosecution's case twenty-seven years ago. 'She got a raw deal. She was railroaded into jail.' "

Yates also interviewed Tsuneishi, who pointed out that "more than 200 Japanese-Americans were employed by the Japanese government in propaganda roles and none [except Iva] was prosecuted."

Yates quoted Tsuneishi as saying: "I don't think she ever thought the American authorities would consider her a traitor. It was very surprising to me when she was arrested and put on trial; very surprising, indeed. I think she was a victim of the war and she was obviously made a scapegoat by the American government. I personally feel very sorry for what happened to her."

Tsuneishi insisted, however, that his conscience was clear and that he had told the truth at her trial, adding: "As for the other prosecution witnesses—well, I'll reserve my comment about their testimony."

And the old colonel added: "The thing that I remember about Miss Toguri was that she was very intelligent, well educated and rather quiet. She never talked too much about how she felt, about what she was doing. I sincerely hope that now she can receive the pardon she deserves and live a happy life."

On the day the first of Yates' pieces appeared, Iva was on the *CBS Evening News* and a new generation saw a little woman in her sixtieth year telling how she had been mishandled by "justice."

Three months later, she was on *60 Minutes*, being interviewed by Morley Safer, who summed up the case by saying: "It was not Iva on trial; it was Tokyo Rose."

A former CIC officer who interrogated her in Tokyo,

George Guysi, appeared on the same program to say: "The State Department abandoned her. . . . She wasn't asked if she wanted to [broadcast]. She was told to do it."

John Mann, the foreman of her jury and the last member to agree to finding her guilty on one count, told viewers: "There was a great deal of anti-Japanese prejudice existing throughout the country, especially here in California, and that had some effect on the jury, of that I'm quite certain. There have been very few months since the trial when I did not think of her and think that she was not guilty, and I am rather sorry that I did not stick to my guns."

Safer concluded the segment by saying: "This year a pardon application is being filed in her behalf. A presidential pardon, we remind you, does not bestow innocence on the pardoned person. Nor can it restore the fine nor the years spent in prison. But in Iva's case it would give back something of great value to her, her American citizenship."

All *60 Minutes* programs draw mail, and letters are read two Sundays later. None of the mail about "Tokyo Rose" was anything but favorable to Safer's defense of her.

Resolutions urging pardons were passed unopposed in the California state Assembly and the state Senate, and in the city governments of San Francisco, Honolulu, Los Angeles, and San Jose. The Los Angeles City Council rescinded its own resolution of December 1948 opposing her return to the United States. Then came the veterans' associations, including the Forty-first Infantry Division Association, whose members had fought all across the Pacific and had taken part in the occupation of Tokyo. After hanging back, nisei veterans' associations began to follow.

Wayne Merritt Collins, the son of Wayne Mortimer Collins, announced the filing of a petition for a presidential pardon on November 17, 1976, calling a press conference at the corner of Seventh and Mission streets in San Francisco, where the old courthouse had stood. Iva Toguri was there, and for once she sounded optimistic: "Times have changed. If the trial was held today there is no way I would be convicted," she said. The petition went to the White House backed by calls from many famous people.

Some of the press, however, was still mired in the myth which it had created, and referred to a possible pardon for the "notorious Tokyo Rose." In retaliation, Senator-elect Samuel I. Hayakawa titled his newspaper column: "The Woman Who Was Not Tokyo Rose." Hayakawa later discussed the petition with Ford.

FBI agents came calling on Iva again, but this time they were self-effacing. They were doing a routine report for the White House on her character and that of her character references. There were predictions that Ford would sign the pardon at Christmas, then on New Year's Day. But nothing happened, and Ford's term of office was due to end on January 19 with the inauguration of Jimmy Carter.

On January 17, CBS said in a news story that Ford would sign the pardon. The radio announcer cited a *Washington Post* article that would appear the following day. Was this a "balloon" by the White House to test public reaction? Wayne Horiuchi, the JACL representative in Washington, called Lawrence M. Traylor, the pardon attorney at Justice, who said he was not allowed to reveal what his recommendation to the president had been.

Then he added: "Don't worry."

Horiuchi, elated, called Uveyda, who decided not to call Iva in case he and Horiuchi had misinterpreted Traylor's remark. But she was anxious, sitting at home by the radio and not going to the store, where CBS already had cameras and lights installed.

Eventually, the next day, she went to work to ease her tension. CBS correspondent Bill Kurtis called Justice from the office above the store and got the break on the news from an attorney there. A full pardon—and this, from a man who had just barely lost an election because of another pardon condemned by seventy percent of the public in polls. He had probably given Iva's petition deep thought before deciding that it was the only decent course which he could take; the fact that there was no serious public opposition must have helped him to make up his mind.

The next day, the elaborately sealed pardon arrived. It said that President Ford "has this day granted unto Iva Ikuko Toguri d'Aquino a full and unconditional pardon," and that he had instructed Attorney General Edward H. Levi to "sign this grant of executive clemency." It was the first-ever pardon in a case of treason.

Some of the Toguri committee were not satisfied. What about restitution? Wayne Collins, Jr. cut discussion short that day by proposing that the committee be declared inactive. This was approved without dissent.

In Matsue, Japan, the writer Fuyoko Kamisaka told a lecture audience that Iva Toguri was going to revisit Japan, where there would be a "joyful reunion" with Felippe in Yokohama and with many old friends. Iva soon denied this. She did write to Ford thanking him for his "compassion and sense of fair play." The Chicago chapter of JACL held a press conference at which she said: "After all these years, it's hard for me to believe it's all over."

Shortly before the pardon, John Leggett had written: "I see Iva's story as a cautionary tale about naïveté—her own and the nation's—and about the vindictive side of patriotism." Leggett said the framers of the U.S. Constitution "were . . . aware that, since the reign of Caligula, treason law has been abused by those in power. That is why they defined it so strictly and, to forestall conviction by circumstantial evidence, added the Biblical requirement of two witnesses to the same overt act. Iva's experience may show how well-grounded was that concern."

17.

The Survivors

KENIICHI ISHII, WHOSE testimony against Iva Toguri on counts seven and eight was not believed by the jury, has now entered his sixties, but he remains tall, handsome, and elegant. The slim Eurasian joined Reuters after his release from the Japanese army and covered the war crimes trials.

He says that, despite his British mother, he was always—unlike his sister—a Japanese citizen and nothing else; so when Tillman came calling with his two armed soldiers, the G-man could not threaten him.

"The nisei were much more vulnerable," he says today.

But a hint of why he gave the evidence which the FBI wanted comes much later in the conversation—he had wanted to come to the United States and gain acceptance into an American university, which would mean getting another visa. He finally received his degree from the University of California at Berkeley.

He said he had studied political science because "it's such an easy subject," and achieved academic honors because "the English-language ability of the Americans was appalling. It was a whiz for me." His only problem: "I had been a spoiled brat, and for a while it was impossible for my father to send me money."

He came back to twelve years with AP, then freelanced and

got into business ventures. From 1977 to 1980, he anchored a television program on foreign affairs, and he still writes a column for *The International Herald Tribune*. He is a past president of the Foreign Correspondents' Club of Japan but lives in a lakeside home at the foot of Mount Fuji, driving into Tokyo in a Mercedes-Benz.

It is in the club that he receives the author, and it is clearly here that he feels most confident and protected, whatever happened in 1949 in San Francisco. He is still proud that Mrs. Cousens mistook his radio voice for her husband's.

Ishii leans back and says that he does not think that any of the nisei at Tokyo radio had any sense of "guilt or treason"; but he remembers Iva as being the most American of them all.

"She was vastly different from the Japanese woman of the time. She stood out." But he does not think her strongly pro-American views caused her to be disliked.

"Unpopular? I don't think so," he says. "Headstrong, yes. Not in tune with the Japanese."

Why had he testified against her?

"I testified that I saw her broadcast. I couldn't deny it. I mean, she wasn't coerced. Not really. It was Major Cousens who selected her. She had the voice he wanted. She could have stayed in the typing pool, but she wanted to help Cousens and the other prisoners."

His fingers begin to tap nervously when he is asked what his sister Mary did at the microphone.

"She only moved from the typing pool to announcing after I left, so I don't know what she did."

To the obvious next question, he says: "I think she'd be reluctant to talk."

After the war and the closure of the English service at NHK, Mary, as mentioned earlier, was reported to be serving meals in a U.S. enlisted men's canteen; but she went on to better things, marrying an American called Fisher who became a professor of Russian history at the University of Chicago, Ishii says. She had become a high school teacher and is now, he relates, living in retirement in Louisville, Kentucky.

Ishii seems more comfortable when the conversation switches to Cousens, Ince, and Reyes. We are speaking in early 1986, and he thinks Cousens died "ten or fifteen years ago." He thinks Ince is dead also.

"I find it very strange that Ince, Reyes, and many others were not put on trial," he says.

Reyes and Ishii were about the same age. Where is Reyes now?

"I don't know if Norman is still alive. I went to his wedding. I heard he divorced in Hawaii. He was a smooth character. His crime was far greater than hers. She at least did not commit treason. I suppose you could say that she was not entirely innocent—you could have got all of them for something. But pressure was brought to bear for a trial."

If there were *double entendres* in Cousens' and Ince's scripts, he says he did not notice them, reminding the questioner that he was nineteen years old at the time.

"Everything was well monitored, and it was Oki's and Mitsushio's job to see to that or else!"

You ask: "Not only Ince and Reyes, but weren't Mitsushio and Oki more guilty than any announcer?"

"Yes. Of course," he says.

You return to the "sabotage" theme. Didn't Mitsushio and Oki and others find her voice unsuitable for radio?

"Perhaps. But they knew nothing about radio."

He is reminded that Cousens compared her voice to a hacksaw, that Ince had said she sounded "like a crow." He professes surprise.

"She had a very sexy voice," he says. "It sounded very sexy over the air. At least, it did to me, at nineteen."

Ishii seems to feel he is being too negative. "She was a very nice person," he says. "I got into trouble after the trial when it came out that she and I had made a number of trips to the POW camp, smuggling in scarce food. At Christmas, we hid the goodies under our overcoats."

Where did the food come from, in his case?

"My father knew war was coming, although he thought it was crazy, so he began to hoard food, and those stocks lasted through most of the war."

He had been with "Zero Hour" from October 1943, a month before Iva's first broadcast, until November 1944. Iva didn't have to put propaganda into her scripts, he says, but he himself did commentaries, so he had no choice. "It was very amusing," he adds with discomfiture.

You ask about the coaching of witnesses. He says Tillman treated them like "performing seals" and that "he had the whip." After Oki, despite the coaching, had been unable to remember anything about the day of a certain broadcast which he was describing, new coaching was hastily introduced for remaining witnesses.

"It went like this: What do you remember? What else happened that day? Get it straight in your mind! Remember the air raid, the trouble getting to the radio station?" Ishii yawns, appalled at the way Americans put a trial together.

He insists that no one at the station ever identified Iva, during the war, as being the "Tokyo Rose" of the American press. He adds, however: "From the description, it certainly sounded to me like Iva. Hers was the only program that stood out. When someone else handled that program, it was dead. Iva had character. At one point, after the war, she was saying that she was Tokyo Rose."

What about the girls with better voices? Ruth Hayakawa? "Possibly." June Suyama? "Too sedate." Miyeko Furuya Oki? Your sister Mary? "I don't know." He hastens to say that he doesn't know if any of these women are alive, although this is obviously not true of his sister and is unlikely to be true of Miyeko Oki, since he and the Okis have remained in touch.

Did she make the "loss of ships" broadcast? "I don't think so. It would have been in the news section of 'Zero Hour.' " Couldn't it have come from another station or another program? "I don't know." If Mitsushio and Oki were under so much FBI pressure, might they not have lied? "I don't know."

He half closes his eyes and recollects: "I did the News from the Fighting Front. Then she came on. Then I did the American Home Front News. Then there was a Souza march. I wish there were some of those recordings left." He pauses to nod at a club member who has just come in, and sips tea.

"She was a good-hearted person," he says. "Look at all she did for the POWs. I think she got a raw deal." But he insists that he cannot feel guilty about testifying, although he was pilloried by both Duus and, he says, another Japanese writer.

Did the program become more propagandistic after Cousens had his heart attack in June 1944?

"I don't know. I wasn't there."

"You were there until November."

"Oh, yes. Well, Reyes was a much weaker personality than Cousens, who was twice his age. Reyes enjoyed his job, though. He'd been a disc jockey in Manila. But his presentations were pretty unoriginal, unlike Iva's. She was a little more than a disc jockey."

You ask again: Why did her colleagues choose her for the sacrifice?

"Some of the other announcers were jealous of her. It may have been jealousy. I was too young to understand."

Kenkiichi Oki was seventy-three when the author called at his Tokyo office in 1986, but he looked much younger. Handsome, trim features smiled from beneath a full head of silver hair. There was not an ounce of extra flesh on his body, which looked like that of a tennis player. It was impossible to guess that he would be dead a few months later, and the writer was startled when Iva Toguri herself gave him the news.

Oki was owner and boss of the Standard Advertising Agency, whose forerunner he had started with the money saved from his witness fees at Iva's trial. "We're a full-service agency—TV, everything. We're twenty-eight years old," he said proudly. On the wall, a map of the world showed where affiliates or corresponding agencies were situated. Oki could spot you into Chicago, right in front of Iva's eyes, or into Sydney, where Cousens' children could watch, even Lagos. Most of the Far East, with the notable exception of Korea, was covered. He seemed to be concentrating on the United States, and if you were put on hold, his telephone would play to you "Home on the Range."

His English was still perfect. On the phone, he had used it firmly to try to dissuade the author from coming, after a secretary had attempted to convince the caller that Oki was "not in." He was to be by far the most reluctant to speak. I had been warned that I would find him tough to get at.

"I decided not to give any more interviews on the Tokyo Rose case after 1976," he said, referring to the *Tribune* articles. He set a time limit of ten minutes, but he was too polite to respect it when his guest did not, and we talked for about half an hour.

The questioning started where that of Ishii left off. How unpopular was Iva Toguri at NHK because of her outspoken pro-American views?

He dodged the question. "She was just doing a job," he said.

He denied ever having said that Iva fitted the Tokyo Rose description. Could the legend have been Ruth Hayakawa? "Perhaps, but I wouldn't know, because I didn't work on Sundays."

He paused. "There were female disc jockeys all over the Pacific."

He was asked about his own supervisory role on "Zero Hour." "I was just a clerk, involved with several shortwave broadcasts. I had nothing to do with editorial content. I was the program manager."

What had his relations been with Iva, with Ishii, and with his boss, Mitsushio? "I don't remember." The staff didn't socialize much, he said. Iva wasn't "very well known—a part-timer, a freelance. She kept very much to herself."

Asked if he thought the prosecution of Iva was reasonable, he said unconvincingly: "I haven't given it a thought." Asked the same question a few moments later in slightly different words, he made the same response. A well-rehearsed performance.

He said he had testified in San Francisco because the Japanese government had ordered him to do so. Asked about his 1976 conversation with Yates of *The Chicago Tribune,* he said at first that he could not remember much of what he had said, only that it had resulted in trouble. But when the relevant interview was read to him, he identified which statements came from him and not from Mitsushio. At first, he did it reluctantly; then he changed gears and pointed out how frankly and honestly he had admitted to acting under threat.

He fiercely denied that his wife, Miyeko, took Iva's place, and insisted once more that she had left NHK in September 1944 to "prepare for the wedding." He added that "of course, she didn't work after the marriage." He said he did not know why she had remained on the payroll until May 1945.

Finally, he went a little further than he had done in 1976 and conceded that yes, Tillman and another FBI agent whose name he had forgotten (Dunn) had rehearsed him as to what to say on the witness stand—but he said again that the order to do anything the FBI wanted came from the Japanese government.

"I didn't think I could refuse the Japanese government."

He was told that one of his former colleagues had said that he and Mitsushio were like performing seals at Iva's trial, jumping to Tillman's command. He looked away, pretending not to have heard or understood what I had said. I realized I had gone beyond the bounds of polite behavior for a conversation in Japan.

"Would you like some more tea?" he asked.

George Hideo Mitsushio lives in an apartment in suburban Toyo-cho. He is a large, jolly man, eighty years old when the author calls. He is in a wheelchair.

He explains that he had a stroke eighteen years before. His right arm stays fixed against his chest, but his speech is unaffected. He volunteers that the stroke was caused by alcohol—"I was drinking too much."

He and his wife, about a generation younger, are sipping tea and watching Kabuki on television. He recalls how he came to Japan because there were no jobs for Japanese-American graduates in San Francisco. His parents remained behind; his father bought grapes from Japanese-American vineyards for Sun Maid Raisin.

By the time of Pearl Harbor, he was already thirty-six, the oldest of the NHK group—three years older than Tsuneishi.

He seems eager to talk. He is old and maimed, and people don't call anymore. He does not, like Oki, regret having spoken out to the *Tribune* ten years before.

"We were rehearsed—we gave prearranged answers," he confirms.

"She was only a part-timer," he says of Iva. "Her real job was typing. The rest of the group didn't know her very well, and she couldn't converse coherently in Japanese."

He is reminded that he testified that she understood everything Tsuneishi said. He gives the awkward giggle of one who is adipose and seated.

"I lied."

Like Oki, however, he claims he does not recall her extensive absences from the station throughout most of 1945, pointing out improbably that she was "not a regular member of the staff" and that her absences could have gone unnoticed.

Perhaps not surprisingly, he rejects the notion that the prisoners burlesqued the program without his awareness, or that Cousens and Iva were in cahoots. Mitsushio says his job was mainly administrative, but that he wrote the "American Home Front News" for Ince to read, until Ince mastered the format he wanted, and some humorous skits, with himself reading the role of the comic Frank Watanabe character.

Asked when he first heard about Iva Toguri's being associated with the "Tokyo Rose" legend, he says: "I think it came out of my own mouth."

Duus and many of her informants claimed that several of the witnesses went to San Francisco for the free trip. Mitsushio agrees only that many nisei welcomed the fact that it proved that they could go back to America. He himself has been back "three or four times" but he has never recovered his U.S. citizenship. He has a son in New York, he says proudly—an executive with Nippon Paint. Mitsushio Senior, until his stroke, worked for Kimberly-Clark's Kleenex division.

He says Iva was "the victim of a legend." Well, yes, the visitor thinks, but also a victim of the cowardice, now twice admitted, of Mitsushio-san and others. The old man smiles broadly, the smile of a Buddhist who knows that all is illusion, *maya*.

His pleasant wife pours some tea and Mitsushio urges the visitor to stay, or to come back soon.

Fred Tillman peers guardedly, as many must have looked at him in the past when they were about to face some awkward questions. The visitor starts by asking about the great variety of voices, including Filipina voices, whom GIs described as "Tokyo Rose." Tillman agrees that they had problems with the GI witnesses.

"J. Edgar Hoover said that report gave him a lot of trouble," Tillman explains. "It became what we called a four-bagger, because there were comments in all four spaces on the pages—both margins and on top and below."

He pauses, as though he feels he is giving too much. "But it's not true," he says, "that it was a loose job, as you're implying. It was set up as a trial brief instead of as an investigative report."

The visitor points out that some of the veterans could remember an "Orphan Ann" as far back as 1942. Tillman says most of the volunteer GI witnesses were rejected for that sort of reason.

"We would give them trick questions. Anyone who says 'yes' to everything is a no-good witness."

The atmosphere on the vineyard at Fowler, near Fresno, is pleasant, if charged with suspicion. But going too easy when questioning an FBI agent would be like talking to an Eskimo in Tagalog. Perhaps the flavor of some of the ensuing conversation comes over better in question-and-answer form.

Q. The Attorney General of the United States said that there was no case against Mrs. d'Aquino and he ordered her released in 1946. Why was the case revived so much later, in 1948?

A. She was originally arrested because she told people she was Tokyo Rose.

Q. Told those two journalists, immediately after the capture of Tokyo, right?

A. Yeah, journalists and others—soldiers. I told her later to shut up, that she could get herself into trouble.

Q. But the Attorney General threw out the case. Why was it revived so much later?

A. There was no real case against her before.

Q. Why was it revived?

A. Because of you people.

Q: The press? Walter Winchell?

A. Yeah. Winchell and others.

Q. I've talked to some of your witnesses, Mitsushio, Oki, Ishii.

A. Who was Ishii?

Q. The tall Eurasian.

A. Oh yes, handsome guy. Very bright, but not to be trusted. What's he doing now?

Q. He's partly retired. He was at one time the president of the Foreign Correspondents' Club.

A. How come?

Q. He was a reporter in the AP bureau in Tokyo for many years. Anyway, what I wanted to ask you is this: when you're preparing a case, you have to make sure that your witnesses don't make asses of themselves under questioning by the defense, especially witnesses who have been brought, at great expense, halfway 'round the world. You have to rehearse their testimony so that they get it right.

A. The FBI never directed witnesses. It's not legal. Only cheap lawyers do that. You know what I mean—they may charge heavy fees, but they're cheap.

Q. Some people say that everyone coaches witnesses.

A. Prosecuting attorneys don't coach witnesses. Our witnesses were not coached! It's the custom, I know, for defense attorneys to coach witnesses.

Q. They themselves say they were coached and co-erced, because they were vulnerable to treason charges.

Some of these witnesses made themselves vulnerable by wishing to return to America—the nisei, I mean. Many, perhaps under duress, had themselves inscribed on the family registry in Japan and had thus become Japanese subjects, during the war, but had never officially renounced their American citizenship. To change citizenship, you have to renounce—

A. Mitsushio had renounced his American citizenship before the war.*

Q. But the others had dual citizenship and could be charged with treason.

A. I think many of them took or kept their Japanese citizenship for family reasons, not from dual loyalty. But all those people who squawk about our putting the nisei into concentration camps forget that those people were Japanese citizens.

Q. The ones who had no choice. They couldn't take U.S. citizenship because of the Oriental Exclusion Act.

A. Don't misunderstand me. I've got Japanese neighbors here—the next vineyard. I've got lots of Japanese friends. In fact, some of my best friends are Japanese. You know, Tokyo Rose was not my most interesting case. Wanna ask me about Baby Face Nelson?

Q. The fact is that some of your witnesses were in an invidious position.

A. Well, they put themselves in that invidious position.

Q. Which you were aware of.

A. Sure.

Q. Was it Colonel Tsuneishi who identified her—Iva Toguri—as being "Tokyo Rose?"

---

*Mitsushio never renounced his American citizenship. He took Japanese nationality only in April 1943. The author did not know this, when talking to Tillman.

A. I don't remember. All this was more than thirty years ago.

Q. In the interrogations which you submitted with your report, he's the only Japanese who says that the person you call Tokyo Rose was Iva Toguri.

A. I don't remember.

Q. Is it your conviction that she was occasionally obliged to insert some news propaganda into her disc jockey patter—that Captain Ince and others wrote propaganda into her scripts?

A. I don't remember. It was Tsuneishi who called it propaganda. All countries call it propaganda. We call it information.

Q. And one of those propaganda items was about a lack of American shipping to get the GIs home.

A. I don't remember.

Q. Surely you remember that that was the basis for the only count on which the jury found Mrs. d'Aquino guilty?

A. Is that the latest Nikon? Have you seen the Leicas the Russians made? Beautiful! You just come back from Tokyo? What sort of uniforms do the Japanese police wear now? Do they still wear those small swords? No?

Q. Did you get the Tokyo bureau because of your wartime report on Japanese-Americans?

A. No. I was an administrative assistant to 'J. Edgar' and I had to make recommendations for appointments. I wanted to get back in the field, so I recommended myself for Tokyo.

Q. You said earlier that the case against Iva Toguri was revived because of Winchell and the press. Do you think that singling her out was unfair or tacky? I'm referring to the fact that no action was taken against her superiors,

Captain Ince and Lieutenant Reyes, even though they were both officers and wrote her scripts.

A. Ince wasn't charged because of the lapse of time.

Q. But there was the same lapse of time with Iva Toguri!

A. So—you prosecute one bank robber and not another! That homosexual Provoo was prosecuted. I'm sorry Rose did such a lot of time. She was a nice girl. But she brought it on herself. They used to execute people for things like that.

Q. So you think maybe eight years was a shade too much.

A. Maybe. But she brought a prosecution on herself. People have been hung [*sic*] for less. Read the trial. She was found guilty. She lost in the appeal court. She lost in the Supreme Court. In treason, you have to have two witnesses, not just one, for every overt act. She must have been guilty. The fact that we didn't prosecute Ince or Reyes doesn't make *her* less guilty. I've had a pimp say to me: "But I only took one girl across state lines; why don't you go after so-and-so, who took about twenty?" And I say, that doesn't make you less guilty.

Q. But not arresting the other pimp doesn't make him more innocent, it only means you settled for second best.

A. Well, that's true. But you can't say you're not speeding at sixty-five because someone else is doing seventy. There were forty-seven Americans in Tokyo during the war who committed treason.

Q. But you only went after one little typist, and Provoo, where the prosecution screwed up the case.

A. Sure.

Some of the rest of the conversation was related in chapter 1. Tillman insisted that all the Japanese witnesses were "forth-

right," that they felt that by being dual citizens they had a right
to help Japan, but that they also felt that Iva Toguri, being
purely American, had "disgraced the Japanese character" by
helping Japan. The reasoning sounded Jesuitical, rather than
Shinto. Tillman said he liked Japan, and threw in a few Japanese
words in a Hollywood accent.

Chainsmoking Dutch Masters, he walked out and posed
for pictures in front of his house and his elderly Cadillac. He
said the vineyard, which he called the "ranch," had been
inherited by his wife. He nodded toward a bedroom window.

"Got a sick girl in there," he said of her.

Of the "ranch," he said: "We gave it to the kid."

The "kid" went to Stanford, made Phi Beta Kappa, and
became a San Francisco stockbroker who sold out to Shearson
Lehman and retired with a "golden parachute," his octogenarian father explained.

Many months later, when the author had discovered the
cloned testimonies of Oki and Mitsushio, he called Tillman to
explain them.

"Maybe they assembled the files wrongly," he said.

Asked if he would like copies to refresh his memory, he
answered with something of a non sequitur: "No, I'd rather
just reply to specific questions." Then, perhaps sensing the next
question, he volunteered that "They weren't interviewed together, I remembered that."

Tillman advised the author to go after Ince, who he said
was more guilty than Iva and who had not been bothered. Ince,
he thought, had been "bought" by the Japanese when he
accepted accommodation at the Dai-ichi Hotel. Brought back
to the subject of Iva Toguri, he said that Morley Safer of 60
Minutes had tried to get him to talk but "I wouldn't play." He
was resentful of George Guysi, the former CIC officer, taking
Iva's side on the program.

Tillman then spoke flatteringly of two of this writer's

books, and said of Safer: "He didn't do a very good job—not as thorough as you're doing." It seemed odd to hear a G-man being sycophantic. I felt uncomfortable. For want of something else to add, I said: "By the way, the army says Ted Ince is dead."

Frederick Tillman obviously doesn't feel that putting Iva Toguri away was his shining moment as a Special Agent-in-charge in the Federal Bureau of Investigation; but then, he doesn't seem too worried, either. He did what he was told to do. G-men don't eat sushi.

The author was unable to trace Felippe d'Aquino, who has retired from his copy editor's job. Iva claims she doesn't know where he is. In a photograph accompanying his interview with Ronald Yates of *The Chicago Tribune* a decade ago, he looked wan and white-haired. He said of the woman to whom he was still married: "You know, I haven't seen her for almost thirty years." In what sounds like a reporter putting the words of his own question into a subject's response, police interrogation style, Felippe is quoted as saying: "An exchange of friendly words might not hurt, but you know it's been a long time and feelings change. The last time I heard from her was in 1956, I guess. We used to correspond about once a month while she was in prison—I wanted to keep up her morale. But then we stopped. It all seemed so hopeless."

Felippe said he feared harassment if he broke his promise to the INS and returned to the United States, but that he would return to testify if there were a new trial. Like others, he used the word "scapegoat" to describe his wife's role.

"All during the war, there was no doubt in anybody's mind that Iva was pro-American," Yates quoted him as saying. "When she was working at Domei, she used to get into terrific arguments with the Japanese Americans who had turned pro-Japanese. In fact, it was all of those arguments which forced Iva to leave Domei. She had made a lot of enemies." He recalled his own fistfight on her behalf.

Felippe went on:

> Iva felt a common bond with those prisoners, because like them she felt a prisoner in Japan. Cousens told Iva not to worry about anything, that he had full control of the whole show and that all she had to do was cooperate. He told her the show was designed to spoof the Japanese, to make asses of them. It was he who coined the term "honorable boneheads" which Iva used so often on the air when referring to Americans.
>
> Nevertheless, I used to warn her about making those broadcasts—I told her somebody might think they were treasonous. But she told me she liked working with the American POWs and that she felt that what she was doing was all right. . . . Being in contact with those American prisoners made her feel at home. . . . The trouble was that a lot of Japanese Americans who worked with Iva at Tokyo radio perjured themselves at her trial to save their own skins. They told lies because they were either bribed or threatened by the American authorities.

Felippe still seemed to fit the description that the wartime Tokyo police gave to the dissident pacifist of being "mild and taciturn." One is reminded that, although the meek may be blessed, they are habitually maltreated. To inherit the earth, they have to wait until they leave it. Interviewed at the time by *The San Francisco Chronicle* about her husband's remarks, Iva said: "Poor guy—he went through hell, too. What happened to me was unfair to him—more even than to me, in a way."

She agreed that he had warned her of the possible consequences of her broadcasts but that she felt they were permissible because they were made at the request of the POWs. Then, she returned to Felippe: "It wasn't his fault. He shouldn't have suffered, too."

Asked if she would like to see him again, she said: "Oh, yes." She said she knew he now lived with a companion, and added: "He deserved to go back to a normal life." After a moment, she went on: "Losing the baby and Phil—it was unbearable. That's one of the reasons I have avoided thinking about it, all these years. I gain nothing by thinking about it. You can't change wrong. You can't bring back thirty years.

"I didn't abandon this country. Wayne Collins used to say it abandoned me, but the nicest thing is still being in a country where you can control your own mind. . . . This has been a reward. But it has been a solitary life."

Today, she sits in the sparse office over her store beside etchings of her father and her brother, Fred, who died in 1960. Both men are remarkable for the gentleness of their features. She seems afraid now to speak well of anybody. Just as she says of the painstaking researcher Masaya Duus "I only met her once or twice," so she says of the artist who did the etchings: "Someone wanted to do them, so I said okay."

She is protective of Felippe's privacy and claims she does not know his address. They are now divorced: "I can't remember when, I'd have to look at the papers." A visitor senses that the odd remark reflects pain, not callousness. Has he remarried? "I haven't the faintest idea." Again, one senses discomfort in what sounds like offhandedness.

This odd vagueness goes for all the painful memories. Cousens died "sometime in the sixties." She doesn't know what happened to Ince. Of Reyes, she says: "I heard he was in Hawaii." She doesn't know which island.

She remains ill at ease with all reporters, even those "on her side." She tape-records the discussion, but it is one of those small Japanese machines which have to be held close to the speaker, and she only records her answers, not the questions. When she goes "off the record" at one point, she switches the recorder off—on herself.

She insists that her karma has not been entirely negative. She has kept up her Japanese, which is now "quite good," and much better than during the war years, when Mitsushio has said that she was "incoherent" in the tongue.

A decade ago, she told Duus that her time in the reformatory in West Virginia "went more quickly than I expected." Today, she says that "my time in prison was not wasted, except financially. I wasted a lot of time when I should have been working. Financially, it was devastating. But it wasn't only a negative experience."

But it was not, the writer suggests, an experience she would have chosen.

"No, I wouldn't have chosen it," she says, "but I learned things from it."

At the door, she seems startled when the visitor, long used to Asia and Europe, gives a slight inclination of the head. She is much too American to return the gesture. She swings around and bustles off to complete another fourteen-hour day in the store. One can hear that gritty voice shouting something to a salesgirl—in the Gracie Allen tones that decreed her karma. Then, she walks up to the office, sits down, and looks at the snapshot on her desk: the late Charles Hughes Cousens, smiling confidently at the sunlight in his Sydney garden.

A few weeks later, Dr. Clifford Uyeda, the person who seems to enjoy her confidence the most, asks the author if he has noticed the photo and what he makes of it.

The author makes the obvious guess: "She's still in love with him."

"Isn't that something?" says Dr. Uyeda.

Postface

LUDOVIC KENNEDY HAS SAID that he thinks most miscarriages of justice are brought about "honestly" by people who really believe the innocent victim is guilty. He was speaking of the three different cases of persons hanged for murder in Britain and later, thanks to his books, given full (alas, posthumous) pardons by the queen, and of the case of Bruno Hauptmann, the man electrocuted for the kidnapping and murder of the Lindbergh baby, whose innocence Kennedy proved in a book which appeared in 1985.

My own, more limited experience has been different. I do not believe that those who brought about the execution of Mata Hari believed that she was guilty—only expendable—and I am not convinced that the persecution of Iva Toguri was conceived in the spirit of justice. The Justice Department and the Counter Intelligence Corps had already acquitted her in 1946.

In any event, what matters is to set the record straight. President Ford did the decent thing and pardoned her, thus restoring the citizenship which the United States promised, under the U.N. Charter, that it would never remove from anyone who had no other nationality.

Now the time has come to go further, and to acknowledge her innocence. The financial and emotional cost of a retrial would be unthinkable, even if so many witnesses were not dead.

The author suggests a joint resolution of Congress, offering Mrs. Iva Ikuko Toguri d'Aquino a national apology. There has never been one before. But then, until President Ford did it, there had never before been a pardon—forgiveness for guilt—in a treason case.

R.W.H.
Tokyo and Washington, 1986–87

Sources and Acknowledgments

FOR READER COMFORT, I have avoided footnotes. Researchers will have noted that the principal primary source is the voluminous FBI file on the "Tokyo Rose" case, which embodies some of the CIC materials. These documents were obtained under the Freedom of Information Act, and are identified in the book. The trial and CIC records are in the National Archives. All oral material obtained from Mrs. d'Aquino herself, and from the other survivors of this historical episode, including Special Agent Fred Tillman, is clearly identified in the text.

By far the most valuable secondary source was Masaya Umezawa Duus' excellent book (*Tokyo Rose: Orphan of the Pacific*; Kodansha, Tokyo, 1979) which is particularly valuable for the interviews with the former NHK "radio girls". The quotations from the Yates dispatches and the Charles Leggett article are identified in the text.

As I have noted, Iva Ikuko Toguri d'Aquino is wary of being famous again. Like Masaya Duus, I had only a few interviews with her. She was always courteous and never discouraging, but she volunteered little. Her caution is easily understandable. I apologize for having felt obliged to refer to this senior citizen quite often in the narrative as "Iva", and even very occasionally as "Toguri" without a courtesy title.

I am grateful to all who consented to being interviewed

and who helped me with my research, particularly to Dr. Clifford I. Uyeda for his patience and assistance on many occasions and his constant encouragement.

R.W.H.

Appendix 1

The cloned testimonies of George Hideo Mitsushio–Nakamoto and Kenkiichi Oki

THESE SWORN STATEMENTS by George Mitsushio and Kenkiichi Oki, taken by SA Fred Tillman and SA "Joe" Dunn on September 24, 1948, met the constitutional requirement for "two" witnesses to an overt act of treason. Readers will see that the testimonies, taken from the FBI files in Washington, bearing the FBI's own underscorings and shown here on facing pages, are identical.

On line 3 of the first complete paragraph of p. 29 in Oki, the witness says "handed him" instead of "handed Mitsushio"—presumably an FBI slip. In the same place, in Mitsushio, the word "him" occupies the space of four letters, implying that they were interviewed together and that the original transcript said "them" before being erased and changed.

APPENDIX 1

MITSUSHIO was interviewed with reference to specific
acts or broadcasts arising from TOGURI's employment at Radio Tokyo in
Tokyo, Japan.

He stated that between the dates of March 1, 1944, and
May 1, 1944, an independent section was organized in the Overseas Bureau
of the Broadcasting Corporation of Japan, which section was known as the
Front Line Section. The Front Line Section was that division of the Over-

seas Bureau of the Broadcasting Corporation of Japan which was charged
with broadcasting or conveying information by radio to American and Allied
troops in the South Pacific battle area. MITSUSHIO stated that he became
Chief of the Front Line Section and that KENKICHI OKI became the Production
Supervisor at the time the section was organized. He stated that the sole
responsibility of this section was the production and broadcasting of
programs known as the "Zero Hour." MITSUSHIO stated that he was given
specific instructions as to the aims and purposes of the "Zero Hour"
broadcasts by his immediate superior, SHINNOJO SAWADA.

MITSUSHIO recalls that at the time the Front Line
Section was organized, they called together a meeting of the personnel
of the Front Line Section for a conference concerning the radio broadcasts. He recalls that TOGURI was among those present. MITSUSHIO recalls
that he specifically restated the aims and purposes of the broadcasts,
saying in substance that the program must be created to attract a large
audience of American soldiers in the South Sea Islands and that after the
large audience was attracted by the program, they were to broadcast
propaganda aimed at creating nostalgia in the minds of the American soldiers
and war weariness among the soldiers in order to discourage them in their
battles against the Japanese soldiers and in order to lower the morale of
the American troops. MITSUSHIO recalls that he gave these instructions
in the English language and that TOGURI made known that she understood
the instructions, saying in substance that she did understand them. He
recalls that at the same meeting he asked for suggestions from the assembled
staff as to how the aims and purposes of the broadcasts could best be
achieved.

MITSUSHIO recalls that one NORMAN REYES, a member of the
staff, made certain suggestions which he prepared previously and suggested
that his, REYES', part of the program would have to do with hot jazz music
or "juke box music." MITSUSHIO recalls that REYES suggested that TOGURI
handle the so-called sweet music on her part of the program. He recalls
that in answer to these suggestions, TOGURI stated in substance that it
was agreeable with her and that she would organize and compose her program
of the type of music that REYES had indicated. MITSUSHIO recalls that
TOGURI assented specifically as to her understanding of the instructions
given by him and the suggestion made by REYES as to the substance of her
program.

SHIGETSUGU TSUNEISHI, then a Major in the Imperial
Japanese Army and a member of the Army General Staff, gave a dinner for
the staff of the "Zero Hour" program on Radio Tokyo in March, 1944 at the
Tokyo Kaikan Restaurant. At this restaurant there were present GEORGE
MITSUSHIO, KENKICHI OKI, SHINICHI OSHIDARI, HISASHI MORIYAMA and IVA IKUKO
TOGURI. At this luncheon Major TSUNEISHI complimented the staff for the

OKI was interviewed with reference to specific acts or broadcasts arising from TOGURI's employment at Radio Tokyo in Tokyo, Japan.

OKI stated that between the dates of March 1, 1944 and May 1, 1944, an independent section was organized in the Overseas Bureau of the Broadcasting Corporation of Japan, which section was known as the Front Line Section. The Front Line Section was that division of the Overseas

 SF

Bureau of the Broadcasting Corporation of Japan which was charged with broadcasting or conveying information by radio to American and Allied troops in the South Pacific battle area. He stated that GEORGE MITSUSHIO became the Chief of the Front Line Section and OKI became the Production Supervisor at the time the section was organized. He stated that the sole responsibility of this section was the production and broadcasting of programs known as the "Zero Hour." MITSUSHIO was given specific instructions as to the aims and purposes of the "Zero Hour" broadcast by his immediate superior, SHINNOJO SAWADA.

OKI recalls that at the time the Front Line Section was organized, a meeting of the personnel of the Front Line Section was called for a conference concerning the radio broadcasts. He recalls that TOGURI was among those present. OKI also recalls that MITSUSHIO specifically re-stated the aims and purposes of the broadcasts, saying in substance that the program must be created to attract a large audience of American soldiers in the South Sea Islands and that after the large audience was attracted by the program, they were to broadcast propaganda aimed at creating nostalgia in the minds of the American soldiers and war weariness among the soldiers in order to discourage them in their battles against the Japanese soldiers and in order to lower the morale of the American troops. OKI recalls that MITSUSHIO gave these instructions in the English language and that TOGURI made known that she understood the instructions, saying in substance that she did understand them. He recalls that at the same meeting MITSUSHIO asked for suggestions from the assembled staff as to how the aims and purposes of the broadcasts could best be achieved.

OKI recalls that one NORMAN REYES, a member of the staff, made certain suggestions which he prepared previously, and suggested that his, REYES', part of the program would have to do with hot jazz music or "juke box music." He recalls that REYES suggested that TOGURI handle the so-called sweet music on her part of the program. He recalls that in answer to these suggestions, TOGURI stated in substance that it was agreeable with her and that she would organize and compose her program of the type of music that REYES had indicated. OKI recalls that TOGURI assented specifically as to her understanding of the instructions given by MITSUSHIO and the suggestion made by REYES as to the substance of her program.

SHIGETSUGU TSUNEISHI, then a Major in the Imperial Japanese Army and a member of the Army General Staff, gave a dinner for the staff of the "Zero Hour" program on Radio Tokyo in March, 1944 at the Tokyo Kaikan Restaurant. At this restaurant there were present GEORGE MITSUSHIO, KENKICHI OKI, SHINICHI OSHIDARI, HISASHI MORIYAMA and IVA IKUKO TOGURI. At this

success of their program. He gave them a general outline of the war
situation at that time and commented that as there were so many landings
of American soldiers on islands in the South Pacific the program should be
effective and that they should increase or continue in their efforts to
reach the American troops. To the best of MITSUSHIO's recollection,
TSUNEISHI pointed out that their program was a psychological weapon against
the American troops. This was a very informal luncheon and none of those
present expressed their feelings concerning TSUNEISHI's praise or encouragement. The program was discussed generally throughout the luncheon, but
details of the conversation could not be recalled.

Major TSUNEISHI attended this luncheon in the uniform of
a Japanese Army Major and his remarks were made in the Japanese language
which MITSUSHIO knows to his own knowledge to be understood and spoken by
TOGURI.

MITSUSHIO further advised that sometime between the dates
of March 1, 1944 and December 1, 1944, the Japanese Army General Staff
invited him to attend a showing of the American movie "Gone With The Wind."
He stated that he attended this movie in company with IVA TOGURI, among
others. MITSUSHIO stated that after seeing this move it suggested to those
present a subject for material for a radio program to be broadcast to the
American troops in the South Pacific Islands, and that he, MITSUSHIO, and
KENKICHI OKI, Production Manager, Front Line Section, directed that a
script be prepared for this broadcast.

MITSUSHIO stated that sometime within the above-mentioned
dates, the exact date of which they do not recall and after the script for
the broadcast had been prepared, the participants in the program were in
the office at the Broadcasting Corporation of Japan and that KENKICHI OKI
gave to them the prepared radio scripts. MITSUSHIO stated that after IVA
TOGURI had been handed the script for the part she was to take on the

radio program and after she had read it, she made the following comments
in substance, the exact words of which he does not recall. He stated that
she said that the program was silly and "corny" and not up to the standard
of their usual broadcast and she desired to go back to the Orphan Annie
broadcast instead of broadcasting that particular script. He recalls that
OKI told her that it was too late to change since they were to broadcast
their program in approximately two hours. MITSUSHIO recalls that they did
actually broadcast the prepared script, the subject of which had been
suggested by the movie "Gone With The Wind" and that TOGURI appeared in
the broadcast, taking the part assigned to her.

MITSUSHIO stated that the above-mentioned program dealing
with the subject material of the movie "Gone With The Wind" was broadcast
at six o'clock in the evening and that IVA TOGURI appeared and participated

in that broadcast and read from the script which had been prepared for her
into the microphone. He said that the program had been prepared to
emphasize the parts of the movie "Gone With The Wind" which dealt with
the discouraging phases of warfare, and that the live participants on the
program spoke words into the microphone announcing different parts to the
sound track of the movie which were played as a transcription. He said
that IVA TOGURI spoke into the microphone, the exact words of which he does
not recall, but he does recall in substance she said that there would next
be played a certain scene from the movie "Gone With The Wind" and asked her
listeners (the American soldiers in the South Pacific Islands) if they
recalled that particular part of the movie.

luncheon Major TSUNEISHI complimented the staff for the success of their program. He gave them a general outline of the war situation at that time and commented that as there were so many landings of American soldiers on islands in the South Pacific the program should be effective and that they should increase or continue in their efforts to reach the American troops. To the best of his recollection, TSUNEISHI pointed out that their program was a psychological weapon against the American troops. This was a very informal luncheon and none of those present expressed their feelings concerning his praise or encouragement. The program was discussed generally throughout the luncheon, but details of the conversation could not be recalled.

Major TSUNEISHI attended this luncheon in the uniform of a Japanese Army Major and his remarks were made in the Japanese language which OKI knows to his own knowledge was understood and spoken by TOGURI.

OKI further stated that sometime between the dates of March 1, 1944 and December 1, 1944, the Japanese Army General Staff invited him to attend a showing of the American movie "Gone With The Wind." He stated that he attended this movie in company with IVA TOGURI, among others. He stated that after seeing this movie it suggested to those present a subject for material for a radio program to be broadcast to the American troops in the South Pacific Islands, and that he and GEORGE MITSUSHIO directed that a script be prepared for this broadcast.

OKI stated that sometime within the above-mentioned dates, the exact date of which he does not recall and after the script for the broadcast had been prepared, the participants in the program were in the office at the Broadcasting Corporation of Japan and that OKI gave to them the prepared radio scripts. He stated that after IVA TOGURI had been handed the script for the part she was to take on the radio program and after she had read it, she made the following comments in substance, the exact words of which he does not recall. He stated that she said that the program was silly and "corny" and not up to the standard of their usual broadcast and she desired to go back to the Orphan Annie broadcast instead of broadcasting that particular script. OKI recalls that he told her it was too late to change since they were to broadcast their program in approximately two hours. He recalls that they did actually broadcast the prepared script, the subject of which had been suggested by the movie "Gone With The Wind" and that TOGURI appeared in the broadcast, taking the part assigned to her.

OKI stated that the above-mentioned program dealing with the subject material of the movie "Gone With The Wind" was broadcast at six o'clock in the evening and that IVA TOGURI appeared and participated in that

- 28 -

broadcast and read from the script which had been prepared for her into the microphone. He said that the program had been prepared to emphasize the parts of the movie "Gone With The Wind" which dealt with the discouraging phases of warfare, and that the live participants on the program spoke words into the microphone announcing different parts of the sound track of the movie which were played as a transcription. OKI said that IVA TOGURI spoke into the microphone, the exact words of which he does not recall, but he does recall in substance she said that there would next be played a certain scene from the movie "Gone With The Wind" and asked her listeners (the American soldiers in the South Pacific Islands) if they recalled that particular part of the movie.

MITSUSHIO stated that he further recalled that shortly after the battle of the Leyte Gulf the Imperial General Headquarters of the Japanese Armed Forces handed him an official announcement concerning the battle of the Leyte Gulf, which announcement reflected that a great number of American ships had been sunk. He stated he received this announcement about five o'clock in the evening and that it was timed just right for them to use in their "Zero Hour" broadcast, and that they were the first to use the news of the Leyte Gulf battle in their broadcast program.

MITSUSHIO stated that on the same day after six o'clock in the evening and before seven o'clock in the evening he saw TOGURI at the microphone in the broadcasting studio and that she in substance made this remark, the exact words of which he does not recall. He stated she said, "Now you fellowshave lost all of your ships. You really are orphans of the Pacific and how do you think you will ever get home." He stated that these words were included by her in her program as a result of the news announcement aforementioned which was given to him by Imperial Headquarters.

MITSUSHIO advised that he recalls sometime between the dates of August 1, 1944 and December 1, 1944 the following incident took place. He is able to place the date of the incident within the above dates since he recalls that the incident took place after the "Zero Hour" program was expanded to a one hour broadcast and before KENKICHI OKI's wife resigned from the program shortly before she and OKI were married. He stated that this incident is further recalled to his memory since a party was arranged which took place immediately following the broadcast and each of the members of the "Zero Hour" program brought food which they prepared before the program and which they ate after the program. He stated that this incident is also recalled to his mind since it is one of the few times that TOGURI stayed in the studio following a broadcast.

MITSUSHIO stated that on this date, between the hour of 6:00 PM and 6:30 PM, TOGURI stood before the microphone and spoke into the microphone saying in substance that "this is your favorite enemy, Orphan Annie" and addressing her listeners as the "boneheads of the Pacific" and/or "you dopes" and further, she said into the microphone in substance that she would play for them over the radio certain recordings which thereafter were played. He also recalled that for a closing theme song that she said into the microphone in substance that she would play the song "Goodbye Now." He recalls that TOGURI was at the microphone for approximately fifteen minutes, and that she also said in substance during the time she spoke into the microphone that she wished her listeners could be enjoying themselves as undoubtedly their folks at home were enjoying themselves.

GEORGE MITSUSHIO recalls that KENKICHI OKI, Production Supervisor, Front Line Section, Broadcasting Corporation of Japan, was present at the time all of the above incidents occurred.

MITSUSHIO further recalls that about May 23, 1945, which date he remembers since KENNETH ISHII visited the studio that day being on his first furlough from the Japanese Army, ISHII visited the office during the afternoon hours at the time when all of the employees were preparing their scripts for the evening broadcast. He recalls that at the time ISHII was in the office that he saw TOGURI seated at her desk and that she was typing words on paper which she was to use as her script for the evening broadcast. He recalls that ISHII engaged TOGURI in conversation for a short time after which she informed him in substance that she had to complete her script for the evening broadcast.

It was recalled by MITSUSHIO that both KENNETH ISHII and KENKICHI OKI were present at the time the above incident occurred.

340

OKI further advised according to his recollection shortly after the battle of the Leyte Gulf the Imperial General Headquarters of the Japanese Armed Forces handed him an official announcement concerning the battle of the Leyte Gulf, which announcement reflected that a great number of American ships had been sunk. He stated this announcement was received about five o'clock in the evening and that it was timed just right for use in the "Zero Hour" broadcast, and that this program was the first to use the news of the Leyte Gulf Battle in their broadcast.

OKI stated that on the same day after six o'clock in the evening and before seven o'clock in the evening he saw TOGURI at the microphone in the broadcasting studio and that she in substance made this remark, the exact words of which he does not recall. He stated she said, "Now you fellows have lost all of your ships. You really are orphans of the Pacific and how do you think you will ever get home." He stated that these words were included by her in her program as a result of the news announcement aforementioned which was given to him by Imperial Headquarters.

OKI also recalls that sometime between the dates of August 1, 1944 and December 1, 1944 the following incident took place. He was able to place the date of the incident within the above dates since he recalls that the incident took place after the "Zero Hour" program was expanded to a one hour broadcast and before his wife resigned from the program shortly before she and OKI were married. He stated that this incident is further recalled to his memory since a party was arranged to follow the broadcast and each of the members of the "Zero Hour" program brought food which they prepared before the program and which they ate after the program. He stated that this incident is also recalled to his mind since it is one of the few times that TOGURI stayed in the studio following a broadcast.

- 29 -

OKI stated that on this date, between the hour 6:00 PM and 6:30 PM, TOGURI stood before the microphone and spoke into the microphone saying in substance that "this is your favorite enemy, Orphan Annie" and addressing her listeners as the "boneheads of the Pacific" and/or "you dopes" and further, she said into the microphone in substance that she would play for them over the radio certain recordings which thereafter were played. He also recalled that for a closing theme song that she said into the microphone in substance that she would play the song "Goodbye Now." OKI recalls that TOGURI was at the microphone for approximately fifteen minutes, and that she also said in substance during the time she spoke into the microphone that she wished her listeners could be enjoying themselves as undoubtedly their folks at home were enjoying themselves.

KENKICHI OKI recalls that GEORGE MITSUSHIO was present at the time when all of the above incidents occurred.

OKI further recalls that about May 23, 1945, which date he remembers since KENNETH ISHII visited the studio that day being on his first furlough from the Japanese Army, ISHII visited the office during the afternoon hours at the time when all of the employees were preparing their scripts for the evening broadcast. He recalls that at the time ISHII was in the office that he saw TOGURI seated at her desk and that she was typing words on paper which she was to use as her script for the evening broadcast. He recalls that ISHII engaged TOGURI in conversation for a short time, after which she informed him in substance that she had to complete her script for the evening broadcast.

OKI advised that both KENNETH ISHII and GEORGE MITSUSHIO were present when the above incident took place.

Appendix 2

The Roll Call at Suragadai

ENSIGN GEORGE HENSHAW claimed to have listed all the prisoners at Suragadai, or Bunka. Some of the men were cooks, orderlies, and other camp "staff." The following were ordered to perform tasks with Nippon Hoso Kyokai, and many of them were questioned by the CIC, the FBI, or by Allied equivalents.

ASTERITA, Joseph John (Joe), Wake Island civilian, from Brooklyn, New York. Minor radio work and cook.

BRUCE, Lance Corporal Donald Carswell, British army, from Glasgow, Scotland. Typed scripts.

COUSENS, Major Charles Hughes, Australian army, from Sydney. Senior prisoner of the camp. His radio work is described in this book.

COX, Major Willistin Madison, Jr., U.S. Army Air Corps, from Tennessee. Second ranking prisoner. Minor radio duties.

DODDS, Darwin H., Wake Island civilian, from Boise, Idaho. Singer and occasional "master of ceremonies" on "Hinomaru Hour," relieving Provoo and Wisner. Participated in "The Postman Calls."

DOOLEY, Warrant Officer John H., Australian army. Wrote commentaries and helped in kitchen.

FUJITA, Sergeant Frank, U.S. Army, from Abilene, Texas. Minor radio duties.

HENSHAW, Ensign George (Buck), U.S. Navy, from Los Angeles. Wrote "Three Missing Men" series, helped with "Saturday Jamboree," spun turntables.

HOBBLITT, Corporal Frederick M., U.S. Army, from San Francisco. "Master of ceremonies," and read POW messages on "The Postman Calls." Worked under Ince, who wrote and directed the program. (Misdescribed in the FBI files as a marine.)

INCE, Captain Wallace Ellwell (misspelled Elwell by Henshaw and Ewell by some others). Radio name: Ted Wallace. His NHK work is described in this book.

KALBFLEISCH, Second Lieutenant Edwin, Jr. Wrote and read political commentaries of three or four minutes' duration, then refused to cooperate.

LIGHT, Technical Sergeant Newton, U.S. Army, from Roanoke, Virginia. According to Henshaw, he was the "stenciling man" and he "prepared all the scripts after they had been written in rough draft form by the various POW writers."

McNAUGHTON, Lieutenant John M., British army, from London. Initially wrote commentaries, then radio dramatizations of stories.

MARTINEZ, Private First Class James Gutierrez, U.S. Army, from Kingsville, Texas. Had minor radio duties and helped in kitchen.

MARTINEZ, Private First Class Ramon Perez, from Laredo, Texas. Disc jockey on Spanish-language program, "Saturday Jamboree." (Not related to James, above.)

ODLIN, Technical Sergeant Walter C., U.S. Army, from Andover, New Hampshire. Wrote commentaries.

PARKYNS, Flight Sergeant Kenneth G., Royal Australian Air Force, from Liverpool, New South Wales. Some writing; appeared on "Australian Hour"; assistant chief camp cook.

PEARSON, Corporal Harry, British army. Scriptwriter and musician. Helped with "Saturday Jamboree."

PROVOO, Sergeant John David, U.S. Army. Chief animator of "Hinomaru Hour" and "Humanity Calls."

QUILLE, Larry W., Wake Island civilian, from La Grande, Oregon. Wrote scripts, but was later relegated to the kitchen.

RICKERT, Corporal Albert Powhatan, U.S. Marines, from Louisville, Kentucky. Typed scripts for Ince and others.

SHATTLES, Stephen Herman, Wake Island civilian, from New Orleans (and Hattiesburg, Mississippi). Wrote and acted in radio dramas, read commentaries, and did mimeographing.

SHENK, Warrant Officer Nicolas, Army of the Netherlands. "Did some writing." Chief camp cook.

SMITH, Radioman First Class Frederick Ferguson, U.S. Navy. Wrote commentaries and typed scripts.

STREETER, Mark Lewis (or Louis). Wake Island civilian, from Ogden, Utah. "Wrote commentaries and dramas and later had his own program called 'Enerjocracy.' "

WILLIAMS, Henry Charles Ralph Fulford (George). British Colonial Service. Refused to cooperate.

WISNER, Second Lieutenant Jack K. (misspelled Wisener by Henshaw), U.S. Army Air Corps (Henshaw mistakenly says Army). Alternated as "master of ceremonies" on "The Postman Calls," and with Provoo on "Hinomaru Hour" and "Humanity Calls," for which he wrote and read "a few assigned commentaries."

After the war, Corporal Pearson used the skills acquired at NHK to get a job as a reporter in Cape Town, South Africa. Quille's work, rejected by the Japanese, enabled him to become a reporter on the Fullerton (Texas) *News-Tribune*. Provoo was convicted of treason but acquitted on appeal; he spent many years in mental hospitals. Streeter was imprisoned, but charges of treason were finally dropped. The wandering Dutchman

Shenk did not go home but stayed on in Tokyo to work for the War Crimes Department of the U.S. Eighth Army. All of the American officers who worked for Tokyo radio were promoted on their return. Corporal Rickert was made a marine officer.

Index